China

Harbin

Changchun

★ Beijing

Xi'an

Shanghai

Taipei

Hong Kong

Taiwan

Me at 3

In *Mulberry Child*, Jian Ping has written a moving, important account of an extraordinary time. And she has done so with grace, acuity and a generosity of spirit. *Mulberry Child* is one compelling read.

Alex Kotlowitz, author of
There Were No Children Here

Jian Ping's poignant and compelling tale of growing up in China during the difficult times of the Great Leap Forward and the Cultural Revolution is an important addition to "scar literature" published in the West about events and people and victims forgotten, buried or silenced by the mainland Chinese and their government over the past four decades. The author shows convincingly how the fortunes and misfortunes of the past shape, inform, educate and haunt each of us. Jian Ping pays tribute to her parents who struggled against tremendous odds in order to realize their own small dreams; that she herself survived to write this memoir, and to tell it with such maturity and wisdom and forgiveness, is a tribute to her family, her generation and her nation. In an unforgettable parting from her parents she recalls she could not find the right words to express her deep feelings of sorrow. Now, at long last, is this memoir, she has found them and blessed not only her parents but each of her readers, too.

Larry Engelmann, author of
Feather in a Storm and *Daughter of China*

Jian Ping is neither a journalist nor an historian, yet in her book *Mulberry Child*, she has managed to combine the skills of both of those professions. She combines the journalist's gift of observation and skillful writing with the historian's eye for detail. The result is a riveting book that ushers the reader to the front row of history as it tells the story of one of China's most turbulent eras through the often tragic, sometimes uplifting but always true experiences of one family—or more accurately, through the perceptive eyes of a girl growing up in 1960s China. Jian Ping is a terrific story teller who writes with both power and precision.

Ronald E. Yates,
Dean of the College of Media at the University of Illinois and former foreign correspondent and author based in Asia

I found this a fascinating and moving story about a child surviving in turbulent times. It is also a touching portrayal of the love that binds a close-knit family whatever the political ideology. Jian Ping's family is a compelling glimpse of the resilience inside a closed and mysterious society about which Americans know little and only now are beginning to learn.

Sharon Stangenes,
Former Chicago Tribune Columnist

MULBERRY CHILD

JIAN PING

MORRISON, McNAE PUBLISHERS

Glasgow, New York, Detroit, Los Angeles

ISBN - 13: 978-0-9794948-6-4
ISBN - 10:   0-9794948-6-9

Library of Congress Control Number: 2008928870

For more information on this book, or for direct sales, please
visit http://www.mulberrychild.com

Cover design by John Apgar
Layout by Richard Cartwright

To my parents, my sisters, and my brother

My Siblings and Me

Contents

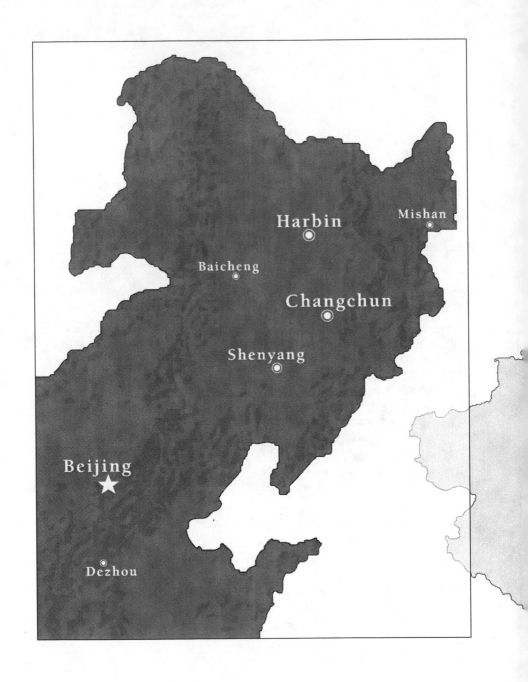

Prologue

My hometown is called Baicheng. It's a small city tucked away in the northeast corner of China, in an area known as the Jilin Province, the old Manchuria. Baicheng borders on Inner Mongolia to the west and the Heilongjiang Province to the north. For nearly half the year, the town is in the grip of cold Siberian winds. Women wore thin scarves like transparent veils to prevent sand from getting in their hair and faces. Men lowered their Mao-style hats to protect their eyes.

Baicheng means "White City," but there is nothing white about it. It's a world of gray: rows of low single-story buildings, narrow dirt roads, a few tar-paved streets, and open sewers. This is where I grew up. For over twenty years, my family—my grandmother, my parents and my five elder siblings—lived in Baicheng's Government Compound.

I remember vividly five mulberry trees growing in the Compound, lining a patch of gravel. They seemed like oversized bushes, their thick branches bent low by the constant winds from Siberia. No one ever took care of them, but year after year, they sprang back to life after remaining dormant each bitterly cold winter. In the spring, they were full of leaves and berries again, just like before. They thrived, enduring not only the trials of nature, but also the abuses of people. As years passed, the trees came to symbolize the hardships of my life in China. And as I learned to endure cruelty and persecution, I grew as strong and as resilient as these trees. Eventually, I managed to leave China and come to the United States. I had to leave my husband and my fifteen-month old daughter Yie behind. A year later, my husband joined me, but my daughter was not able to come until three years later.

I had gone through more than two decades of hardship and wandering in China and it had taken me a long time to adjust to this new life, this new world in the United States.

And then, one day, I saw a mulberry tree at the edge of a park in suburban Chicago, its leaves glimmering in the sun. The magnificent sight surprised me.

I thought about planting a mulberry tree in my own back yard. I searched every nursery, but I couldn't find any.

"It's a weed. No one carries it," a nurseryman told me. "No one wants it."

I wanted it. I dug up a two-inch seedling emerging at the foot of the tree in the park and planted it in my yard. Within a few years, it grew tall and spread wide. I could no longer reach the top to harvest the berries. The birds got most of them. Soon, I noticed small mulberry plants springing up all over my flower and herb garden. I pulled out these young trees I didn't want, but their roots went deep. When I broke the trunk of one, it bounced back, like a stubborn thistle. Their strength continued to amaze me. Their dark green leaves and purple fruit reminded me of the few innocent years I had as a child. Along with my older siblings, we used to pick the leaves to feed our silkworms, and we watched in awe as they transformed themselves and started producing delicate, white threads.

I harvested the fruit of my tree. It tasted like blackberries, but softer and sweeter. Street vendors in China often sold the berries at markets, but once they ripened, they became too soft, too difficult to handle. Their juice left stains on the hands and lips of those who touched it and turned their tongues purple. My neighbors smiled at me when I picked them. They stayed away from them. The berries splashed the windshields of their cars.

My own daughter Yie, who called herself "Lisa" upon entering school, showed no interest in the berries either. I asked her to taste them. She said no.

"Please," I said. "You'll be surprised."

I put a bowl in front of her.

"No way," she said. "They are for birds, Mom."

She pushed the bowl aside. She preferred fruits from the supermarket. I thought of telling her the story of my mulberry trees, and our ordeals in China, but I hesitated. I wasn't quite ready yet to face my past.

But one day, Yie was writing a greeting card to my mother and father back in China, her grandparents. She was struggling with an English-Chinese dictionary.

"Send them my regards," I said.

"Okay," she said, scratching her head with the back end of her ballpoint pen.

When I looked at her writing, I froze. She had written the word "大家," meaning "everyone," as "大象," meaning "elephant." I realized that our own language had become foreign to her. In her desire to become American, she shied away from anything Chinese.

I went outside to my tree, touching its bark with my fingertips. The rustling of the leaves took me back to the barren land of my childhood. It felt like a door was opening.

I decided to tell her my story.

Our story.

Jian Ping

Mother and Me 1961

Chapter One

First Hurdles

1

I wasn't supposed to be born. My mother didn't want me, not at first. She tried to get rid of me, but I was stubborn. In the end, it was the summer rain that brought me into this world, two months premature.

It was a rainy day in June 1960. Early in the morning, my mother, Gu Wenxiu, was on her way to a local university in Changchun, the capital of Jilin Province. Jilin is a rugged and vast region in the northeast of China, with stifling hot summers and bitterly cold winters. Mother was seven months pregnant. She ignored my impatient movement inside her. For several weeks now, she walked to work rather than ride the bus. She didn't want to expose her oversized belly to the rush hour jostling. Passengers elbowed their way onto the bus, and those who climbed in last were pushed from behind, so the driver could close the door. Many people rode bicycles. My mother walked.

In the drizzle of that particular morning, she took a shortcut on a side street. She heard the patter of rain on her umbrella and quickened her pace. Suddenly, she felt the shift of a slippery object under her right foot. Before she could regain her balance, her body fell backward. She landed heavily on the ground. The rain and mud on the street splashed all over her.

Passersby came to her assistance. She was in pain and couldn't move. She was carried to the People's Hospital of Jilin.

Shortly before midnight, I was born. I was as helpless as a small kitten, unable to open my eyes or make a sound.

2

Mother was only thirty-two and already had five children.

In the 1950s, the Chinese Government encouraged families to have as many babies as possible. There were no contraceptives, and abortions were severely restricted. When Mother realized she was pregnant again, she decided to have an abortion. She had worked too hard to become a teacher. She was new at her post, and couldn't afford to take time off.

She went to the hospital shortly after the Chinese New Year. The temperature had dropped to 25 degrees below zero Fahrenheit. The snowfall over the past two days covered the ground. That day, the sky was gray and the strong wind cut into Mother's face. She shivered with cold and slightly bent her body forward. Her mind was going over the same question again and again:

What am I going to tell the doctor?

She sighed deeply as she entered the People's Hospital of Jilin. She shook off the snow on her shoulders and scarf. The small lobby was not much warmer than outside, and the pungent smell of disinfectant made her nauseated. She took off her cotton-padded mittens and wiped her shoes on a floor mat. She proceeded to the registration window and took a number.

This was the second time she had come to the People's Hospital for an abortion. She had been there the year before, and the procedure was difficult and painful. There was a lot of blood, and it had taken her a long time to recover. Could she endure another abortion? And what would the doctor say? Maybe if she lied about her medical history, it might be easier to obtain the procedure.

She sat on a bench in the hallway, waiting her turn, her fingers clutching the piece of paper with a number printed on it. When she looked up, she saw a pregnant woman slowly approaching. The woman was staggering, leaning on the arms of a man for support. The couple sat beside her. The woman let out a moan. The man turned to Mother.

"She is in pain," he said quietly, as if he was apologizing. Mother stared at the woman's pale face.

At that moment of doubt, Mother decided she would tell the doctor the truth.

When Mother's number was called, she slowly stood from the bench. She was fearful and nervous. She nodded a brief farewell to the couple and then went into the doctor's office, taking small, careful steps.

She took a seat across from his desk.

"Do you have any other children?" the doctor asked. He was a middle-aged man, and his voice was soft and caring.

Mother nodded. "Yes."

"How many?"

"Five."

The doctor raised his eyebrows. "Five?"

Mother nodded. "Four of my own and a stepdaughter."

The doctor gave her an appreciative nod and made a note.

"You should be grateful."

"I am."

"Chairman Mao says: 'Man is the most precious of all beings. The source of all miracles.'"

"Yes," Mother said. Mother didn't need another miracle. She was still young, and she wanted to pursue her teaching career.

"How old are your children?"

"The youngest is six. The oldest is ten."

"And your stepdaughter?"

"Twenty-one."

Her first two daughters, Yan and Ping, were born in 1950 and 1951. After that, she decided to avoid pregnancy. She had other plans for her life: She wanted to go back to school and become a teacher. But it wasn't that easy. At the time, giving birth to many children was considered a patriotic duty. The Communist Party held up the fertile women of Russia, who had ten or more children, as role models. So Mother took the issue of birth control into her own hands. After her second child, she turned to Chinese herbal remedies, but they had no effect. She became pregnant a third time. She had just enrolled in an intensive study program. If she managed to complete the course, she would finally have a middle-school diploma, which she needed to attend college. A pregnancy was out of the question.

One day, she stopped by the playground at a corner of her campus. She climbed the parallel bars and started swinging. Perspiration soon glistened on her forehead. She pressed on, ignoring the caresses of the gentle breeze that drifted through the open campus. She was determined. She closed her eyes and picked up speed. She swung faster and faster, then let go. She could feel herself flying through the air. With a heavy thump, she landed rather painfully on the dirt ground.

She had her desired miscarriage, but she nearly died from the heavy loss of blood. She suffered from severe anemia, and the resulting dizzy spells often made it unsafe for her to walk. She was forced to take off a whole semester to recuperate. During the next two years, she became pregnant twice more, giving birth to Binbin, a son, in 1953 and Wen, another daughter, in 1954. Each time, she managed to stay in school until the last minute. Her classmates, especially the young men, constantly teased her. They put cushions under their shirts and imitated her awkward waddle.

Mother was the oldest student in school and served as Party Secretary for her class. Her job was to represent the Communist Party, the highest institution in China. The younger students looked up to her. She was a big sister to them. She joined in their laughter, but deep inside, she was very much concerned about her frequency of pregnancy.

After giving birth to Wen, she and Father obtained abortion permits. Precaution and herbs had failed them. Mother managed to finish the four-year program over a period of six years, and with Father's support, she went on to college. By the time she fulfilled her dream of becoming a teacher, she had undergone four abortions. In early 1960, with Wen, her youngest child, about to start school and her new teaching job lined up, she had more reasons than ever to end her latest pregnancy.

She told all this to the doctor.

When she was finished, the doctor said: "I don't think you should have another abortion."

Mother's eyes grew wild.

"The device we use can be quite harsh on the body," the doctor continued. "You are putting yourself at great risk."

"I know," Mother said. Normally, abortions were performed without anesthetics. The memory of the pain made her shudder, but she was willing to go through it again. Anything was better than another child.

"I'm not afraid of the pain," Mother said, but her voice betrayed the lie.

"You don't understand." The doctor raised his voice slightly. He sounded serious. "I'm not talking about the pain."

"Please." Mother begged. Tears welled up in her eyes. "I've just started my teaching job... I can't be distracted by the repeated morning sickness and maternity leave. The time is all wrong..." her voice trailed off.

The time had never been right. She clenched her fists under the table, trying to maintain her composure.

"Listen to me," the doctor said. "You might bleed to death. It's too much of a risk." He stood up and paced back and forth in the room. When he came back to the desk and sat down across from her, he said with finality: "I won't do it."

Mother blushed deeply, and then she cried. The doctor averted his eyes. Mother was shivering. She lost control. Tears streamed down her face.

Feeling her helplessness, the doctor said: "If you want, I can recommend having your tubes tied after this birth." He cleared his throat. Looking into Mother's eyes, the doctor said firmly: "But no more abortions."

Mother looked away. She sat without speaking for a while. Then she stood up to leave.

"Thank you," she said, her voice heavy with resignation.

She left the room and the Hospital and slowly walked home. All the way she could feel me kicking inside her. All the way she cried. The wind stung her face. She vowed again and again that there would be no more children after this pregnancy.

She decided that after my birth, she would go through with the tube tying procedure. She contemplated doing this before, but was afraid of the operation. As it turned out, her fear was warranted. The day after giving birth to me, Mother undertook the operation. The tubes were easier to locate right after giving birth, and the operation usually took about fifteen minutes. Unfortunately, a trainee operated on her. At that time, small operations such as tube tying used local anesthesia, which was injected into the incision area. It was effective for about only forty minutes. The trainee turned the simple operation into a two-and-a-half-hour nightmare for Mother. When the anesthetic wore off, Mother felt the excruciating pain as the trainee stirred and pulled her insides. Mother screamed. Her usual strength and endurance disappeared. Five nurses rushed to assist. They tied her to the operating table with belts, and then each took a position to hold her limbs and head, preventing her from moving. More anesthetic might cause poisoning and would not prevent pain in the internal organs. The trainee pressed on, his forehead covered with perspiration, his hands shaking. Mother begged to have her incision sewn up and for them to let her be. Nobody listened to her. By the time her tubes were tied, Mother's voice was gone and her eyes had no more tears. Her body twitched with each jab of the needle and each pull of the suture. When the stitches were finally done, Mother's sweat from the pain and struggle had soaked the entire table.

3

After my premature birth, I was placed in an incubator. For a week, I clung to life, supported by intravenous tubes. When I opened my mouth, no sound emerged. And I couldn't draw milk from the feeder.

Mother was allowed to see me just three times a day. Only then, watching me struggle to stay alive, did her love for me arise. One day, as she stood by my cradle, her hands over the incision from the operation, she made a promise: If I survived, she would breastfeed me and make me a strong child.

And I did survive.

After the first three weeks in intensive care, I was moved to a regular ward. At the end of July, tiny and weak though I was, I was well enough to be discharged from the hospital. Mother carried me home. Nainai, my grandmother who had been living with our family for five years, welcomed me with open arms. In the Chinese tradition, family members were, and still are, identified by their positions, not by their names. Nainai was the term for paternal grandmother.

Nainai set up an old cradle by her bed. She took me under her protection. My bruised body, dotted with the tracts of three dozen needles, triggered a tender feeling in her heart. She had raised four children of her own and had helped bring up several grandchildren. Never in her life had she seen such a tiny, pitiful looking baby.

"Poor Jian is the size of a kitten," she said to Mother. "In fact, a kitten's meow is louder than her cry."

Mother agreed. "It's a miracle she's made it so far," Mother said, holding me in her arms. "She hasn't gained much weight yet."

Because of my ill-timed arrival and poor health, I received special care and attention from Mother and Nainai. The close bond I had with Nainai must have started right there and then.

I continued to struggle for life, and frequently suffered from mysterious high fevers. Mother stood by me, breastfeeding me, in the hope of making me stronger. It was very hard for her. She had resumed her busy work schedule, leaving early in the morning and returning late in the evening. She fed me before breakfast, and during the day she pumped milk from her swollen breasts. Only when she got home after a day's work, usually about nine in the evening, was she able to let me eagerly suck until her breasts emptied. During the long hours of work, the milk accumulated, which was quite painful for her.

1960 was a devastating time for most Chinese. It was the beginning of the so called "three-year famine." The famine was caused by ill-advised political movements and natural disasters, compounded by the withdrawal of Russian aid. There was a severe food shortage throughout the country. Our family suffered. Everyone was hungry all the time. While it wasn't much, city residents still received their rationed grains, but people in the countryside were starving to death by the tens of millions. To make what little grain they had last longer, they mixed it with tree leaves, weeds, and plant roots. Soon, even edible tree bark was stripped clean. In many places, the countryside became barren. Unable to survive, many peasants fled their home villages. Among them were my uncle Desheng, Father's older brother, and his wife. Driven by hunger, they dug up weeds, mushrooms, anything that could stop the rumbling of their stomachs. Malnutrition and poisonous weeds turned their bodies into balloons. They both succumbed to hunger despite having made their way to the northeast.

Against all the odds, I survived.

But there were many challenges. When I was five months old, Mother had a severe breast infection. She had a high capacity for enduring pain, and so continued to breastfeed me. She also maintained her regular teaching schedule, determined not to interrupt her students' studies so soon after returning from her maternity leave. Since she only had time to feed me twice a day, milk accumulated in her breasts, exacerbating her infection. She refused to take antibiotics, fearing the medication would be passed on to me through her milk. Soon, a ring of scabs surrounded her right nipple, cracking open every time I put my hungry mouth to it. She stared at me, as if my tiny, soft mouth was a sharp knife. She shivered with each movement of my lips.

But she persisted. She wiped away the perspiration on her forehead and fought back her tears. Each time she finished feeding me, her blouse was soaked with sweat.

She resolved to walk to school again, as in the days when she was heavy with her pregnancy. She could no longer take the sharp pain caused by the bouncing of the bus. Every day, she carefully cradled her right breast with her left hand to stabilize it as she slowly made her way back and forth to school. She endured this ordeal until one day, suffering from a high fever, she collapsed during a lecture. An ambulance took her to the same hospital where I was born. She was operated upon right away. Several doctors worked on her for hours and extracted a small bucket's worth of dark liquid from her right breast. The odor was so strong that it stunk up the whole wing of the hospital.

The doctors told her she was lucky to be alive. Acute blood poisoning might have cost her life if she had delayed treatment for one more day. They shook their heads in disbelief. How could an intelligent, educated woman choose to ignore such a serious infection? How could she put up with such terrifying pain? Mother smiled weakly at their inquiries. She had made a promise to build my strength with her milk, and she had wanted to maintain her schedule with her students. She wanted to hold on until the end of the semester, counting each hour of the remaining days.

Her pain, however, did not subside with the operation. Her breast felt hollow where it used to swell, and the constant pain was like the stab of a knife. Even turning around in bed became a challenge.

"Young lady, I know how painful it is to have a breast infection," said an old woman in her ward. "If screaming or crying can give you relief, go ahead and do it."

Mother shook her head. That wasn't her way of dealing with pain. She sank her teeth into her lower lip instead and never made a sound.

That ended Mother's breastfeeding, at a time when my life seemed to entirely depend on it.

While Mother was recovering in the hospital, Nainai took on the full responsibility of caring for me. She nurtured me at home, teasing me with her fingers until I learned to drink from a plastic nipple on a milk bottle. She held me in her arms whenever I cried, which happened often.

Slowly, with her care and love and constant attention, I grew.

Then, in my ninth month, I had another brush with death. One of my worrisome high fevers persisted and eventually turned into pneumonia. Several doctors took turns administering a variety of antibiotics, to no avail. The high fever would not recede, and my labored breathing finally became inaudible. When my eyelids became motionless and my body turned cold, Mother thought I was gone. She moved my bedding to the floor in a corner of Nainai's bedroom and prepared to lay me to rest the following day, but Nainai refused to let me go. She held me in her arms throughout the night, dripping water into my tightened mouth and calling me to come back.

"Jian, my little Jian," she rocked me back and forth, talking softly the whole time as if I could understand her words.

In the morning, before the break of dawn, when Mother tiptoed to Nainai's room, Nainai's smiling face greeted her. I was fast asleep in Nainai's arms, and my chest rose and fell slightly with the rhythm of my breathing.

"It was the most beautiful sight I had ever seen," Mother recalled.

She pressed her face against Nainai's cheek and thanked her.

"Jian is a survivor," Nainai said, putting me gently in my mother's arms.

Nainai's eyes were red from lack of sleep, but she was happy. She was right. I had overcome the first hurdles in my life.

Laolao and Mother in 1964

Chapter Two

Mountain Girl

1

Mother came from a very poor family in a mountain village in Mishan, in the Heilongjiang Province. The area is in the far northeast corner of China, near the Russian border. It is remote, but starkly beautiful. In the summer and fall, the mountain slopes are full of wild mushrooms, fruits, and nuts. My mother and her younger brothers used to gather them as supplemental food for the family. The winter was long and brutally cold, and spring always short. In the 1930s when Mother was a little girl, China was in the middle of a civil war. The Communists, under the leadership of Mao Zedong—the founder and first ruler of the People's Republic of China—were struggling to overthrow the strongholds of the old regime, the Kuomintang, led by Generalissimo Chiang Kai-shek. In addition to this civil strife, the northeast of the country was under Japanese occupation.

Laoye, my maternal grandfather, was a sharecropper. He supported his family by working a small piece of leased land. From time to time, he had to sell his services as a hired laborer to make ends meet. Laoye's family originally moved to Mishan from the Shandong Province. He had grown up to be a tall and handsome man, but he was not strong. He tired easily. Since his family was poor and lived in a remote mountain area, he never went to a doctor.

Laolao, my maternal grandmother, came from a family of nine daughters. Only four of them lived to adulthood. At a time when most Chinese women bound their feet—the smaller the feet, the prettier and the more sexual the women were considered to be—none of Laolao's siblings conformed to the custom. They all grew tall and exceptionally beautiful. With their fair complexion and large eyes, they looked Russian. They did their work for the family just like boys, until each of them was married. When Laolao and her siblings were young, their father used to get furious with them. He always found fault with them and lost his temper at the slightest provocation. He couldn't stand the fact that all his children were girls. When his ninth daughter was born, he threatened to throw the baby out of the window.

"Another girl!" he screamed. His wife wept and held the newborn in her arms day and night, afraid that he would toss her into the trash. He needed a son, because in China it is the sons who take care of their parents in old age. In the end, he simply adopted his nephew, but as it turned out, he didn't get along with his nephew's wife. So, in his old age, he ended up living with his daughters after all, first with Laolao and then with his youngest daughter. They dutifully took care of him, but constantly complained about his attitude toward women.

Laolao suffered from acute nerve pain. It came unexpectedly, like hot needles. Sometimes, the pain would render her immobile for hours. Whenever that happened, Laolao curled up in bed and didn't allow anyone to come close. She moaned, but she endured. She emerged only when the pain subsided. She accepted her suffering as a matter of fact and never complained about it. Laolao often furrowed her eyebrows into a knot, leaving three deep lines between her eyes. She had a will of iron, and orchestrated the household with order and control. She also had a bad temper, and when infuriated, she could fly into a fit, cursing and crying until she exhausted herself.

Laolao gave birth to four children. My mother was the oldest, and she looked exactly like Laolao. Luckily, she was healthy and strong. She started helping Laolao with household chores and cared for her little brothers when she was just a child. Mother admired Laolao's resilience and strength, but she was also afraid of her, especially her hot temper. She always obeyed Laolao without question.

Mother attended several years of elementary school and received good grades. When her family could no longer afford her tuition, she dropped out, abandoning her dream of becoming a schoolteacher.

2

Mother's childhood was spent in the shadow of Japanese occupation. Although the full scale war against Japan didn't break out until 1937, the northeast of China had been in the hands of the Japanese since 1931. For years, Japan had wanted to control China's vast resources. In the mountains where Mother lived, they heard about the atrocities of the Japanese Army. They burnt entire villages, they conducted chemical experiments on Chinese men and women, and they killed Chinese peasants as if they were slaughtering animals. But Mother and her family didn't see any Japanese troops. Only after 1937—when Japan increased its number of soldiers in China and set up a large military base at the foot of their mountains—was their village visited by Japanese soldiers. Life changed overnight. Mother watched in horror as the young men in the village were ordered to gather and then herded away. They were supposedly being sent to work, but none of them returned to the village. Older men were not safe either.

Since Mishan was near the Russian border, the Japanese arrested and executed anyone whom they suspected of being a Russian spy. Men disappeared without a trace. Laoye moved around with caution, doing his best to avoid any encounter with the Japanese. Women were no better off. Rape and murder were common. During the day, the women in the village stayed in their homes. They were constantly looking over their shoulders, prepared to flee at any moment. At night, many chose to sleep in a barn instead of their home, hiding behind haystacks or pig feed. They were always scared. Japanese soldiers frequently burst into houses and raped the women. No one could protect them. If the men dared to interfere, they could be killed right on the spot.

Mother and Laolao confined themselves to their tiny cottage. When they had no choice but to go out to run errands, they covered their faces with black charcoal, to hide their beauty. Everyone lived in constant fear.

One night, a banging at the door awakened Mother's family. Laoye ran to check. Two Japanese soldiers were standing outside the cottage. They were so drunk they could hardly stand, but each carried a rifle. Laoye risked his life by keeping them at the door, talking to them, delaying them.

"Nü Ren," they uttered in broken Chinese. The word meant "women." They were demanding Laoye hand over the women in the house.

Laoye pretended he couldn't understand them. He turned to Laolao and urged her in a hushed voice:

"Wake up the kids and get out!"

As he spoke, he tried to engage the soldiers' attention with exaggerated gestures. Mother's youngest brother Wenqing was only three months old. Laolao was afraid he would cry so she hid him behind a pile of homemade quilts. She put on a rabbit fur hat to cover her lustrous hair and placed Laoye's hat on Mother's head. Then, grabbing Mother in one hand and Wensheng, her older son, in the other, Laolao led them toward the door. They bent low as they moved, their bodies trembling with fear. Mother's legs buckled when Laolao told her to get out first. She had turned ten that year and was completely paralyzed, only two feet away from the soldiers. At Laolao's urging and pushing, Mother got down on all fours and crawled between the parted legs of the soldiers, with Wensheng trailing closely behind. Laolao crawled out last, barely able to squeeze her larger frame through the narrow space. They ran to their next-door neighbor, looking for shelter. Once inside, Laolao broke down. Mother and Wensheng clung to her, one on each side, and they wept. They feared the soldiers would kill Laoye and the baby. The neighbor blew out the candle and told them to be quiet.

The soldiers lingered until daybreak. Once they realized there were no women in the house, they demanded that Laoye retrieve them from their hiding place. Eventually, it dawned on them that they should be back at their base before sunrise. They hurried away, but not before kicking the front door off its hinges.

This wasn't the only encounter with Japanese soldiers. The second time, the family was prepared. When they heard the soldiers approaching from the distance, they fled. They managed to escape, but they couldn't live in their cottage anymore. The very next day, they packed their meager belongings and moved in with a relative in a nearby village.

At fourteen, an age at which girls were drafted by the Japanese Army to do maintenance and cleaning work, Laolao feared for Mother's life. Many young women were raped or turned into sexual slaves for Japanese soldiers. They called them "comfort women." The only way to delay this fate was to stay in school. Mother had an uncle living in Mishan City where there was a middle school. He was a landlord and agreed to let Mother stay with his family. Even though the uncle was a wealthy man, Laoye had to deliver a bag of grain each month, to pay for Mother's room and board.

Mother attended the middle school for nearly a year. The school principal was Japanese. Each morning, the students greeted him in Japanese. They gathered in the playground to listen to his speeches. Loyalty to Japan was an absolute duty. Before they returned to their classrooms, the students had to face the portrait of the Japanese Emperor and bow three times. The portrait was always placed in the direction of Japan. The principal was fluent in Chinese, but he would not allow anyone to speak the language to him. Each day, one of the students collected all the homework from the previous day and delivered it to the principal. Upon entering the office, the student had to give an oral report in Japanese. Anyone who failed to speak Japanese was punished by being made to kneel outside the office building, even in the dead of winter. Mother learned enough Japanese to get by. She was always scared when she had to face the principal. The Chinese teachers were subjugated. Since the students' command of Japanese was minimal, the teachers were allowed to conduct their classes in Chinese, but they had to swear an oath of loyalty to Japan. It was forbidden to discuss current events, which led to the subjects of Japan's invasion of China, or Chinese heritage and sovereignty. Mother constantly feared for her life. She was a slave. Like most of the other students, she learned to cope with the situation by showing no emotion, but deep inside, she hated the Japanese.

A year later when the Japanese Army started withdrawing from the region, Mother returned home. At the end of World War II, the Japanese surrendered unconditionally and finally left China. By then, Japan had maintained control over northeast China for fourteen years. The people in Mother's mountain village were relieved. They could finally mourn their dead. Those who had fled the village returned home, but Mother's family didn't have time to rejoice. They were fighting a constant battle against poverty and hunger.

3

In 1947, the Communist Army marched into their village. Even though the Japanese invaders had withdrawn, China was not at peace. A civil war had long been raging between the Communists and the Kuomintang, the old rulers of China. Their Generalissimo, Chiang Kai-shek, had been trying to eliminate the Communists since the 1920s, but by 1947, the Kuomintang were losing ground, and the Communists were about to drive them out.

The peasants were cheering the Communists on as an army unit, officials and soldiers, marched into the village and settled among the peasants. They helped the locals establish a council and encouraged them to join or support the new government under the Communists. The head of the unit was a Mr. Wang. He was a tall and thin man in his early forties. He was always seen smoking a pipe, and the nicotine from the tobacco had stained his teeth. Wang moved into my grandparents' home, one of the poorest in the village. Many times, he helped Laoye with his fieldwork during the day, and when darkness fell, he gathered the family members around the oil lamp and told stories of the Communist Army and Mao's revolutionary ideas.

"Do you know why you are so poor?" he asked.

Mother spoke up. "It's our fate," she said. "It's predestined."

Wang puffed on his pipe. "Who told you that?" he asked.

"My mother."

Wang stood up and tapped his pipe against the sole of his shoe. Then he looked around and said:

"This is what you've been taught. But it's not true. You're poor because you're being exploited."

A murmur rose from the family. Wang gave a slight smile. "That Zhao, the landlord in your village, is exploiting you."

Zhao was a pleasant, pudgy man. It had never occurred to anyone that he was the enemy. But Mr. Wang had a point. They had all borrowed money from Zhao before, and had to pay him back with high interest. He owned the majority of the land and other properties in the village. Everyone seemed to have relied on him for support or help.

"Zhao would not be a rich man without you and the other peasants," Wang continued. "The land reform movement will take care of that."

Mother's eyes radiated excitement.

Each time Wang talked, Mother listened intently. She timidly asked questions about the lives of the young women in the "liberated areas." She was excited to learn about an organization called the "Women's Association," which taught women to read and write, and tackled issues such as domestic abuse and women's rights. In addition, the Women's Association encouraged mothers to get their sons and husbands to join the Communist Army. When Mother heard all this, she could hardly wait to join the revolution.

When her local government eventually formed a Women's Council, a branch of the Women's Association, Mother not only applied to become a member but also said she wanted to work on staff. With Wang's recommendation, she was accepted. She soon found herself enthusiastically participating in the "land reform movement." The properties of landlords, their land, their houses, their furniture, and other belongings, were confiscated and redistributed among the poor. This was not done by peaceful means. The landowners were often brutally beaten, and many were executed.

Zhao was shot to death at close range after a large rally meeting. His execution was meant to relieve the peasants' anxiety, enticing them to participate in the "land reform movement" without fear of repercussions from the old regime. Moreover, it made clear who held the power over life and death. The villagers were shocked and excited at the same time. They charged into Zhao's home, and those of the other rich families, "confiscating" their properties and belongings. When Mother joined the Women's Council, she participated as well. She and a group of the Council members focused their attention on Zhao's two wives.

The first wife was an older woman in poor health. She didn't seem to care whether she lived or died. They couldn't get her to talk. After a few beatings, they left her alone. Instead, they focused their attention on the younger wife. She was pretty and she liked to dress up. They whipped her with a belt. They wanted her to tell where she had hidden her family treasures. At one point, a woman passed the belt to Mother. Feeling the weight of the leather in her hand, Mother shivered. She had never raised a finger against anyone. Besides, she knew the young widow in front of her might as well be herself. Two years before, when she turned eighteen, Zhao had noticed Mother's beauty and wanted to marry her as his third wife. He had sent a go-between to her family. Laolao was infuriated. She gave a flat no and sent the go-between running. "Third wife?" she said to Laoye. "There is no wife here. There is only concubine!" she said, slamming her fist on the table. She turned to Mother: "Remember, we are poor, but we have dignity. I won't let you live like a slave in a rich man's house as long as I'm alive!" Laolao's firm stand put an end to the marriage proposal. Otherwise, Mother shuddered at the thought that she would be standing side by side with this woman, being beaten and humiliated.

"Go on," a woman tapped Mother on her shoulder. "Beat her. Get the truth out of her!"

Mother came back to reality, but she couldn't raise the belt.

"We are lenient to those who confess," she said loudly, reciting a policy set by the Communist Party. "Tell us, what else are you hiding?" She tried to avoid taking action.

"Confess. Tell us." Several women shouted around her.

"Please, have mercy," the young widow begged. "There is no more."

"You liar. How dare you!" More women joined in.

"What are you standing around for?" A Council member shouted at Mother. "Teach her a lesson. She is a liar. But she can't fool us!"

Mother felt she had no choice. She lifted the belt and landed it on the woman's back. Her scream made Mother tremble. To hide her weakness, Mother lifted the belt and hit her again. Then again.

The young widow gave in. She could no longer endure the pain and led the group to the backyard, where they dug out a set of silk bedding, as well as some jewelry. Mother felt sick and excused herself. The young widow's screams echoed in her head. She felt torn. Was it right to beat her? To use so much violence against the landlords? If she had become Zhao's third wife, would she have deserved such torture? The idea of revolution collided with the morals her parents had instilled in her. Earn an honest living, be kind and righteous, they had always told her. She felt she was not revolutionary enough. To avoid conflict, she volunteered to go deeper into the mountain areas to recruit council members, away from the gatherings where beatings were routine.

The impoverished situation of Mother's family quickly changed, however, thanks to the land reform. Since they were among the poorest in the village, they received a small plot of land and a two-room cottage. Having worked as a hired laborer since he was twelve, Laoye was thrilled to have a place of their own. He fully supported my mother and Wensheng, his two oldest children, who were working for the newly established government, allowing them to move to its local headquarters. It was not an easy decision. Mother, twenty at the time, was Laolao's major source of domestic help. She took care of her younger brothers, cooked for the family, and tended to Laolao when she was debilitated by her attacks. Wensheng, Mother's eighteen-year-old brother, was Laoye's right hand in the field. Their two younger brothers, ten and seven at the time, couldn't do much to help. Instead, they made themselves useful by gathering branches and grass from the mountains for cooking and heating.

Laoye's health deteriorated. When he started coughing up dark blood, he realized he was suffering from consumption. Soon, he could no longer work, and was grateful that the newly formed Village Council took over tending his land.

In the fall of 1948, six months after he learned of his illness, Laoye passed away. By then, this tall and handsome man had been reduced to eighty pounds, a mere skeleton. Mother and Wensheng returned to the village for his funeral.

Before Wensheng joined the local government, he had sworn brotherhood with eleven young men in the village. It was a tradition in the village for the men to bond and look after one another. Wensheng was the youngest among the group. When Laoye passed away, Wensheng's sworn brothers gathered together. They chipped in money to buy a wood coffin for Laoye and hired a handyman to carve flower patterns on the front of the coffin, a symbol of well-being for the dead. They observed the seven-day wake. Then, with hired trumpet blowers leading the way, Wensheng, the oldest son, along with his sworn brothers, carried the coffin to the burial ground. Everyone was supposed to wear coarse white linen, but Laolao couldn't afford it. She bought a large piece of linen and cut it into two-inch wide and three-foot long strips. Each member of the family and the pole bearers tied a strip around their foreheads, and another one around their waists.

Laolao howled.

"Poor husband. You suffered so much and died so young," she chanted between inconsolable crying. "What do you expect me to do with the children?"

Mother supported Laolao, tears running down her face. Besides mourning the loss of her father, she was worried about Laolao and her two younger brothers.

After the funeral, the chief of the Village Council approached her and Wensheng and told them the village would continue to help their family.

"You can concentrate fully on your work," the chief said. "There is nothing for you to worry about at home." His assurances, and the generous assistance her family had received, made Mother more dedicated than ever to the cause of the revolution. She worked feverishly and visited many women in the mountain areas, helping them to form a support network.

"If it weren't for the Party, our family would have starved to death," Mother used to tell us when we were children.

To her, each day was an opportunity to show her gratitude, to "add new bricks to the communist construct," as the Party line went. Her needs and those of her family became insignificant in this grand cause. The Party wanted everyone to be "utterly devoted to the cause of revolution without any thought of self." Mother took pride in doing so and readily purged any "split-second flash of selfish thought."

In 1949, less than a year after she joined the revolution, Mother was admitted into the Communist Party. This was considered a great honor. Not just anyone was allowed to join. Those who were chosen had to prove themselves first. Mother was thrilled. At the time, to protect the safety of Party members, the initiation ceremony was held in secret, and Party membership was not made public. After all, the "class struggle" between the poor and the rich was raging, and the Communists had not secured full control. They didn't want to subject their members to potential danger.

Mother joined six other young men and women in the pledging ceremony. It was a warm day in late summer. Mother received the notice, and went after work to a small room in the county's administration building. The room was lit by a large lamp. A table was standing at the front of the room. The small window was covered with a blanket. The local Party Secretary stood across the table and faced the new members.

"You are the most outstanding young men and women in our county," the Party Secretary announced. "You carry the future of China on your shoulders."

He looked each of them in the eye, as if to do a final check of their dedication. He was pleased by their solemn expressions.

"Now, raise your right hand and repeat after me," he said. Then he continued: "I volunteer to join the Communist Party of China and would like to commit myself to the following under oath."

Mother, along with the rest of the group, eagerly repeated the pledge, echoing the words of the Party Secretary:

"Make a life-long commitment to the cause of Communism,
Put the Party's interest above everything else,
Abide by the Party disciplines,
Fear no difficulties and always work for the Party,
Work as a role model for ordinary people,
Preserve the secret of the Party,
Keep faith in the Party,
Be tenacious and never betray the Party."

With the last few words still echoing in the air, the new Party members shook one another's hands, tears welling up in their eyes. They were ready to die for the revolution.

Mother had taken her pledge to heart. The charged political atmosphere of the time only fueled her enthusiasm. Only after her retirement, decades later, did Mother acknowledge regret. By single-mindedly devoting herself to Party work, she had largely missed watching her children grow up. She treated her children like a schoolmaster treats her students, without ever openly showing love and affection, as if she was afraid she'd turn us into little bourgeois, sentimental brats. Our family stood solid and stable, even later, during the most turbulent years of political storms. She was firm like a pillar, but she hardly ever showed any loving emotion. It was a considered a sign of weakness. Mother taught us by example that we should be composed and strong at all times.

Mother and Father in 1951

Chapter Three

A Semi-Arranged Marriage

1

The revolution opened a window into a new life for Mother. Her work at the Women's Council exposed her to a larger world, and she embraced the extended view with passion. She was young and pretty, and she soon found herself the center of attention among her male comrades, but she kept her distance from them. She knew Laolao wanted her to marry a local man, properly introduced by a matchmaker.

Mrs. Zhang, Director of the Women's Council, however, had other plans for her. Zhang was Mother's supervisor. Mother got nervous whenever Zhang talked about fixing her up with a husband.

At the time, most of the officials were bachelors. Some had been on the move with the army for years on end, far away from their previous families. When they finally settled in an area, they found themselves in their late twenties, thirties, or even forties, without any women in their lives. And even though there were female comrades working side by side with the men, there were not many. The army and the government were still male-dominated worlds. Most of the men, abiding by tradition, did not court women directly. That was seen as inappropriate and impetuous. The proper way was to seek the help of a go-between. These go-betweens, or "Hong Niang," were usually elderly women or the wives of high-ranking officials. Mrs. Zhang took pride in her ability to match the young men and women working at various levels of the County Government. She certainly didn't see herself as a traditional matchmaker. It used to be that the parents decided marriages, and that the newlyweds had no say in their own fate. Sometimes, they didn't even meet until their wedding. Zhang felt she was quite modern by helping young men and women establish their families. She liked Mother and often joked about introducing her to a man who would match her beauty.

One day, she called Mother to her office and showed her a list of the young men working at the County Government.

"Times have changed," Zhang said. "Women are no longer victims of arranged marriages." Then she handed her the list. She wanted Mother to set a good example and get married right away. She only needed to pick a name. Nothing more was required. Mother stood in front of Zhang, feeling paralyzed. She was afraid that when Laolao learned of this, she would fly into a tantrum. Mother was a beautiful woman, and Laolao had already been approached with two marriage proposals. One of the young men was short, and the other, with his weather-etched face, looked much older than his age. Neither of them was interesting to her. And neither was satisfactory to Laolao, who said no to both candidates. She wanted to take her time to select the best young man for her only daughter.

Glancing at the list, however, Mother's heart skipped a beat. There was one name she recognized.

But she said: "I need to discuss the issue with my mother first." She put the list on a table. Tempted as she was, she was concerned about Laolao's reaction.

"Are you going to listen to the Party or your old-fashioned mother?" Zhang asked. "Are you an independent woman or not?"

"I am."

"Then make a choice," Zhang said. "You should always listen to the Party," Zhang concluded.

Mother stared at the floor and nervously twisted her fingers as Zhang went on. She had never gone against the wishes of Laolao and was afraid to upset her, especially now, a widow caring for two small children. By the same token, she had never done anything to disobey the Party either. Her thoughts went back and forth. When Zhang eventually ceased talking, the silence in the room made Mother's duty-bound heart even heavier. She was caught in a dilemma. She wanted to explain, but words failed her. She couldn't bear the thought of upsetting Laolao. This was about her future. She couldn't possibly exclude her mother from the decision. Seeing Mother's face turn from red to pale, Zhang came around the table and put her hands on her shoulders.

"You shouldn't be so worried about your mother," she said. "If necessary, I can go talk to her."

Zhang's touch and soft voice tipped the scale. Mother sat down and took a deep breath. With Zhang's encouraging look, she timidly raised her hand and pointed a finger at the name "Hou Kai." She set her right forearm on the edge of the table to stabilize her trembling hand.

She had never talked to Kai in person, but had noticed him at several meetings, where he had given speeches. One time, on her way to such a meeting, she and a couple of female colleagues took a ride on a horse-drawn cart. As they were chatting on top of the haystack, they noticed a handsome young man approaching them on a bicycle.

"That's Kai, from the Zhiyi District," one of them murmured. The women, including Mother, stole glances at him.

Kai caught up with their cart, acknowledged them with a friendly nod and pressed on. He was going to the same meeting.

"What a handsome fellow!" one woman said as soon as Kai was beyond earshot. Her remark triggered giggles among the group.

Mother's heart pounded.

Kai's handsome face and confident manner had caught her off guard. In her short career, several young men had showed interest in her, but no one succeeded in creating a ripple in her heart. Even Mr. Wang, the official who lived at her home and first introduced her to revolutionary ideas, didn't meet her fancy. One day, Wang expressed his desire for her. Fortunately, Laolao was the first to say no. Wang was over forty, more than double Mother's age, and Laolao was shocked when Wang sent a go-between to talk to her.

"I won't allow my daughter to marry anyone who is not from here," Laolao said.

Laolao rejected the marriage proposal as diplomatically as she could. After all, Wang had done a great deal to help her family. She said she didn't want her daughter to be taken away. And that was bound to happen if Mother married an official.

"The Government could send an official anywhere, at a moment's notice," Laolao said. "I can't bear to live without my daughter nearby." Looking at the go-between, she added: "Besides, Mr. Wang is too old for her."

As soon as the go-between left, however, Laolao burst with indignation.

"What an official he is!" she said to Mother. "He is older than your father. He ought to be ashamed of himself."

She paced around the room, fuming at the thought of the amorous Mr. Wang. Ever since then, Laolao turned a cold shoulder to Wang, and he soon moved out.

Mother was relieved. Wang's small and slanted eyes always made her nervous. Wang, however, didn't stop his pursuit. More than once, he directed his bodyguard to bring Mother items such as a blanket, eggs, and clothing that only an official of his rank had access to. Mother refused to accept any of the gifts. Each time, she insisted the bodyguard take them back. At work, she did everything in her power to avoid Wang. The situation lasted for several months before Wang finally gave up.

It was different with Kai. Whenever there was a meeting, Mother was keenly aware of his presence and longed to see him, albeit at a distance. His distinct Shandong accent never failed to perk her ears up in a crowd. Mother soon learned that Kai had come to Mishan with the Communist Army and was Party Secretary of the Zhiyi District, a different division in Mishan County. He was the most handsome and eloquent young man she had ever met. Kai's image lingered in her mind.

Director Zhang wasted no time in presenting a list of women to Kai. His finger hovered over the list for only a moment, and then, without any further hesitation, he chose Gu Wenxiu, my mother. From the first time he had seen her sitting in the front row of a meeting, he was drawn to her beauty.

Two days later, when Mother was called into Zhang's office again, she was shocked to see Kai sitting in the room. Her face turned red, betraying her embarrassment. She timidly shook hands with him as Zhang made the formal introduction and then sank into a chair. She didn't dare lift her eyes. This was happening too fast. She hadn't had the chance to go home and talk with Laolao. Mother could hear the pounding of her own heart.

Kai didn't say much either. Seeing Mother so shy and embarrassed, he got up and brought her a cup of tea, trying to put her at ease. Zhang laughed and clapped her hands, once more delighted with her own matchmaking skill. She took out two forms.

"These are the official marriage applications," she said. Then, with a satisfied smile, she gave one form to Kai and the other one to Mother.

"You two make a handsome couple," she said. "You are born for each other."

Then she rubbed her hands together.

"Let's get started. Your applications will be sent to the Heilongjiang Provincial Government for approval. This will take two to four weeks. Once approved, I'll set up a wedding for you," she said.

Mother couldn't say anything with Kai sitting five feet away. All she could think about was Laolao. Once the application form was submitted, everything would be final. Out of the corner of her eye, she saw that Kai was already filling out his form. Zhang gestured to her to start. When Mother made no movement, Zhang held out a pen. Mother didn't want to offend Kai, so she took the pen and slowly started writing, beginning with her name in the first line.

The next day, she took some time off work to go see Laolao. There was no way around it; she had to tell her. The journey to Laolao's home village was seven miles, but the walk felt too short for her. Her hands trembled as she opened the door.

Surprised to see Mother in the middle of a week, Laolao asked if everything was all right.

"Yes," Mother found herself saying. "Everything is fine."

She helped Laolao do her laundry, swept the two rooms clean, and mopped the kitchen counter, but she couldn't bring herself to tell her. Late in the afternoon, still unable to break the news, Mother said goodbye and left. Five hundred yards down the road, she stopped. She pulled herself together and turned back.

Laolao was watching her through the window. She knew her daughter had something on her mind.

"So, what is it?" Laolao showed no surprise when she come through the door again.

Mother told her everything, in one big rush of words, pouring out of her mouth like water. She was afraid she would lose her courage if she paused.

Laolao's jaw dropped. She couldn't believe what her obedient daughter was telling her.

"So this is what the revolution is teaching you, eh?" she yelled. As Mother had feared, Laolao flew into a fit. In her mind, Kai was completely unacceptable as a son-in-law. For one thing, he was too old, by a whole eight years. Second, Laolao suspected Kai might already have a family somewhere else. Many of the senior officials had been in arranged marriages before they joined the army. Third, as Laolao said before, she didn't want Mother to marry any official who might take her away. But most of all, Laolao's pride and dignity had been wounded.

"The only way to get married is through a matchmaker!" she shouted. "That's the way it has always been. What's the world coming to? Now the Communists are making decisions over the head of my daughter?"

Mother explained to her that as a free thinking, modern woman, she had to obey the Party. Laolao reminded her that free thinking women obeyed only their mothers. She yelled and wept. When Mother showed her a photo of Kai, she threw a glance at it and then tossed it aside, saying it probably was taken years before. "Don't use a young face to fool me," she cried.

Laolao threatened to disown Mother if she married Kai. In the end, Mother left home in tears. A quarter of a mile away, on the mountain trail, she could still hear Laolao crying, screaming at the sky, asking why she was being punished like this.

Director Zhang was adamant in her stance and in the end, Mother remained committed to her choice. When their marriage applications were approved, Zhang organized a simple wedding ceremony, along with another couple, whose marriage was also the result of her maneuvering. Coincidently, the other bridegroom was Wang, the official who had courted Mother for months. Mother was surprised to learn Wang's bride was a year younger than herself.

Their wedding took place early one evening, after a full day of work. The District Government had allocated twenty yards of blue fabric to them, especially for the occasion. Mother had made a set of "Mao suits" out of the fabric as her wedding dress, and a pair of matching shoes, using the same fabric. It was the fashion of the time, for both men and women, to wear plain suits in the style of Chairman Mao, the founder and father of Communist China. The Sunday before Mother's wedding, Laolao's youngest sister, Mother's Laoyi, had come for a visit. She took Mother for a haircut and shed tears as she waited for her at the hairdresser's.

"You poor thing," she said. "Even a concubine would be married in more style." She didn't come to the wedding, not wanting to upset Laolao. Also, she didn't want to see how weddings were conducted under Communists. One pound of candy and two pounds of apples were the only luxuries at their ceremony.

Despite their comrades' cheers, Mother was keenly aware that Wang was staring at her coldly. At one point, the two newlywed couples were near each other, and Mother felt someone hit her hard on her back. She staggered and turned to look. She saw Wang right behind her.

"You, Wenxiu!" he hissed in her ear.

She was appalled by his behavior, but she said nothing. The incident left a shadow in Mother's heart, and she always avoided Wang until she left Mishan with Father a year later.

Mother didn't mind the simplicity of the wedding. She would have considered anything more elaborate as out of line with the Party's principles. She was disappointed; however, that no one from her family was present at the ceremony. For months, Mother avoided going home, not wanting to face Laolao's explosive anger, but she adored Kai and was happy about their shared simple life.

2

Father was soon promoted to the position of Governor of Mishan County and Mother was transferred to the County Government. She was assigned a job as a typist, a much-in-demand position, since very few people could read or write. The few years of schooling she had received served her well; however, she had never touched a typewriter before. A Chinese typewriter used metal plates to hold the characters. Each character was molded on a tiny lead block, the order dictated by its composing particles and frequency of usage. The typist had to move a handlebar to locate the exact character, snatch it up, and land it heavily on the carbon paper wrapped around a roller on the top. If a character was not on the plate, the typist would have to locate it from one of several other plates and put the tiny lead block in place. As soon as the character was typed on the paper, the typist would then take it out and put the original character back again. A large plate contained up to two thousand characters. Their small size made it very difficult to read. The typist had to memorize the layout of the plate.

Mother was overwhelmed by this ocean of words, many of which she didn't recognize. She took out a dictionary and embarked on a mission to memorize them, starting with the most frequently used ones. Before she was ready, she was given a confidential document that could only be typed by a trusted Party member. She promised to finish the task on time. When she made little progress in the first two days and the wastebasket was filled with crumpled paper, smeared with mistakes and corrections, she packed her bedding and camped out in her office. She pounded at the machine day and night for a week, typing and retyping until she got a clean page. She finally emerged from the room, looking terribly pale, but proudly waving the document in hand. However, she was suffering from severe insomnia. She was sent to a hospital and put in a dark room, listening to the sound of a waterfall to be lulled to sleep. She found no rest. In her mind, she continued to wrestle with the layout of the characters. She could not take her mind off the typewriter. She returned to work three weeks later, and the insomnia would follow her for the rest of her life. The typewriter had devoured her sleep.

In 1950, a year after their marriage, Father was transferred to the Northeast Bureau headquartered in Shenyang, capital of the Liaoning Province. To ensure they could relocate together, Mother was assigned a job in the same bureau. Shortly before their departure, they went home to bid farewell to Laolao. It was the first time for Father to meet Laolao. By then, Laolao had become reconciled to her daughter's marriage. When Father finally showed up at her door, Laolao was surprised by his good looks.

"I told you the photo was recent," Mother murmured to Laolao. Laolao smiled.

"You look like a college student, not an official who spent years in the Army," Laolao said to Father. She finally accepted her son-in-law.

As Laolao predicted, Mother moved out of the mountain area with her husband. She was assigned to work in the Organization Department, a division of the Northeast Bureau that managed all the dossiers of the government employees and was responsible for checking employees' backgrounds. Mother took her job seriously and worked with dedication and enthusiasm, ever appreciating the opportunities the Communist Party had given her.

Chapter Four

Another Family

1

It was in 1950, in Shenyang, a few months after giving birth to Yan, her first child, that Mother found out her husband had another family. He had been married to another woman previously, and on top of that he had a twelve-year old daughter named Wei. Father had never been particularly forthcoming about his past. When Laolao had warned her that he might already be married, Mother had dismissed the idea. One time, after they got married, Mother playfully asked him:

"Do you have a family in your hometown?"

But she used the word "family" in an ambiguous manner, where it could easily mean something quite innocent.

"Yes," Father said in an equally lighthearted manner.

"What does she look like?" Mother asked. She was venturing into dangerous territory, and she wasn't certain if she wanted to hear the truth.

"She looks just like you," Father said.

His answer was just as ambiguous as her half-hearted questions. Mother didn't pursue this line of questioning any further.

Then, in 1950, Father introduced her to his daughter, Wei. He had brought her back to Shenyang after visiting his hometown. Mother was shocked.

It was a rainy day in late spring. Mother returned home from work, finding her husband in the kitchen with a village girl. He was looking for something for Wei to eat.

"Who is that?" Mother asked in surprise.

Father turned to face her, but couldn't bring himself to answer her. Instead, he turned to Wei.

"This is the new mom I mentioned to you. Go ahead and call her Ma."

Wei hid behind Father and shook her head.

"Call me Ma? What are you talking about?" Mother asked, her eyes moving back and forth between Father and Wei with astonishment.

"I'll explain it to you," Father said. "But let me get Wei settled first."

Father took Wei by the hand and walked her to the second bedroom. The small room was the living quarters for Yan and her nanny. There was no space to set up another bed for Wei. Father told the nanny to keep Wei there for the moment and hurried back to Mother.

He sat Mother down at the dining table and closed the kitchen door. He told her the whole story.

2

It turned out Father had an arranged marriage in 1937, when he was sixteen. He was the youngest of four siblings in a poor peasant family in a village in Wuqiao County. It was located on the border of the Hebei and Shandong Provinces. He was the only child in the family to receive an education.

Father grew up in the midst of chaotic fighting between local bandits and warlords. When Japan invaded Northeast China in 1931, Father was only ten. He witnessed refugees pouring in from the three northeastern provinces, and saw his mother opening their door to them, providing room and board to those who were fleeing south. Father was too young to grasp what was going on, but he heard plenty of stories about the atrocities of the Japanese.

In the following years, the ruling Kuomintang tried to eliminate the Communist Army, instead of fighting the Japanese, their common enemy. In 1936, under pressure to fight the Japanese, Generalissimo Chiang formed an uneasy alliance with the Communist Army. Chiang, however, had a hidden agenda. He was hoping the Japanese would wipe out the Communists. He called his policy "first inner peace, then outward resistance." It would soon prove disastrous, with more and more territories falling into Japanese hands.

During this time, the people in Father's home village were left to fend for themselves, fighting against local bandits and warlords who looted the peasants' grain and other possessions, all in the name of resistance against Japan. Father was very lucky that Yeye, my grandfather, supported his schooling during this unsettled time. In July 1937, full-scale war against Japan broke out. The Japanese Army captured Beijing and marched south at record speed. Father was at a middle school in Dezhou, the largest town near his home village. Father and many other students felt the call of patriotism, but there was hardly any news on the Anti-Japanese War. Newspapers took days to arrive, if they arrived at all. Father and the other students relied mostly on rumors, which made them even more nervous. When the sound of explosions in the distance reached their school, indicating the approach of the Japanese troops, nobody could sleep or eat anymore. Concerned about the safety of the students, the administrators shut down the school before the arrival of the Japanese and sent all the students home. No place was safe, but anything was better than keeping hundreds of defenseless children in one place, facing the risk of being captured, or worse, slaughtered.

Father returned to his home village and helped Yeye with work in the fields. He kept in touch with his classmates, and together they explored the option of joining an army to fight the Japanese. It was during this time Yeye accepted a marriage proposal on his behalf, from a family in a nearby village, the Yins. The bride-to-be was Baolian, six years Father's senior.

Mr. Yin, Baolian's father, was a sesame oil vendor. His second son was Father's classmate. Yin had met Father before and was impressed by his good looks and dogged persistence in his studies. Yin's family came from Daliudong Village, about six miles from Yeye's home. Baolian was the only daughter among four siblings, and she was the apple of her father's eye. At the time, young women were usually married around the age of eighteen, but Mr. Yin couldn't find any man he deemed good enough for his daughter. With the looming threat of Japanese troops arriving at any moment, Yin was very worried about her safety. He asked Father's Uncle Tian, whom he had known for years, to serve as a go-between for a marriage proposal. Tian lived in the same village as Mr. Yin, and he felt the marriage was a good match. He gladly presented the proposal to Yeye. Yeye hesitated, saying that Father was still too young. Tian worked on him, telling him Baolian's father was a hardworking, honest man and it was an honor that he didn't mind that Yeye and his family were so poor. As an additional incentive, Tian offered to pay for the musicians and promised to arrange for Mr. Yin to pay a carriage that would bring the bride to Yeye's family. The father of the bridegroom normally covered these expenses.

"All you need to do is to prepare a dinner," Tian said.

It was a generous proposal. Yeye couldn't refuse. Within three days, everything was arranged and the wedding took place. However, everyone was afraid of attracting the attention of local bandits on the six-mile journey to the other village. They decided on what was called a "silent procession." The musicians followed Baolian's carriage without blowing their trumpets.

Father had never given any thought to marriage before and knew nothing about married life. Out of respect for Yeye, he accepted the situation and on his wedding day, he dutifully did as he was told. Baolian, like Father, simply obeyed her parents, as a good daughter was expected to do. She was illiterate and her bound feet were so small that she had difficulties walking steadily.

When all was said and done, Baolian and Father settled in Yeye's house and helped Nainai, my grandmother, with her weaving and cooking. The marriage, however, didn't change Father's determination to join an army.

A year later, when the Eighth Route Army, one of the major forces under the Communists' control, happened to pass by, he ran into them and immediately enlisted. He asked a fellow villager to tell his family his whereabouts. At that time, the Eighth Route Army was fighting a guerrilla war, moving swiftly from place to place, and avoiding large-scale battles against the Japanese. They had limited manpower and resources, and they needed to choose their attacks carefully.

Before taking off with the Army from the local assembly area, Father went home to bid farewell. He saw that Baolian had gone to visit her father during his absence. He borrowed a bicycle from a neighbor and rushed over to say goodbye. It was a windy day. It took Father an hour to cover the six-mile dirt road. Baolian silently shed tears when she saw him, but said nothing to prevent him from leaving. Mr. Yin, Baolian's father, begged him to stay. When Yin stepped out to fetch some dates that had been blown down from the trees by a gust of wind, he carefully locked the front gate. Concerned that the Army might depart without him, Father sneaked out a side door and left. Baolian didn't tell him she was pregnant. She didn't want him to worry about her. Or maybe she didn't know at the time.

Over the next decade, Father fought first in the Anti-Japanese War and then the Civil War between the Communist Army and the Kuomintang Army, moving from one province to another, while his family lived under the occupation of the Japanese and the regime of the Kuomintang. If word of his serving in the Communist Army had been leaked, the entire family could have been executed. To protect them, Father posed as a merchant and occasionally sent a letter home from various places to let his family know he was alive. There were a few years when even this sporadic communication with his family was cut off, and Nainai heard rumors that he was killed. She set up a hearth for her son and burned paper money for his lost soul.

When the situation permitted him to write again, Father reconnected with his family. He learned he was the father of a daughter and wrote to request Yeye and Baolian not to subject the child to foot binding. He also asked them to ensure the child would receive an education. For ten years, Baolian and their daughter Wei lived mostly with Yeye and Nainai. Baolian was quite capable of carrying out household duties. While Nainai fed the pigs and helped in the field during the day and weaved at night, Baolian cooked three meals a day and made clothes for the entire family with home-woven fabric. She was a lonely and quiet woman. When the busy harvest season was over, she would go to her father's place, where she didn't have to work so hard. She was always short tempered with her daughter Wei, the only person toward whom she could vent her frustration. Mindful of Father's request, however, Baolian urged Wei to learn how to read and write. When Wei turned eight, Yeye sent her to school, but she didn't like to study.

Most of the children in the school were boys. They used chalk and stone boards to write, but being poor, Yeye had no money to buy her the necessary school supplies. Wei was embarrassed to go to school each day empty handed. She had to borrow study tools from others to do her homework. Baolian yelled at her when Wei showed any reluctance to go to school and never hesitated to pinch Wei when she brought home bad grades.

Baolian wanted to bring up a child who would make her father proud upon his return.

Then, to everyone's surprise, Father wrote Yeye a letter in 1949, asking for permission to divorce Baolian. He stated he had no feelings for her, and the arranged marriage should be dissolved. Yeye and Nainai strongly opposed it, and, in an attempt to protect Baolian, didn't tell her of Father's request. Seeing no solution, Father had the Mishan County Government send a letter to the Wuqiao County administration to seek an annulment. Complicated marriage situations like Father's were very common among army and government officials at the time, and many of these arranged marriages ended up in divorce, creating a wave of separations immediately following the establishment of the new China. Many officials remarried without bothering to get a divorce. The country was going through a regime transition and there was no established legal system in place to settle civil matters. Ultimately, Father went ahead and married Wenxiu without having received any response from Wuqiao County.

In 1950, upon learning that Father had settled in Shenyang, Father's older brother Desheng came to see him. Yeye was seriously ill and Desheng urged Father to return to the village immediately. Father took a week off and left with Desheng. It was his first visit to his hometown since his departure at eighteen. It was also the first time he met Wei, his twelve-year-old daughter. During the few days of his visit, Wei observed her father from behind a door or hidden next to Nainai. Having never uttered the word before, she couldn't walk up to her father and call him "Ba," but she was curious and would not let him out of her sight. Baolian was still living at Yeye's house, but remained in the periphery when the impending death of Yeye took center stage. Father was cordial but distant to her. No one had told her of Father's second marriage. Desheng, the only person who had seen Mother, didn't breathe a word.

When Father eventually got Wei to talk to him, the first thing she asked for was money to buy chalk and a stone board for school. Realizing that education in the village remained rudimentary, Father sat down with Wei and offered to take her with him to Shenyang.

"I'll get you real pencils and paper there," he said. He felt responsible for her and wanted to provide the best education he could afford. Baolian encouraged her to leave with her father. Life in the countryside was very hard, and getting out of the village was her daughter's only hope for a bright future. Was she also expecting to join them later? Wei recalled years later that if she had known Father had married someone else, she would not have left with him. It was on the train, shortly before arriving in Shenyang, that Father told her she had a new mother and a baby sister. Wei was at a loss.

Mother was equally confused. Wei, her stepdaughter, was eleven years her junior.

3

Mother was furious when she heard the whole story. She cursed Father and blamed him for not telling her the truth. She stormed into her bedroom and wept. Dinnertime came and went. She didn't move. She heard Father setting up a temporary twin bed in the hallway. When he came in for bedding sheets, Mother looked out at Wei. She was small for her age, thin, and timid. Her hair was so overgrown that it hung down over her eyes and face. She was wearing a pair of baggy homemade pants and a coarse fabric shirt that made her stand out as a village girl.

When Father bid her goodnight, Wei sobbed. She had always slept with her mother or Nainai on a big Kang bed and was scared to be left alone for the night. Despite her mixed emotions, Mother pitied the poor child. The big city and the new adults in her life must be very intimidating. Mother wiped her own tears and stepped out of the bedroom.

That evening, Mother ended up settling Wei in her own bed and sending Father to sleep in the hallway. But no matter what she said to her, Wei kept quiet. She would only shake or nod her head in response to Mother's questions. She wouldn't call this new woman "Ma."

Mother kept her anger toward Father to herself. There was no privacy in the small apartment, and she didn't want to make a scene when Wei was within earshot. She settled for giving Father the cold shoulder.

The next day, Mother took Wei shopping. In addition to a school bag, a couple of pencils and a notebook, she also bought Wei a pair of pants, shoes, and a flower-patterned blouse. Once home, she gave Wei a haircut, shortening her hair to right below her ears and cutting her bangs above her eyebrows. Wei started to look like a student. Father enrolled her in the third grade of a public school. He kept her behind one grade, giving Wei time to catch up with her studies.

Gradually Wei warmed to Mother. Not long after Wei's arrival, Mother found she was pregnant with her second baby. She suffered from severe morning sickness. At that time, the government was run under the "supply-meets-demand" system, in which officials didn't receive salaries, but their family needs, including their food, clothing, the care of their children, and other living expenses, were all covered by the government. Meals were served at canteens, which were divided into "large," "medium," and "small" categories. People ate at the canteen appropriate to their rankings. Father, with his higher position, was entitled to eat in the "medium" canteen, which had better food than the "large," but not as good as the "small." Only the very top officials were entitled to have their meals at the "small" canteen. Father could bring his children there, but not his wife. Mother had her meals at the "large" canteen. Seeing that Mother couldn't eat much, Wei brought her meals home and exchanged them with Mother's. In the evenings, Wei fetched Mother a basin of warm water so she could soak her tired feet before retiring for the day, but she wouldn't address Mother directly, and when cornered, she would use the pronoun "You" to speak to Mother.

"What can I bring you?" she asked, avoiding the term "mother."

"What do you call me?" Mother snapped sometimes, only to be met by Wei's silence.

One day, Wei, having never before used running water and a sewage system, dumped tea leaves into the sink and blocked the narrow pipe. Water soon accumulated as she did the dishes. She was worried Mother would yell at her, or worse, spank her. To her surprise, Mother cleaned up the mess and explained to her how the sewage system worked and why she should throw leftovers or used tea leaves into the trash, not the sink. Wei was very touched by Mother's patience and tolerance. She promised Mother she would not make the same mistake again. After that, for the first time, Wei called her "Ma." Mother and Wei learned to accept and care for each other, but for a long time, Mother would not forgive Father.

4

In 1953, Baolian came to visit her daughter. She missed her. She didn't realize Wei's departure would mean their permanent separation. Father told her about his marriage before he left the village and requested an official divorce. Baolian cried. She had sensed it coming because Father hadn't come to her since his return for the visit. But she didn't protest, nor did she agree. "I'll think about it," she said. After Father left with Wei, Baolian moved back in with her father. She was no stranger to divorce. Her second younger brother, who left the village at about the same time as Father, but joined the Kuomintang Army, had gone through something similar. He remarried in the city and left his country wife. Baolian witnessed the entire process. When it came to her own divorce, she took it in with her usual silence and tears. She remained silent for nearly two years. Then, she decided to visit her daughter and settle the divorce. One of her younger brothers accompanied her on the trip. She didn't complain, nor did she ask for any compensation. The only request she made to Father was to be kept in his family. Her father was exceedingly ill, and it had become more difficult for her to live at his house.

Father put Baolian and her brother up in a small hotel. Baolian signed the divorce papers, but asked to be allowed to stay. Two months before her arrival, Mother had given birth to Binbin, her first son. Baolian suggested that Mother dismiss the nurse for her baby and let her take care of the child and the household chores. After all, in the old days, Chinese men used to have a wife and several concubines. Baolian was willing to stay in the background, living close to her daughter and relieving her father of the burden of providing for her.

Mother was shocked when she heard this. Her barely suppressed feelings flared up all over again. She felt responsible. Had she deliberately ignored the implications of the exchange she had with Father about his other family? Would she have made the same choice if she had known the truth? She wasn't sure. Feeling guilty, she decided to have a talk with Baolian, asking for her forgiveness. She wanted to tell Baolian that times had changed and she couldn't possibly live in the same household as an ex-wife. Mother dreaded her self-appointed mission, but knew she should no longer avoid facing reality.

There were many similar incidents at the Northeast Bureau. Abandoned wives came from the countryside and made scenes, their small children trailing behind. Baolian had been very discreet and had never made a fuss. Mother felt appreciative of her manners. The two women had never met face to face.

Mother gently pushed open the door to Baolian's room. She was relieved that her brother was not there. She stopped dead in her tracks at the startled face of an old woman. Baolian bore a timid look on her weather-etched face, and her bound feet were so small that she staggered as she stood up from the edge of the twin bed. Baolian seemed much older than her years. She looked vulnerable and out of place. Baolian managed to steady herself. Tears started running down her face. Mother was rendered speechless.

Foot binding was officially banned in 1911, when the Republic of China was established. Mother knew some young girls continued to have their feet bound, especially in the Shandong Province. Many parents were afraid they would never be able to marry off their large-footed daughters if they abandoned the tradition. Baolian was one of the girls caught in this cruel custom. Looking at Baolian's tightly wrapped feet, with large, pointed toes and arched soles, Mother's heart sank. She swallowed her words and sat down on a bare wooden chair across from Baolian. The two women looked at each other, shedding tears for their mutual misfortune and pain.

"It was the time of war and the tradition of arranged marriage that had created this," Mother eventually said. "Please don't hate me or Kai," she continued. When Baolian remained silent, Mother added: "We were all victims."

A mixed feeling of dignity and pity overwhelmed her. Mother returned home from the hotel and proposed to Father that she leave the family with the new baby, letting Baolian move in and care for the two older children and Wei. Mother said she could make a living on her own while Baolian would have to depend on someone else for survival. Father dismissed her proposal as pure madness and managed to calm her down.

Finally, Baolian returned to her village and lived with her father. After Mr. Yin passed away, her younger brother became the head of the household. He had the obligation to care for his aging mother, but not a divorced sister. He was kind to Baolian, but his wife was unhappy about the situation. Life was hard enough for them without the additional burden of providing for Baolian. Eventually, her brother sat down with her.

"You don't have a son," he reasoned. "You can't rely on your daughter to support you in your old age. The only sensible solution is to get married."

Baolian shed tears again. It was hard for her to imagine that she, once the proud daughter of a loving father, had to be married off as an abandoned woman, but without any other option, Baolian consented. In 1954, a year after her official divorce, Baolian quietly married a peasant, an older widower who had two daughters in a nearby village. She lived there the rest of her life. She died in 1987, after suffering a stroke.

When he learned of her death, Father borrowed two hundred Yuan from payroll and sent it to Wei to cover the expenses for Baolian's burial. Wei went back to her village and made all the arrangements to put her mother to rest.

Father at a Conference

Chapter Five

Banishment

1

After he left Mishan, Father's career went smoothly. For three years, he worked in the Northeast Bureau in Shenyang. In 1953, when the Bureau was dissolved, Father was transferred to the Municipal Government of Changchun and appointed Deputy Director of Light Industry. Changchun, meaning "evergreen," is the capital of the Jilin Province. It was north of Shenyang. Except for the pine trees that were planted in the metropolitan area, there was nothing green in the city.

Mother, committed to her studies, didn't move with him. To support Mother in her endeavors for a middle school diploma, Father took the three children—Yan, Ping, and Binbin, aged one to four—with him. He put them all in a boarding nursery. At the time, most of the officials' children were sent to nurseries or boarding schools, with the expenses covered by the government under the so-called "supply-meets-demand" system.

Every Sunday, the Administration Office of the Municipal Government sent a big bus to pick up my older siblings and the other neighborhood children at a designated street corner, taking them to their respective nurseries or schools. Each Saturday, the bus brought them back and dropped them off at the same spot. From there, they walked home.

Over the weekends, when Yan, Ping, and Binbin were home, Father played the role of both parents. He mended their socks, washed their hair, and occasionally walked with them to fetch food coupons in a nearby grain store, where the family's food allocation was registered. The boarding nursery, which was a great help to him, also came with its problems. It was very crowded and the living conditions were poor. All my three siblings were infested with lice. They constantly scratched their bodies and heads. Each weekend, after washing their hair, Father used a "Bizi," a comb made of fine bamboo strips, to filter through their hair, section by section, getting rid of the lice and their eggs. The tight comb pulled their hair, making the process painful and time-consuming, but it was the only effective way to get rid of the lice. As for their shirts and sweaters, Father simply threw them into the boiling water in a metal basin, eliminating the lice in one stroke.

Another issue was food. The servings at the nursery were too small, but the children couldn't ask for more, since the portions were rationed. When they returned home over the weekends, they were like hungry wolves, gulping down anything Father managed to put on the table.

In December 1954, shortly before giving birth to Wen, Mother moved to Changchun, much to Father's relief. She found it impossible to manage in two cities, especially with another child. So she transferred to a similar school in Changchun, delaying her studies for the diploma by another semester. After Yeye passed away in early 1955, and Nainai came to live with us, she went back to school. Nainai provided the help Mother and Father desperately needed at the time.

Nainai took care of Wen. When my other three siblings came home for the weekends, she watched them as well. It was not an easy task. My three older siblings were energetic and adventurous. When they were not running around the house, they were playing on a nearby college campus or at an adjacent park. Nainai couldn't keep up with them. Once, Binbin climbed on top of the wall surrounding the house. Inside the yard, the ground level was high and the wall was not very tall, but outside, the street was on a much lower level. Binbin fell head first off the wall, onto the street side. When Yan and Ping ran through the front gate and reached him, they found him lying unconscious on the sidewalk. A large bump was on his forehead, and blood was seeping from his wound. They carried him home, and dumped cold water on his head. Binbin was unconscious for ten minutes.

Another time, on her way to school, Ping and her classmate Li walked across a frozen pond. People working at a nearby medical center had been taking large chunks of ice from the pond back to the hospital, so they could keep their medical supplies properly cold. Refrigerators consumed too much energy and were rarely used. Ice cubes from the pond came in handy in the winter. Ping had seen workers break the thick layer of ice and haul the large chunks away, but she didn't give much thought to it. That morning, she slid over the ice and challenged Li to a race. Suddenly, she heard a loud pop, like a crisp explosion of popcorn at the street vendor's portable oven. She noticed the ice around her breaking away. Before she could utter a sound, the ice sank under her weight, plunging her right into the cold water. Instantly, her cotton-padded jacket and pants were soaked. The cold water felt like needles poking into her body. She yelled at Li not to come close. She kicked hard and tried to grab the ice in front of her to climb up, but the thin ice kept breaking upon her touch. Li stood on the solid layer, too scared to make a move. There was no one else in sight, but Ping didn't panic. She shouted to Li to go to school and ask for a day of absence for her. It didn't occur to her she was in any danger.

She struggled in the water toward the hardened ice. Her body shivered, and her teeth chattered convulsively, but she kept pushing forward. By the time an adult happened to pass by and noticed her, Ping had managed to pull herself out. "I'm okay," she said, declining the adult's offer of assistance. She tucked her wet schoolbag under her arm and started running toward home. Within a matter of minutes, her clothing and schoolbag turned to icicles. She called out to Nainai, pounding on the closed door. Nainai's jaw dropped when she saw Ping. She pulled her inside and quickly stripped off her stiffened clothing. She wrapped Ping in a blanket and soaked her feet in warm water. Having only one set of winter clothes, Ping stayed home for the day. Mother lived at school and only returned home on Sundays, and Father was busy with his work, coming home late each evening. They didn't have any time to get involved in their children's daily life.

Later, Yan, Ping, and Binbin each attended a different school. Weekend was the only time for them to be together. They always looked forward to it. One Sunday, Mother sent Yan to a neighborhood store to buy a bottle of soy sauce. She asked Ping to go with her. Once in the store, they heard a salesgirl telling another customer that a young man hanged himself on a tree in the park. They ran home to tell Binbin, and out of curiosity, the three rushed over to the park. They had heard stories about the "Diao Si Gui," meaning "hanging ghosts," and now they wanted to take a look at a real one. A "Gui," a "ghost" or "spirit," was scary, but fascinating. There were many ghost stories about people who died an unnatural death. For example, those who died of hunger were called the "E Si Gui," "hungry ghosts." It was said that their spirits remained on earth, searching pots and containers at night for food, making terrifying noises, but this was nothing compared to the "hanging ghosts." Death by hanging was one of the most brutal ways to die. Their ghosts lingered behind in our world, filled with rage, seeking justice or revenge. My siblings wanted to see what that looked like.

The corpse had been cut from the tree and placed on the ground. It was in full view of a gathered crowd. Everyone was stunned into silence. The only sound was the weeping of the dead man's mother and sister. My sisters and brother pushed through the crowd and found themselves right in front of a thin, gray-faced body. This was no ghost! My siblings were shocked. They simply stood there, motionless. The mother was holding her son's pale, dead face in her hands, refusing to let go.

"My son," the mother wept. "How could you do this to me? I didn't send you to college for this!" she wailed. The crowd stirred. It was very difficult to get into college. The dead man must have been brilliant. College graduates were in high demand and had a bright future. Why would he kill himself? In hushed voices, some of the adults exchanged sympathetic words.

The mother cried and cried, and her voice got coarse and low. Her daughter knelt beside her, sobbing inconsolably. After a while, an eerie silence came over them. The mother's mouth was wide open, but she was too exhausted to utter anymore sounds. Her large gaping mouth looked like a dark hole. It was all Ping could gaze at.

Ping was traumatized. As brave as she was, she never fully recovered from the shock. All three of them suffered from nightmares for weeks to come. They were too scared to ever go back to the park again, but the impact on Ping was most severe. She was always afraid to be alone in a room, and she developed the habit of looking over her shoulders, as if someone was always standing behind her. Even as an adult, she couldn't vacuum a room without turning sideways, so that she could see the entire room. For the rest of her life, the dead man and his mother would always be with her.

2

In 1956, Father was sent to the Central Communist Party Institute in Beijing to study for a year. When the Anti-Rightist Movement started in 1957, his stay in Beijing was extended for another six months. By the time he returned home, a year and a half later, Mother had entered college, and each of his children was much taller than when he last saw them.

The Anti-Rightist Movement was a political campaign started by Chairman Mao to persecute right-wing elements, especially intellectuals and non-communist members who dared to criticize the Communist Party and the government. At first, Mao invited all citizens to point out any flaws or failures within the Party. He said: "Let a hundred flowers blossom and a hundred schools of thoughts contend," encouraging people to speak up; but when they did speak up, and the criticism became too severe for his liking, Mao saw it as an attack against the Party. He struck back, calling his early strategy a measure to "lure the snakes out of their caves." Those who had made comments about the Party were now labeled rightists. They were criticized, stripped of their positions, and exiled to the countryside for reeducation by hard labor. Over a period of two years, more than half a million people were labeled rightists. It was not uncommon to hear of people committing suicide or see entire families ruined. Twenty years later, the government admitted that these persecutions had been excessive and rectified their cases. Only six remained as rightists; but for many, the "rehabilitation" came too late.

The movement surged with new vigor in 1959. There was increasing tension to finger rightists. The government even implemented a quota. Some people participated enthusiastically, anxious to prove their loyalty, while others accused their colleagues behind their backs. Meetings were held to produce the necessary number of rightists. It was said that if someone went to the bathroom during one of those meetings, he might well return to find himself labeled. Father had witnessed many officials in the City Government purged and sent to the countryside for reeducation, without any justification. He was concerned about his own future. He knew of a deputy mayor who had been trying to get him. The mayor's wife worked with Father in the same department, and their disagreements over a number of issues had created an undercurrent of tension between them. Father was afraid she would use her husband's power to crack down on him. Father was new in the City Government, and he knew that he was more vulnerable than the local officials who had deeper roots and stronger political alliances.

An accident that happened at a power plant set the stage for his fall. The plant was under the Light Industry's jurisdiction. A newly built electricity tower had collapsed in a storm and a broken piece of metal pierced the belly of a worker, killing him instantly. The engineer who designed the project was immediately criticized and conveniently accused as a rightist. During the investigation of the accident, Father reportedly made the remark that the Anti-Rightist Movement was wrong if an accident would so quickly render a professional a rightist. Such a statement was enough to convict him. It was immediately reported to the City Government. The case was taken very seriously. Father explained the situation to the authorities, proclaiming his innocence, but his voice was buried under waves of accusation. A special committee of the City Government requested he conduct in-depth self-criticism and attend denunciation meetings. He felt wrongly accused, but he obeyed orders.

Facing the potential end of his political career, and, worse, the danger of being persecuted as a rightist, Father asked for a job transfer. He volunteered to leave his position, to manage one of the state enterprises in Changchun. Such a move, he figured, would satisfy the authorities and allow him to remain in Changchun where his family had finally become settled. However, the Jilin Provincial Government decided to send him to Baicheng, a poor and remote region in the far west corner of the Province. He was to stay in the government, serving as Director of the Light Industry in Baicheng. It was an unofficial demotion, or rather, banishment, but Father took the job without complaint. Having been a soldier, he had long learned to follow the Party's directive without hesitation.

In the spring of 1961, Father took the train and left for Baicheng by himself. He bought a ticket for a soft berth. When he got to the train station, he found it was so crowded that he couldn't even get on to his car. Passengers, mostly peasants, carrying large and small parcels, filled the seats and jammed the passageway. Father barely made his way on board before the train blew its loud whistle, and with a heavy click, started moving. He was stuck in the passageway for three hours. Even the toilet was packed with people. Using the facility created a chain reaction and required considerable effort. Father was not able to secure a seat until he changed to another train heading for Baicheng at a connection station. He had no idea that public transportation was so horrific. As a government official, he felt disconnected with the daily life of ordinary people. He felt responsible. For the rest of the trip, he stayed in the hard berth car. The steam engine puffed and choked, making many stops along the way. It took him nine hours to reach Baicheng. By the time he stepped onto the platform at the Baicheng station, it was nearly midnight.

The train station at Baicheng was a small, two-story building. It was already locked up for the night. Father followed the crowd and walked to the street by the side of the building. Five or six dim lamps lit up the station and the area before the building. Beyond that, all Father saw was darkness. Father hadn't notified anyone at the Baicheng Prefecture about his arrival. He didn't want to create a scene of welcome and didn't want to bother anyone so late at night, but he didn't expect Baicheng to be a large village. There was no public transportation. Father stopped a passer-by and asked for directions to the Baicheng Government Compound. He threw his small duffel bag over his shoulder and started walking.

All the passengers from the train soon vanished into the night. He was grateful there was no cloud in the sky. He was the lone traveler on the dirt road. It was eerily quiet. All he heard was the crunching of dirt under his feet. With the moonlight as his guide, he followed the road. He saw that the buildings on either side of the streets were low, one-story structures, all in the same color of mud gray. There were only three or four street signs at main intersections. Eventually he arrived at the Baicheng Government Compound.

The metal gates were shut and locked. Father walked to a side plank door and tried to open it. It didn't move, so he pounded on it. Five minutes later, a man's sleepy voice responded. The gatekeeper was in his fifties. He pushed the door ajar and poked his head out. He was not happy to be awakened in the middle of the night.

Father introduced himself. There was a guesthouse for visiting government officials in the Compound and he was supposed to stay there until the rest of the family could join him. The gatekeeper eyed him with suspicion. New Director of the Light

Industry? Walked alone in the dark all the way from the train station? He had never seen any official do that.

"Nobody told me to expect an official tonight," he said.

He wouldn't let Father go to the guesthouse.

Father didn't argue. It was one o'clock in the morning. He was exhausted.

The gatekeeper told him to wait in the reception area if he wanted to. There was a long bench there for visitors. Father accepted the offer. He put his duffel bag at one end of the bench and used it as a pillow. His stay in Baicheng would be difficult.

Chapter Six

Country Boy

1

Father came from a poor peasant family in the Shandong Province, the youngest of four siblings. For years, Yeye worked the field as a hired laborer, while Nainai spent long hours at home, spinning and weaving clothes. Through hard work and frugality, they eventually managed to gather enough money to purchase two acres of land. Father's oldest brother, Desheng, started working with Yeye in the field. Desheng, twelve years older than Father, was thin, and his large eyes seemed to sink in their sockets. He and Yeye shared the burden of supporting the family. Father's two older sisters helped in ways that they could. They joined Nainai in her weaving, a major financial resource for the family. No one could read and write. Tired of begging others for help when it came to dealing with paper work, Yeye sent Father to a village teacher. He was eight years old. Father was fascinated and studied hard. A few years later, when Desheng and Father paid a visit to their Uncle Tian during the Chinese New Year holiday, Father's ability to write and calculate impressed his relatives. One of Tian's sons was a school teacher. He recognized Father's talent.

"You are doing well," his cousin said. "Why don't you attend my school after the holiday?"

He told Father and Desheng that there was no charge for tuition and room, and students were responsible only for their own food, which was measured in bags of grain.

Desheng, who never had the chance to study, wanted his young brother to get an education. When they returned home,

Desheng talked with Yeye at length, and eventually persuaded him to let Father attend school.

After the New Year holidays, his cousin stopped by with a donkey and took Father, his bedding and a bag of grain to school. Father had traveled on this road numerous times before, but he had never before felt so excited. He chatted along the way, asking endless questions about the students and the teachers at school.

Father did well in his tests on arithmetic, reading and writing, and was placed into the fourth grade. He studied hard and made friends with a group of older students. He soon found himself involved in their effort to oust the school principal. He didn't know that at the time there was a struggle going on between the local teachers and an outsider principal who had been sent by the Education Bureau. The experience gave him the first taste of victory. People can make a difference if they stand together, for better or worse.

Two years later, Father and a group of others went to Dezhou, the largest neighboring town. There was a two-year normal school that provided free education for future teachers. But more than a thousand applicants showed up for the one hundred openings. They weren't even able to reach the door to submit their applications. The other alternative was the regular middle school. It charged a hefty fee of thirty silver yuan for tuition, but there were plenty of applicants as well. Again, more than one thousand students competed for a total of one hundred and thirty admissions.

Yeye was not supportive of Father's pursuit of further education, but he didn't stop him from taking the tests. As Father made his utmost effort at the examinations, Yeye prayed at home for his failure. When the test results were posted at the school a month later, Father was thrilled to see his name on the list, but his excitement didn't last long. He was concerned about the tuition. He took his time on the long journey home, pedaling slowly on his borrowed bicycle. He struggled hard between his desire to study and his duty as a son to help support the family.

Halfway home, he ran into Chen, his older sister's husband. Chen was a chubby man. He always looked serious, but he was kind. He ran a small business in the village, selling daily necessities from food seasoning to sewing materials. Chen was the wealthiest person among Father's relatives. He was delighted to hear about Father's success and patted him on his shoulder. "You brought honor to our family," he said.

Father did not respond.

"I'm not sure if I should go," he said slowly. "It's very expensive."

Chen paused in the middle of the road and was silent for a moment.

"Why don't you come with me to my house?" he finally said.

Father followed him. Once inside his house, Chen went straight to a cabinet and took out ten silver yuan out of a box that was hidden behind a pile of clothes.

"Take this. It will help put you to school," he said, wrapping the money in a piece of white cloth.

Father bowed to him, carefully placing the package into his pocket. As soon as he turned the corner from Chen's house, he jumped on his bicycle and pedaled as hard as he could, his heart pounding with excitement. He stopped a block away from home, giving himself a few minutes to catch his breath and wipe off his sweat.

He avoided Yeye's anxious gaze as he stepped into the house and quietly placed the bundle of silver yuan on the table. The money was still warm with his body heat.

Then, in a subdued voice, he told his father about the test results and his encounter with his brother-in-law Chen. Yeye listened, his eyebrows furrowed into a deep knot. Father followed Yeye with his eyes. Each move, each gesture would determine his future. When he finished speaking, Yeye gave out a sigh and squatted down at the door. He stayed there for a long time, his head lowered, and his eyes cast on the ground. Father held his breath. He felt guilty for putting Yeye in this awkward situation. But Father had a thirst for knowledge. He knew he had to go to school. Now that the results had been made public, it would be a disgrace to the family if Yeye didn't allow his youngest son to attend school. There were several hundred households in the entire village, but only a dozen or so young men attended school. It was an honor to be accepted into a middle school. It meant the person had talent. And Yeye was as proud as he was poor. Eventually, he stood up. Looking at Father, he gave only the slightest nod, but it was as if a large stone had fallen off Father's heart. Yeye gathered all his family savings together and told Father he was willing to borrow the rest from his relatives, to send him to school.

Father went to the middle school, elated. He was determined to study hard and excel, making his father proud. He wanted to be a teacher or find a career that would help support the family. Nearly all the students at school came from wealthier families. Father's coarse clothing revealed his poor family background. When he visited his classmates at their homes, their parents often greeted him with remarks such as "Are you also in school?" or "Your father let you do this?" Sometimes, they sounded genuinely surprised, and other times, there was an undercurrent of contempt. Father took it all in. Out of courtesy, he either changed the subject or pretended that he didn't quite understand, giving a response that was a little off the track:

"Yes, I like school," or "I'm doing well in school."

Yet deep in his heart, these remarks were a reminder that he had to become an outstanding student. That he must bring honor to his family. Against all odds, he achieved his goals. He was the only boy from his village who had become a high-ranking official. Later, he would help many of the other villagers.

But in 1937, the Japanese invasion put an end to Father's studies. He was forced to return to his village.

It was during this time that he entered the arranged marriage.

Not long after that, he left with the Eighth Route Army.

2

During the early years of the Anti-Japanese War, Father changed from a patriotic young student to a devoted Communist. When he was in school, he read numerous newspaper articles about the "Ri Ben Gui Zi," meaning "Japanese Devils," massacring civilians. In one incident, the Japanese Devils marched into a village and killed the entire population of more than 1,200 people. In another, they used Chinese peasants as guinea pigs to do chemical tests. Photos of their disfigured bodies and infected skins were unbearable to look at. The worst atrocity happened during the "Nanjing Massacre," after the fall of the city in December 1937. Within a matter of days, a quarter of a million people were killed, including women and children. The brutality of the Japanese shocked him and filled his heart with hatred for the invaders. Once he joined the army, Father became a dedicated soldier. The blood that was shed by his comrades on the battlefields made him more determined to defend his country.

Most of the people in the army were illiterate. Sometimes even commanders needed others to read orders to them. Having received a few years of schooling, Father rose quickly through the ranks, and soon joined the Communist Party. He moved from unit to unit, and by the end of his second year, he was running an operation in the Special Intelligence Unit; but then, something happened that changed him forever.

The year was 1940. Father's intelligence unit was operating in the Japanese-occupied territory in the Shandong Province, gathering information from the enemy camp. The Communist Headquarters had just won over Mr. Feng to their side, a Kuomintang officer in the Security Bureau, a local police station. It was a clear spring day; Father and Feng went to the market, mingling in the crowded streets. Father's mission was to hand Feng safely to another secret agent who would escort him back to his Kuomintang base, to work undercover for the Communists. Father and Feng reached the place where they were supposed to meet their contact. Neither of the men spoke. Each of them was wearing a black hat and a pair of brown gloves. Both items were signals. A tall man, dressed as a market vendor in a blue coat, recognized them. Father left Feng with him, and didn't say a word. A few days later, news reached the Communist Headquarters that the Japanese had arrested Feng. Father immediately took up the task to investigate the case. He arranged to meet the agent in the blue coat, whom he had last entrusted Feng to. He chose a remote cemetery for an evening meeting. After dark, the man in the blue coat finally came. He looked nervous. He had put on a pair of glasses to hide his face. He brought a young man with him, no more than a teenager. Father was surprised to see another person. Contact in the underground network was restricted to a one-on-one basis. It was to protect the people involved as well as preserve the structure of the network.

"He is my messenger," the man in the blue coat introduced the young man. "The road from town was too dangerous to travel alone," he added, sensing Father's alarm.

Father nodded. He led them to a secluded area in the cemetery. The dirt mounds of graves were scattered around them. Those that were neglected by the living had grass and weeds sprouting from their piles of earth. The others, those that were tended to, had offerings in the front. Their dirt mounds were kept clean of plants. The air in the cemetery smelled of decay, and the wooden plaques serving as tombstones shook with the wind, making creepy noises. A pile of fresh dirt indicated a new burial, not far from their meeting spot, and they saw the ashes of burned paper money scattering around. A plate of steamed buns was placed at the foot of the wooden name plaque. Paper money and food were supposed to protect the dead from poverty and hunger in the next world. Father looked over the surrounding, making a mental note for a possible retreat in case of trouble. Aside from the Japanese patrols and the Kuomintang soldiers, there were also bandits lurking in the countryside, robbing and killing people.

"Give me a full report of what you know about Feng's case," Father said. He intended to finish the questioning quickly. It was a violation of safety rules to bring a third person to a meeting, and Father was suspicious.

"I escorted Feng to his base as required," the man in the blue coat said, clearing his throat. "I finished my mission," he continued after a pause. "What happened afterwards was beyond my control."

He told Father the local police chief at the station didn't trust Feng, and his visit home in the countryside made him more suspicious. "It must be Feng's own fear and lack of experience that gave him away," the man in the blue coat told Father.

Feng was a middle-aged man and struck Father as reliable and sophisticated. He had provided information to the Communist network before. He was patriotic, and he hated the Japanese. Father couldn't believe he would blow his cover.

"Feng is a key contact. Headquarters is planning to have him rescued," Father said.

Before the meeting, Father had met with Li, Director of his unit. Li revealed in no uncertain terms that they should come up with a plan to find out where Feng was kept and attempt to get him out. There were two prisons in the surrounding areas. The one run by the Kuomintang police was not well guarded. The other one, guarded by the Japanese, was more difficult to deal with. Both prisons held many civilians, captured Communists, as well as common criminals.

As Father made more inquiries, the agent in the blue coat grew agitated. "When did you learn of Feng's capture? What did you know about Feng's circumstances? Who else is involved?" Father bombarded him with questions.

The agent started to stammer, and Father became more suspicious, but before he could take any action, the tall agent gestured to his companion. All of a sudden, they leapt onto Father. One of them attacked him from behind, grabbing his waist and arms, and the other came from the front and went for his legs. Father realized they were turncoats. He kicked the young man in the face, knocking him backward, but the man in the blue coat held him tight. Father fell. They wrestled on the ground. They tumbled next to a grave, and Father grabbed the wooden name plaque and smashed it on the agent's head. The eroded wood crushed into pieces. The agent gave out a cry, more out of frustration than pain. As his young companion regained his balance and came to his assistance, the agent picked up a rock and bashed it against Father's head. Stars danced in front of him. He passed out.

When Father regained his consciousness, it was in the middle of the night. He realized the two traitors had dragged him behind the fresh grave. His hands and feet were tied, and his mouth was gagged with a piece of cloth. He couldn't move or make a sound. Throughout the night, the two traitors took turns watching him. As soon as daylight broke on the horizon, they brought him to the local police station, where he was interrogated.

Father refused to answer any questions. They beat him. In the afternoon, the local police turned him over to the Japanese.

The Japanese tortured him. His clothes were stripped away and his body was covered with bruises and lacerations. Every time he passed out, they poured cold water over him, to bring him back to consciousness. The two turncoats were also present. Father heard them talk with the Japanese via an interpreter. He realized they didn't know his exact position in the underground network, and so he decided to play dumb. He insisted he was just a messenger and didn't know anything. The Japanese pointed to the sign above the door that said: "Xian Bing Dui," the Military Police Station, and demanded he confess and cooperate. Father pretended he was illiterate and dim-witted. Frustrated, they beat and interrogated him off and on for three days and nights. His nose was broken, his face and eyes were covered with so many bruises and cuts that his head was a bloody mess. Even his front teeth were loose from the beatings.

But he didn't break.

On the third day, enraged, one of the Japanese knocked him out with a heavy blow on the side of his head, leaving him permanently deaf in his left ear. They dragged his body to a prison cell. Father wasn't alone. He saw other unfortunate souls in there, as ragged as he was. Over the following few days, his entire body was burning with a fever. He relied on his fellow prisoners for survival. They helped him to a thin porridge made of red sorghum husk, littered with sand. The only source of salt was a few pieces of pickled turnip. Food was so scarce that everyone was suffering from constipation.

Along with the excruciating physical pain came the mental suffering. He saw with his own eyes the darkness that came when a nation lost its sovereignty and liberty. He could see the grim future ahead. Right then and there, something in him changed. He became resigned to his own death. At that moment, he lost all fear. It was replaced with something else, something darker. He hated the Japanese with all his heart. He was prepared to die for the freedom and independence of China.

When further interrogation didn't bring the desired results, the Japanese decided to keep him in jail indefinitely. One day, during a brief period when the prisoners were let out for fresh air, Father saw Feng. His forehead was covered with a large scar, and he was limping. The man had apparently been tortured. They nodded to each other, and as their path crossed, Feng whispered to Father that he didn't reveal anything. But someone among the prisoners saw the incident and reported it to the Japanese immediately. Father and Feng were both interrogated and beaten again. It infuriated him to realize there were collaborators even among the prisoners.

The prison smelled of blood and mold. The thin blanket he picked up in the cell was stained with blood and infested with lice. The screams and howls from other prisoners, especially a few women down the hall, scraped every nerve in his body. Hunger was constant. The wounds from the beatings hurt him with every move, making it a daunting task to lift his arms and legs. Father watched silently as dead prisoners were pulled away. He resigned himself to death. In some way, he even welcomed it. All that he had left was to die on his feet, to not give in.

His hunger, pain, and rage kept him awake. He was deprived of sleep and suffering from exhaustion. Then, a fellow prisoner gave him the butt of a cigarette. Yeye had always been opposed to smoking, saying it was no different than burning money. Father never smoked in his life. To his surprise, after the initial cough that nearly choked him, he felt a sense of relaxation. He took another drag and inhaled. When the cigarette butt was gone, Father was able to fall asleep. He became a heavy smoker the rest of his life. When I was a child, I used to see Father crush tobacco leaves with his hands and moisten them with liquor. With a large family to support, he couldn't afford to buy packaged cigarettes. He made his own. He bought bundles of tobacco leaves that cost little, stuffed the crushed leaves into a small rectangular bag, and carried it with him all the time, along with a small deck of paper. Whenever he had a chance, he would take out his gear and roll himself a cigarette, sealed with his tongue.

During the Cultural Revolution when he was kept awake at night to write self-denunciation, his cigarettes again functioned as his sole companion and comfort. Even when he suffered from tuberculosis in the early 1970s, at a time when he was banished to work in a coal mine, no doctor or family member could persuade him to stop smoking. To show his defiance, Father would light a cigarette with the burning butt of another.

In 1940, when he was on the verge of collapsing from lack of sleep, smoking calmed his nerves and helped him maintain his sanity. Sometimes he even traded his meager portion of food for a few cigarettes.

Father kept track of time in the prison by counting the grains that had been stuck to a broom. Each day, he put one piece of grain into his pocket. After a while, he would empty the grains into his palm and count them. When all the grains from the broom were gone, Father lost track of time. Days eluded him. Time became meaningless. If he was to survive, he swore he would fight the Japanese to the end of his life. He was nineteen.

At that time, Japan not only invaded China, but also spread its armies to several other countries in Southeast Asia. They couldn't keep up with the supplies and maintenance to their troops. In the fall of 1940, the Japanese army in Shandong announced they would draft a thousand Chinese to provide transportation and maintain horse stables for their troops in the south. They had a tough time enlisting enough young men. Those whose families had money bought their way out. Short of hands, they used prisoners. Father was one of them.

He and his group were sent to Shanghai. Only after his arrival in the outskirts of Shanghai did Father realize it was already November and he had spent six months in prison. The fresh air was chilly and energizing. He had never been so aware of the open air he breathed. It felt like a miracle, an affirmation of life amidst all his despair.

Father worked in a stable. He could see Japanese guards standing on raised platforms. They carried machine guns and took shifts watching everyone's moves. Winter in Shanghai was damp and cold. His thin layer of clothing and blanket were not enough to keep him warm. He soon fell ill. When he became too weak to stack the hay and move the water buckets in the stable, he was sent to a camp for the old and sick, a place where people waited for their deaths.

Around this time, US forces were launching air raids on Shanghai, and the Japanese armies were struggling to maintain control on the ground. With more pressing situations to handle, the Japanese decided to dismiss the people in the camp, who were of no use to them. They issued each of them a travel pass, a bamboo tube for water, and a pair of worn-out Japanese shoes, and then they put them on a train heading north. It was bitterly cold. Father kept himself from freezing by lying between two men who had thicker blankets. He saw dead bodies taken off the train each time it pulled into a station. By the time the train reached Shandong, he could hardly walk on his own. He was starving, and his body was covered with open sores.

He had to beg for food and slept on hay stacks, or under the eaves of villagers' houses. He counted the steps he managed to cover, taking a break when he made it to fifty. By the time he reached the village where his comrades were stationed, no one recognized him. Fortunately, his director Li was still there. Li and his comrades cautiously welcomed him. When he had a chance to look at himself in the mirror, he didn't recognize that dark, scar-faced person. His long hair was in disarray. He realized his nose had settled back twisted and his once evenly-lined teeth now looked like saw-teeth. For the rest of his life, these wounds would serve as a reminder of his sufferings at the hands of foreign invaders, and reinforce his commitment to the revolutionary cause.

Li put him with a local family, who were trusted supporters of the Communist Army, to heal and recover. He managed to get a large piece of pork and chicken to help nourish him. His comrades each donated some money from their meager allowance to assist him to obtain living necessities. Father was touched and felt right at home. He bought extra food, and of course, a carton of the least expensive cigarettes. He shared them with his comrades. Meanwhile, Li used the Communist underground network to check on Father's whereabouts and to find out what he had done and said during his capture. Father learned that Li's unit had tracked down the two turncoats who had betrayed him and Feng. Li had them executed. Father's capture by the Japanese resulted in the suspension of his Communist Party membership. It took Li and his group several months to clear his records and restore his membership. Father waited patiently. Nothing could change his devotion now.

When he resumed his position in the Communist Army, Father moved with his unit all the way to the Heilongjiang Province in northeastern China. After the surrender of the Japanese at the end of World War II, the fight between the Kuomintang and the Communist became a full-scale civil war. Chiang Kai-shek's Army eventually lost ground, and the Communist Army took control over large rural areas and established local government in these newly taken territories. Since local governments at all levels urgently needed capable officials to fill in leadership positions, Father volunteered to leave the army and join the local Mishan County Government. It was in Mishan that he met Mother.

Family in 1958

Chapter Seven

The Government Compound

1

The northeast of China was well known for its dark, fertile soil and the abundance of produce such as soybean, corn, and red sorghum. Somehow, that richness managed to escape this deserted corner. In and around Baicheng, it was common to see large pieces of land filled with gravel, or rendered infertile by alkaline and salt. In early spring or late fall—when the fields were not blooming with corn, red sorghum, or millet—one could see large patches of soil covered with a white, frost-like crust. Drainage in these areas was very poor. Puddles of water were everywhere, making it impossible for crops to grow.

A year after Father's departure for Baicheng, Mother and the rest of us joined him in this small town. The government arranged for Mother to work at the Normal College of Baicheng. We moved from our comfortable two-story house in Changchun to a barely furnished four-room apartment in the Government Compound of the Baicheng Prefecture. In the living area on one side of the Compound was a row of four single-story, red brick apartment buildings. The space between each building had been turned into gardens where the families grew vegetables. Standing apart from this area was a simply constructed low brick building. It looked as if it had been added as an afterthought. It contained four apartments. Clustered together in each of these apartments were four small rooms—a kitchen and three bedrooms. There was no bathroom or hallway. That was where our family settled. Father seemed to have gotten used to Baicheng, which looked like a large village rather than a town, but Mother was shocked, and my older siblings were not prepared to face the shabby living conditions, especially the lack of a toilet. They had never used an outhouse before.

But my parents, both coming from poor families, didn't complain, nor did they allow their children to grumble. We learned how to heat water on the stove and wash ourselves in the kitchen behind the door. After all, my parents had committed their lives to the revolution. In the years to come, no matter what the circumstances, their devotion to the Party would never waiver. Father worked with the same enthusiasm, and Mother plunged herself whole-heartedly into her new teaching job.

My sisters and brother, aged seven to eleven, all attended the same elementary school. Their old friends, their old lives, were gone forever. But if they felt any regret about the move, they kept it to themselves. I was too young to have any regrets. Every day, I crawled around Nainai and slept by her side, safe and comfortable under her care.

The well-protected Government Compound covered an area of a hundred acres and was separated from the outside by a six-foot brick wall in the front, and eight-foot mud walls on the other three sides. Barbed wire was set on top of the walls. I took my baby steps in the Compound, and eventually I began running around.

All the office buildings and the top officials' families were located in the Compound. A team of civilians took turns guarding the large front gate day and night. Once the Communist Party was in power, they built tall walls to separate themselves from the ordinary people they had sworn to serve. The higher the rank, the more exclusive and better protected the government offices and officials were, exemplified by Chairman Mao who had his office and living quarters set in the former palaces of Emperors.

Father was one of the top officials in Baicheng. Although he was assigned as head of the Light Industry, his high ranking put him at the same level as a deputy governor. The Compound was home to fourteen families. Though not luxurious by today's standards or what we had enjoyed in Changchun, we all had running water, radiators, and a telephone, all rare items in a private home. The city outside the walls was an expanse of low mud buildings, or single-story red brick apartments, a world completely foreign to me. While my older siblings made friends with their classmates and occasionally visited them outside the Compound, I didn't see the conditions they lived in until I was old enough to attend school. A typical residence was a two-room apartment, with low ceilings, hard dirt floors, and a Kang bed, shared by the entire family. In the northeast of China, the Kang—made of adobe blocks and lined with zigzag grooves below the surface—was the bed for the entire family, sometimes three generations. It was constructed from wall to wall, and connected to a large stove in the next room. Packed in this room, a multifunction space that served as kitchen and storage, were a big earthen jar for water, a pile of wood or coal, and some grains and vegetables. And of course, the large adobe stove. All of the family meals, whether soup, a stir-fried dish, or a bowl of rice, were cooked in a deep pan, which was permanently mounted on the stove. A hand-operated bellows blew wind under the pan and kept the fire burning. In the winter, smoke from cooking heated the Kang and warmed the room. One had to be careful—too much heat could burn the bedding. Homemade quilts served as cushions against the hard surface. In the summer, all the bedding was removed so the heat could dissipate, and the quilts were replaced with bamboo mats to keep cool. The entire family ate their meals sitting lotus-style at a removable low table on it.

As a toddler, I ran within the secluded walls of the Compound as if it were a playground. The most important structures were two office buildings, each three stories tall. Father had an office on the second floor of a brick building painted white, which we called the White Building. The other building still had its original red brick color. We called it Red Building. Other structures in the Compound included a two-story guesthouse for visiting government officials, as well as two canteens. To save money, most of the employees ate at home, but all the officials' families, including us, ate at one of the canteens. Most of Father's salary was spent on our meals. Our supply of food was strictly limited by rationed coupons, but the canteen sometimes managed to obtain extra supplies of grains. Occasionally, fish and meat from the countryside were served, but that required additional money. We grew our own vegetables and even raised a dozen or so chickens for their eggs.

There was a fenced daycare center behind the White Building. In the courtyard were sandboxes, a wooden slide, and a swing. Many employees sent their children there, from newborn babies to six-year-olds. I often watched them through the fences and wondered what it would be like to have so many friends, but I was happy to be with Nainai.

Cherry trees, lilacs, and low bushes separated our living area from the office buildings, with two dozen or so of large poplar, elm, and willow trees lining the dirt walking trails. Next to this wooded area stood the furnace room, with a tall chimney that towered above all else. Its height fascinated me, making me wonder what it would be like to view the world from far above. The large furnace provided heat for the radiators in every office and residential apartment. In the winter, the temperature could drop to 30 degrees below zero.

The Wan Building next to the trees on the office side was my favorite with a curved roof of arched gray tiles, and a courtyard filled with a variety of trees. From a distance, the steeply curved roof and its straight lines of tiles looked like plowed rows in a field. Up close, the first round tile of each row revealed a monstrous face—the guardian of the buildings. But such craftsmanship was becoming a lost art. It was seen as a feudal idea, the superstitions of the old society. Superstition had no place in the new China. The children of the Compound spent many hours at the Wan Building. We kicked shuttlecocks, played jump rope, and hide-and-seek games in the courtyard. We picked dates and cherries before the fruits were ripe and climbed the lower section of the buildings to reach swallows' nests. In the middle of the entrance hall stood a ping-pong table. I hit my first ball on that table and played there many times afterwards.

When I was young, it never occurred to me to ask how the Wan Building had gotten its name and why nobody talked about it. For many years, the Security Bureau used the Wan Building as its offices. Only when I was well into my adulthood did I find a record of its history. The Wan Building was the residential house of a warlord named Wan Fulin, the wealthiest person in the area. It was built in 1926. Originally, the whole complex consisted of eighty-five rooms. In 1949, Wan fled to Taiwan with his family, along with what was left of the Kuomintang Army and the government officials. He died there two years later. Wan was condemned as an enemy. No additional information about him or his family was given. Now the building has been remodeled and preserved as an historical site. A large metal plate mounted on a platform in the middle of a room states that Wan Fulin was a local heroic general who fought against the Japanese.

A prominent feature of the Government Compound was the barbed wire on top of the surrounding walls. Over the years, the wire rusted away or was torn. Broken glass was attached to the top of the wall, or, in some cases, black tar that would stick onto a climber's clothes or skin. Mostly children from the surrounding neighborhood climbed over the walls to explore the secluded compound. The civilian guards kept an eye on them and always chased them out quickly. Mr. Fan, a man in his early sixties, was the most aggressive guard. He yelled at these children and threatened to beat them with a club. Sometimes, the children living in the Compound climbed over the walls as well, to take a short cut on their way to school.

Since there was no toilet in our apartment, we had to use an outhouse next to the Compound wall, half a block from our door. It was nothing more than a big pit covered with pieces of nailed wooden boards and surrounded with four brick walls and a triangular roof. From time to time, I ventured there with Nainai, but didn't dare step on the board. I was afraid I might fall through the hole. When winter came, even Nainai would not risk going there with her bound feet. We used a potty inside and threw the waste to the thick pile of snow accumulated in the vegetable garden behind our apartment. My sisters and brother used the toilets in the White Building on their way in and out of the Compound. Other times, they went to the pit toilet without any fuss. It was no worse than the ones they had to use at school.

2

Later, with Father's promotion—first to Mayor of Baicheng, and then Deputy Governor of the Baicheng Prefecture—our family moved to one of the regular apartment buildings. We had more and larger bedrooms, and most importantly, an indoor toilet. There was also a small separate room, which had a built-in bathtub, but there was no hot water. As soon as we settled down in our new home, we tended the large garden behind our apartment. We grew corn, tomatoes, cucumbers, eggplants, green beans, peppers, and green onions. There was never room for any flowers except for sunflowers, which were grown not for their beauty but for their edible seeds. Pots of junipers or pine trees, which symbolized longevity, were the only decorative plants in the city. Flowers were a symbol of bourgeois sentiment, and were eliminated from our lives. Besides, the severe shortage of food in the early 1960s had trained everyone to be pragmatic. Every corner of the garden had to be fully utilized. Only years later did I realize that our garden was a very important source of supplemental food for our family.

Father took the lead working in our garden, from planting, weeding, and fertilizing to watering. The most challenging job was to collect human waste from the outhouse, to be used as fertilizer. Each time Father rolled up his sleeves to scoop up the human waste, he asked us to join him. None of us children wanted to have anything to do with it, but we couldn't say no. When the partially fermented waste was stirred, it stank so badly that our stomachs were seized with waves of nausea. I hid inside the apartment. My older siblings followed Father's footsteps. They made faces to one another and sometimes blocked their noses.

"Smelly waste is a treasure," Father said. The behavior of his children made him realize they had forgotten their family roots as peasants.

"No delicious food can be produced without manure," he told us. He decided to use this opportunity to train us.

He started with Yan.

"You attended the best nursery and best elementary school in Changchun," Father said to her. "Working with human waste is the best way to cleanse petit bourgeois habits."

Yan followed Father's instruction. She put up her best face, but she hated the chore. Ping and Binbin got their turn as well. They gagged but didn't dare complain or slow down. If Father didn't mind the disgusting waste splashed on his pants and shoes and smeared on his arms, how could they?

I was the only one who was spared. I enjoyed watching Father work in the garden. As the season progressed, his complexion turned dark, and he looked strong and healthy. I followed him when he weeded the eggplant and tomato plot or watered the green beans. Our favorite produce was corn, which occupied the majority of the garden. In late fall, as soon as corn was ripe enough to be picked, Nainai would boil the large ears in a big pot, covering the top layer with corn shucks to keep in the flavor. The fresh, sweet smell of corn filled the room, making our mouths water. We bit the corn off the cob while it was piping hot and stuffed ourselves to our hearts' content.

At the time, the strict food ration system allowed each person up to thirty-one pounds of grain per month, with a child's portion starting at nine pounds. We picked up our food coupons at a grain store. As my older siblings grew into teenagers, their monthly rations became less adequate. Other food items, including fish, pork, chicken, beef, soybean products, and even cooking oil were all rationed; each allocation was less than two pounds per person per month, with cooking oil limited to five ounces. Without much protein and oil in our diet, we felt hungry not long after filling our stomachs with grains. My older siblings, especially Binbin, were always looking for food.

Nainai used all her skills to help us cope with the food shortage. In early spring, she collected flowers from elm trees and tender willow leaves. Elm flowers had a sweet taste and could be mixed with cornmeal to make porridge or steamed buns. But willow leaves were bitter. After dipping them in hot water for a quick boil, Nainai soaked them in cold water overnight to get rid of their bitterness. Then she added some seasoning and made a tasty cold dish. Dandelion was another source of food. We used to run all over the Compound to dig them up and eat the greens as salad. Nainai was creative in her cooking. She added white flour to cornmeal when she made stuffed buns. Each of us received only two pounds of white flour per month, and Nainai had to use it sparingly. Without the white flour, the rough cornmeal wrapper wouldn't hold together. The stuffing consisted of chopped Napa cabbage or turnips, mixed with carrots and green onions. Every once in a while there would be a touch of ground meat, but the buns always tasted delicious to us. Many times we waited by the steamer and rushed them to the dining table as soon as they were placed in a bowl. Binbin boasted that he once had eight of those fist-sized buns in one go. Years later when we had plenty to eat, we tried to make them with Nainai's recipe. We found them tasteless and hard to swallow.

Despite our lack of material things and food, however, we did not feel poor. I marvel today at our blind satisfaction. Ideological campaigns created miracles in our mind. Our parents always reminded us to be appreciative of what we had and made us feel grateful for being born in the new China.

"My family only had one overcoat," Mother repeatedly told us. "We had to take turns to go out in the winter," she said.

We touched our cotton-padded jackets and pants, feeling most fortunate that we did not have to suffer in the bitter cold. At school, my sisters and brother received the same message.

"Children in the capitalist societies are starving. You are so lucky to be born under the red flag of China," their teachers reiterated the statement until they had the images of the poor, starving children engraved in their hearts.

They were asked to compare our current life to those who had lived "in deep waters and burning fires" of the dark, old society before 1949. Films and picture books described how landlords tormented their tenants. A black-and-white cartoon film featuring a mean landlord mistreating his farm tenants made an especially lasting impression on me. Several times, my sisters took me to a large movie theater to watch this film. In the dark auditorium, we gazed at the black and white screen, mesmerized by the image and story. In order to get the farmhands to start working early each day, Zhou the landlord—nicknamed "Killer Zhou"—sneaked into his chicken coop and imitated the crow of a rooster in the wee hours of the morning. Soon enough, the sleeping rooster was aroused and started crowing at the top of his lungs. The landlord then jumped up and knocked on the doors of the farmhands.

"Get up, get up!" he yelled. "The rooster is crowing. How come you are still in bed, you lazy bones?"

No one could afford a watch or a clock. The poor tenants had to drag themselves out and start their long, hard workday under the stars, or in pitch darkness. The cartoon generated much hatred toward the landlord in me. I learned that, along with capitalists, landlords were members of the exploiting class. I never questioned why Killer Zhou needed to get on his fours to imitate a rooster's crow in order to get his hired laborers to work, but I was scared of the old days. It was not until I was a second grader when it finally dawned on me that the "dark, old" society so often presented to us actually had daylight and sunshine, just as we did. For years, the image in my mind had been of a life actually lived in pitch darkness.

3

During my years of growing up, I always wore hand-me-down clothes. My happiest moments were when I received a new blouse or a pair of new pants at each Chinese New Year. Nainai always made shoes for us, in the old-fashioned way. The flattened front looked like the head of a catfish, while the sole, sewn with tight stitches, was as stiff as a wooden board. The thick string used for stitching was made from hand-woven hemp. I remember working with Nainai for hours on the edge of the Kang bed, twisting and blending the coarse fibers until they became even strings. I wore those homemade shoes all through elementary school. They were called Lao Tou Xie, "old man's shoes," and belonged to a past era. Our next-door neighbor Mr. Wang, Director of the Administration Department, continued to tease me about them.

"Where are your old man's shoes?'" he asked when we ran into each other, laughing and winking at me.

I disliked these clumsy looking shoes, but I was ashamed of my vanity. I never dared voice any objection to wearing them.

We, like most of the people at the time, took the Party's call for "working hard" and "living simple" as our motto. Instead of making us feel poor, it gave us a sense of spiritual triumph. Father, despite being a high-ranking official, wore patched shirts and jackets, though more out of necessity than choice. One of his dark blue winter jackets lasted him for more than ten years. The collar wore out, the elbow had layers of patches, and the color of the entire jacket faded. Each year, Mother carefully took it apart, washed the outer layer and the inner lining, and then put the cotton back in and sewed it together. We looked up to Father as our role model. In our mind, material things and physical needs were insignificant in the pursuit of a higher cause. To endure hardship for the benefit of others was noble and heroic, and the grand cause made self-sacrifice gratifying. Some people even went so far as to deliberately sew patches to the elbows or knees of their new clothes, as if it were a shame to be able to afford anything new. It was called "Jian Ku Pu Su," living an industrious and plain life. It was a form of make-believe, but to us, it was a gospel.

Compared to many people, especially those in the countryside, our life in the Compound was indeed affluent. Every year, ten or more people from Father's village turned to us for help. They were distant relatives, or Father's middle school classmates or their children, or Nainai's old neighbors. Father was the only one from the village who had become a high-ranking official. They all came to him at times of crisis. Perhaps money for a difficult season, or a job in the city, or settling an entire family somewhere in the northeast to survive. Father always received these requests with great hospitality, regardless of our own situation. Many times, he borrowed money from his own payroll to provide for others. He felt obligated. He was sorry that the people at his home village were still so destitute, more than a decade after Communist rule.

Mother was never thrilled to see these people, but she understood their situation and Father's obligation to help them. She received them out of sympathy. She took out our worn-out clothing and gave them to take home when she knew they had children of our age, but the villagers had no clue that our family was consistently in financial difficulties, too. In their eyes, we were rich. Once, Shikai, one of Father's nephews, came to ask for money. It was at the end of the month, and Mother only had five yuan left. She took out the five yuan bill and handed it to him, hoping he would leave soon. She had no resources to provide extra food for a grown man who ate three times more than us. "That's all you are going to give me?" Shikai asked, feeling humiliated. Mother apologized, saying that was all she had at the moment. Shikai threw the money to the ground. "Who do you think I am? A beggar?" he yelled at Mother before storming out of the apartment. Mother was stunned and hurt. She was taking a risk by giving away all the money she had.

Mother often found herself in such impossible situations. One day, an old man in rags was brought to our door. He introduced himself as Director of Education at the Dezhou Middle School, which Father had attended as a young man. Father was not home. He was leading a group of government employees in the countryside, carrying out a political campaign called "Four Clean-ups," a movement to purify politics, economy, organization, and ideology, but the old man wouldn't hear any of that. He insisted on meeting with Father, even when Mother offered him money.

Mother had no choice but to ask the Administration Department to notify Father. In the end, they sent a jeep to bring him home. When he arrived, he didn't recognize his school director, who used to be well-dressed in a long gown and was proud.

"I know I've been a nuisance," the old man said, holding Father's hands tightly as he stepped into the door. "But I have to see you."

Father was shocked. His old school director was covered with open sores. His rags were smelly and his hair tangled and dirty.

"Let's have something to eat," Father said. He learned the old man hadn't touched much food since his arrival. He insisted on seeing Father first. "Have some food and tell me what's going on," Father said.

Nainai made a dish of stir-fried eggs with tomatoes, and another with string beans, all from the garden. She frowned as Father served the old man a small cup of Baijiu, strong white liquor made of red sorghum. Father served it only when he had guests.

It turned out the old director was on his way further north. He wanted to join his son who had become a lumberman in the forests of the Heilongjiang Province. He didn't have much money. So he packed all the paintings and scrolls of calligraphy that he had collected over the years and went on the road. He sold them all, one after another, dirt cheap, and eventually he had run out of everything. He was already in the Jilin Province, more than half way to his destination. He came to Father.

He asked Father for fifteen yuan, saying that it would be sufficient to last him the rest of the journey.

Father promised he would get him the money. The following morning, he bought the old man a train ticket to Heilongjiang.

"You are a good brother," the old director said as he placed the money Father gave him into his bag. Father had to go back to the countryside. He dropped the old man off at the train station.

"I wanted to see you," the old man said, turning to take another look at Father on the platform. "I know I won't be able to pay you back in this life," he continued, his voice choking. "I hope I will see you in the next."

He boarded the train, wobbling as he climbed the metal stairs.

Father never heard from him again.

Years later, Father made the comment how devastated he was at seeing his old teacher in such a sorry state. "The Communists have turned my school director into a beggar!" he said. That was the only time I heard him say anything negative about the Communist Party.

4

Father's village had an unusual reputation. It was known as an "acrobat village," traditionally the hometown of many performers. In the old days, they performed at local fairs, but fairs and performances were banned in the new China. During the famine years in the early 1960s, many young men left the village, hoping to join one of the government-run performance troupes. Most of the time, their aspirations didn't lead them anywhere. They were lucky if they found work as handymen. Nonetheless, each of them thought he had a chance. Every year, two or three young men from Father's home village would come and ask him to place them in a performing troupe.

Once, when I was four or five, I saw two of the young men from the village practice juggling in the yard, throwing five clubs in the air and catching them. I was impressed. To demonstrate their abilities, the two jugglers insisted on giving a performance for my parents. They each rolled up their sleeves and set up their stage in Binbin's bedroom, which also served as a living room when we had guests. They moved two chairs from the dining area and stacked them. One of the performers tilted the top chair to an angle and held it tightly. The other one climbed up. Slowly, he put one hand on the back of one chair and the other hand on the edge of the other chair. Then he lifted his legs up. His body trembled. I was looking on with trepidation, afraid he might fall. So was Mother. After several attempts, he finally succeeded. Mother was relieved when he came back down.

"That's enough," she said.

"Wait, you have to see the next one," said the one who was holding the chair. He rushed to grab his clubs. He stood in the middle of the room and started tossing the clubs, first three, and then four. The fourth one hit the ceiling. It chipped off a chunk of paint and bounced back down. Mother gasped. The young acrobat tried to catch the falling club. He lost control, and all of them came raining down. One after another, they hit with a loud thud, leaving dents in the wooden floor. Mother put her right hand over her mouth, a startled expression on her face. Father remained calm, smoking a cigarette in his chair, a slightly bemused expression on his face.

"I'm so sorry," said the juggler. "Let me try that again."

"It's quite enough, thank you," Father said.

Mother got up and quickly left the room. It seemed that I was their only interested audience.

The next day, Father bought them each a train ticket and sent them home, with a small amount of money tucked into their pockets.

Over the years, Father helped dozens of people in various ways, but he had to send the majority home with nothing but kind words. He was not supposed to play favorites with people from his village. He was criticized once for getting one of his nephews a job in the city, and he had to resettle him to the countryside.

Most of the people who came to Father for help were peasants. They climbed onto the Kang with their shoes on and spat everywhere, sending their phlegm flying through the air as if to show off their aim. When they saw there was no dirt on the wooden floor to absorb their spit, they smeared it with the soles of their shoes, making an even bigger mess. The front of their clothing shone with accumulated stains, and they wiped their noses with their sleeves. I pitied them. Compared to them, I realized our life was very privileged and affluent. I chatted with them and showed them around the Compound. My heart was full of gratitude for what we had. I knew our family was lucky, as Father and Mother often said. I ran around the Compound like a happy princess.

Me and Cousin Xizi

Chapter Eight

A Free Spirit

1

The preschool years I spent in the Government Compound were the most carefree times of my life. Although bouts of pneumonia or high fever still plagued me, I was a restless and energetic child. Nainai was my constant protector and accomplice. She wanted all her grandchildren to be happy and allowed us, especially me, to run free when we were in her care.

My early childhood was filled with playtime at the two-story Wan Pagoda, with Nainai mending our clothes under the shade of a large willow tree, a sewing kit on her lap. She watched me from a distance. Several other children at the age of four or five and I loved to run up and down the pagoda. Shaded by a nicely curved roof and a few tall elm trees, the pagoda was an ideal spot for games on a hot summer day. Gentle wind breezed through the open space on the second floor, and despite the chipped surface, the concrete siding, slightly over a foot in width, was smooth. They became our makeshift slides. We challenged one another to run up its steep slope, testing our courage and balancing ability. Upon reaching the top, we slid down, laughing with delight and triumph. Nainai kept changing the patches sewn to the bottom of my pants, but never stopped me from tearing them. When Mother caught me risking life and limb at the pagoda, she would point to a scar right above my front hairline, a reminder of a fall against the stairs when I was a toddler, and tell me to behave, to be a good child.

"Look at that portrait," Mother pointed out to me. "That is Chairman Mao, our great leader." She said patiently, as if I could understand.

"All the children should listen to Chairman Mao," Mother continued. "You, too. I expect you to be Mao's good child."

I looked at the portrait of Chairman Mao and liked his fatherly look. His large eyes and smiling face looked friendly. I nodded and promised Mother I'd listen to Chairman Mao.

"That means to obey rules and follow instructions," Mother added. She would remind me again and again, whenever I stepped out of line.

Sliding on the narrow concrete edges of the pagoda staircase was certainly not good behavior. I was well behaved whenever Mother was around, but once she was out of sight, which was most of the time, I ignored her rules. The thrill and joy of these spontaneous games brought me repeatedly back to the pagoda. Nainai rarely interfered. She believed children should run free and just be themselves.

Nainai cared for Wen and me during our preschool years, sparing the two of us from attending boarding nurseries. Nainai was a small woman, barely five feet tall. As far as I could remember, her hair, forever tied in a bun in the back of her head, was always white. She seemed ancient to me. Her back was hunched from years of hard labor, and her eyes, which must have been large and beautiful when she was young, sank in their sockets and had a dull look—the onset of cataracts. All her teeth had long since fallen out, a result of poor nutrition and lack of proper care. Without teeth for support, her mouth curved in, giving an impression that she was always smiling. Nainai was soft-spoken and patient. No matter what my siblings and I did, she never raised her voice or lost her temper. Sometimes, when we started quarreling among ourselves, which could end with one or two in tears, Nainai would step in and mediate. But she would not report our unruly behavior to Mother. As a child, I was always afraid of Mother. She had high expectations of us and was always very strict. But Nainai set no rules and passed no judgments. Whenever we were together, I played and laughed without restraint.

Nainai came from a poor peasant family and had never received any education. She was the oldest of five children. From an early age on, she shared in the family responsibilities such as caring for her younger brothers and sisters, cooking for the family, and weaving clothes. Growing up in a village in the Shandong Province where Confucius came from, Nainai learned to observe the virtues traditionally defined for women: as a young girl, a female should obey her parents; as a married woman, she should put the interests of her husband and children first; as a widow, she should serve the needs of her son and his children. Nainai's life mirrored each of these three stages.

Father used to tell us stories about Nainai back in the village. As a small boy, he'd wake up each day seeing Nainai at her spinner, and go to bed each night bidding goodnight to Nainai, who was sitting in the same spot, weaving and spinning. Her day consisted of cooking for the family, feeding the pigs they raised, and weaving. Yeye would take the pigs and fabric to sell at the local market. This was how they made most of their living. Through their persistent effort and frugality, they were able to save enough money to purchase two acres of land, but their land meant more work for Nainai, for she readily joined forces with her husband and her older son in the fields during busy seasons. Sometimes, when Yeye was too busy going to the local market or tending to the family's crops, Nainai would also go to the hillside to collect tree branches for fuel and carry them home in a big bundle on her back. As the youngest, Father followed her everywhere and was always amazed by Nainai's inexhaustible energy and strength. Heavy work such as hauling buckets of pig feeds, weeding in the field with a hoe, or getting bundles of tree branches home was challenging enough for a grown man, but Nainai did them all. And all she had to stand on were her tiny, bound feet, barely four inches long.

As if that was not enough, Nainai also extended her generosity and care beyond her immediate family. Her sister died young and left behind two small children, aged five and three. Nainai took them in. She had four children of her own, and was having a hard time to meet all their needs, but she took her two nephews home without hesitation. "As long as my children have food to eat, you will have food in your bowls," she told them. For five years, she looked after them. Only when their father got remarried and their stepmother was willing to care for them did Nainai let them go. Years later, when Father joined the Eighth Route Army, Nainai often opened her door to the underground Communists who needed temporary shelter. When Father left, they were living under the ruling of the Kuomintang and the Japanese. If she was caught assisting the Communists, she could have been executed. "Our son might be out there getting help from some family as well," she would tell Yeye, persuading him to help these young men.

Ever since Nainai came to live with us, she was the key figure who held the family together. During the extended period when Mother attended school, Father was the sole breadwinner. With so many children to support, it became a challenge to make Father's salary last to the end of each month. Nainai managed the finances of the household, utilizing her skill of frugality. By the time I was toddling behind her heels, Nainai had become an indispensable part of our family. "We would not have pulled through these difficult years without Nainai," Father often said to us, ever appreciating Nainai's contribution.

2

Nainai's most prominent physical feature was her bound feet. Like most of the women of her generation, Nainai had her feet bound when she was six. In her time, foot binding for women was the norm and in the Shandong Province, the custom was strictly observed. Women without bound feet ran the risk of becoming unwanted old maids. Young girls usually had their feet bound at the age of five or six. Nainai was no exception. To me, her four-inch long small feet looked like a pair of scared mice. Their backs arched high, heads pointed down, as if ready to flee at any moment. Instead of springing away, however, Nainai wobbled when she moved around. Her crippled feet were disproportional. Her heels were round and much too large, because they had to support the entire weight of her body. Her soles were narrow and arched. And her toes, the most heart-wrenching sight, had been folded under and flattened.

"My mother bound my feet when I was a little girl," Nainai said. She told me her story many times. "It was supposed to be for my own good," she sighed, shaking her head.

I often put my small hands against her feet, alarmed at how unbelievably small they were. Sometimes, I tried to put my feet into her shoes. I couldn't. The pointed front was too narrow even for my feet.

"I remember how my mother tightly wrapped a wide, long cloth around each of my feet," Nainai said. "She told me it would hurt, but that it had to be done. She said no one would want to marry me if I grew up with large feet. It would mean life-long suffering. All the girls my age went through the same procedure, so I didn't object, but nothing prepared me for the excruciating pains." She paused, going back in time and space. I listened to her, wriggling my toes. I couldn't comprehend the horror she went through.

"When my toes were bent, it sent waves of pain through my entire body. I screamed," Nainai said, her voice controlled and low. Whenever she brought up the subject, tears came to her eyes. After eight decades, she was still emotional about it. Each time she washed my feet, Nainai would playfully stretch my toes, telling me what a lucky girl I was. To ensure the desired form of her bound feet, the wrappings were tightened every day and she had to walk on her folded toes. Many girls suffered from infection. In a severe case, it could lead to a girl's death.

"My mother beat me with a stick and chased me to move around the house. She did what her mother had done to her when she was a little girl. She cried with me and wiped my tears, but she wouldn't allow me to sit down. I limped around during the day, and at night, the burning pain kept me awake and restless, especially during the first few weeks. I begged my mother to let me be and told her I'd rather be an old maid all my life. Little did I know twenty years later, I would do exactly the same to my own two daughters."

I found her stories hard to believe, but her tiny feet were real. Four out of the five toes on each of her feet were folded under and rolled inward. They appeared nearly flat after years of tight wrapping and pressure, and the two big toes, though intact, never grew to their full length. Each morning, I watched Nainai wrap her feet, and each evening, unwrap them. She washed her feet carefully in lukewarm water before retiring for the night. If she neglected to do so, a rotten smell would seep out. The layers of wrapping left no room for her feet to breathe.

Every morning, Nainai carefully laid her wrapping cloths flat by her side, a long, white strip for her feet, and an equally long, black one for her ankles and calves. She first secured the white strip around her toes, looping around one foot then the other with measured caution and pressure—too tight would hinder her blood circulation, and too loose would make walking more painful. One circle after another, she moved slowly as if performing a ritual. Eventually she would tuck in the end under the last loop. The black strip picked up where the white one left off, going all the way up to her calves. She also covered the lower section of her homemade baggy pants underneath. I watched her do this every day, and years later when she could no longer take care of the wrapping on her own, I helped her. Nainai's bound feet were a reminder of the limitations and boundaries that women used to live under. For years, I took Nainai's submissiveness and amiable manner as a sign of weakness, not strength. I felt she was a victim of the old society and the conventional value system, and I didn't want to follow her example. Mother's leadership role and career were glorious and significant in my eyes. Yet, despite my choice of role model, it was Nainai I leaned on for help and comfort. "Nainai," I called out numerous times every day. To me, the endearing sound of Nainai, a common term for paternal grandmother, was very special and befitting only to her, my grandma alone. Even my parents used the term to refer to her when they talked to us. Nainai was the consistent presence in my life, the first person I saw in the morning and the last one I clung to before falling asleep at night. Mother's appearance at my bedside in the evening was welcome, but not essential. Nainai was the one I expected to tuck me in and hold my hand until I drifted into dreams.

In her quiet way, Nainai instilled in me a free spirit. Political jargon didn't mean anything to her. To be kind and caring, in many cases at the expense of her own interest, was Nainai's principle of life. As a little girl, I indulged myself in Nainai's protected world of freedom. I was her little darling, regardless of my faults and errors. She let me run loose in the Compound, as she had done to her own children in the country village. A bump here or a bruise there was part of a child's growing up. She readily used her country remedies to heal the minor wounds.

3

The gated Government Compound was a safe place for children. There were no paved roads within the residential area. Near the office buildings, the tar-paved narrow streets were marked by footprints or bicycle tracks. There were only a few cars and jeeps in the fleet of government vehicles. They were parked in a garage next to the Wan Building. My brother Binbin and his friends liked to hang around the garage, watching the drivers fix their vehicles and learning the mechanics from them. These vehicles were reserved for the officials' use, and Father forbade us to get a ride or make any request for personal use. These cars were driven by professional chauffeurs and always moved slowly in the Compound.

Nothing posed any threat to the children in the Compound. Most of us, in the care of our grandmothers, wandered freely. We checked back with them occasionally, while they sat under a tree or in front of someone's yard, sewing and chatting. I often played with Wuzi, a boy from next door. Wuzi was a year younger than me, and was from a large family. Like mine, his brothers and sisters were much older than he was. So we became friends and playmates. Wuzi was a timid, quiet boy and followed me everywhere. We played jump rope, kicked shuttlecock, or made paper cut-outs of various patterns. One summer day, getting tired of our routines, I schemed with Wuzi to go play in a park only a few blocks from the Compound. We had been there with our older siblings before. In the park was a man-made pond surrounded by many trees. We went out from the back entrance and reached the park without a problem. In the middle of the week, few people were there, and we played at leisure, throwing pebbles to skip on the water surface, building sand castles on the small beach, and venturing into the shallow water to get our feet wet. When we finally felt hungry and saw the sun setting in the west, we cleaned our hands in the water and walked back to the Compound. My skirt was wet and my sandals were covered with sand and mud. Wuzi held his soaked shoes in his hands and walked barefoot. We had a great time. The moment we stepped into the Compound from the back, however, someone called out to us.

"There they are!" A tall woman rushed over, followed by a few more adults from a distance. "I'll call their parents," another voice shouted.

It turned out we had been gone for more than six hours. When we didn't show up for lunch, a search began. Everyone was alarmed when our grandmothers couldn't find us anywhere in the Compound. Our parents were notified and the city's police department and many government employees were engaged in the search. Nainai changed my dirty clothing and patted me on my cheeks, saying I had made her sick from worrying. Mother was furious. The search for us had troubled so many people. Despite her relief that we returned safe, she was embarrassed by what we did—we were lacking in discipline. In no uncertain terms, we were forbidden to leave the Compound. And after that I never did.

4

Mother was absolute about discipline. I would learn the hard way that her absolute dictates extended to the table. I always hated ginger. The popular opinion was that it added a refreshing flavor to stir fried dishes and dumpling stuffing. It stimulated blood circulation and drove the chill out from the body. When someone in the family suffered from a cold, the first remedy Nainai or Mother applied was a drink made of ginger. The patient had to drink a large glass of hot water simmered with fresh ginger, sometimes sweetened with honey, when available. After drinking the concoction, the patient would go to bed, and sweat under a thick layer of cotton padded quilt. Afterward, the symptoms of the cold were reduced. I refused to take any of that drink.

The pungent smell of ginger nauseated me. If the ginger was sliced and put in a dish, I picked out every piece of it. If it was minced, and inseparably mixed into the vegetables, I simply refused to touch the dish. On the few occasions when I happened to chew on a slice of ginger, I gagged. I ran off to spit out the mouthful of food in the yard. There were always a few chickens wandering around, eagerly awaiting my spill from my mouth.

My dislike of ginger was not widely appreciated. However, Nainai accepted my objection. No ginger drink was forced down my throat, and when it came to cooking, she put aside a portion of a dish or dumpling stuffing, before adding any ginger. However, Mother refused to do any of that whenever she was in the kitchen.

"Ginger is good for you," she said. She considered my stance on ginger the behavior of a spoiled brat. She demanded that I eat what was on the table and was determined to set me straight.

I decided to make a stand against Mother. One Sunday, when Mother was home, she prepared lunch, putting plenty of ginger in the two stir fried dishes, one being string beans, and the other green pepper with sliced potatoes. The produce was from our garden and I had enjoyed picking beans and peppers with Nainai in the morning, but the strong smell of ginger permeated the air, ruining my appetite. I walked away from the lunch table.

"I'm not going to eat anything with ginger in it," I said, but I kept my head low, and didn't dare look Mother in the eye. When I felt hungry in the afternoon and was about to come out of my self-imposed isolation, Nainai came to my rescue. She brought me a boiled egg, a treat for special occasions. I peeled off the shell carefully, not wanting to lose any of the egg white to the shell. I relished each bite of the warm egg. Later, when dinner was ready, I saw slices of ginger mixed with eggplant and Napa cabbage. The ginger seemed to stand out in my eyes, more than the usual portion. I took it as Mother's retaliation. I stole a glance at Nainai.

"Don't ask Nainai for help," Mother said. "I've asked her not to spoil you."

Mother's voice was calm, but firm. I gave up my silent plea and left the dining table the second time that day, this time with tears running down my face. I felt my rumbling stomach was almost ready to take in anything, but I walked away, slowly. I was hoping Mother would call me back. She didn't.

I shut myself in my room. If only Mother could come after me. I lay down on my stomach and tucked a pillow underneath. I waited, and eventually fell asleep. When I woke up, I noticed my room turning dark. All I could think of was food. I felt starved and unloved. I started to cry, hoping my tears would move Mother. I kept an ear out for the sound of footsteps in the hallway, and saved my energy, sobbing only when someone was within earshot. Finally, I heard someone approaching my room. Then I turned on the faucet, but it was Nainai, offering me a few pieces of biscuit. She did not want to undermine Mother's discipline, but didn't want to see me go to bed on an empty stomach. This time, I declined the offer, despite being hungry. I wanted Mother to change her mind or at least to come to me in person.

"Food is on the table if you want to eat," Mother's voice startled me. It was shortly before bedtime. My heart started pounding and my hopes ran high. I rushed to the door and was about to swing it open when I heard her say, "It's all flavored with ginger!"

I froze. Tears flooded my eyes. I heard her walk away. The door to her bedroom gently shut. Mother had retired for the night. I cried bitter tears. I resented her tough stance. When it came to children and discipline, no point was too trivial for Mother to make.

I didn't test Mother's formidable willpower again, but I stayed away from ginger as much as I could. Years later, when I was in college and had to eat in the cafeteria where all the dishes and dumpling stuffing were seasoned with ginger, I found myself no longer nauseated by it. At the time, I wondered how much of my reaction was actual dislike and how much was simple defiance against my Mother's refusal to recognize my needs. Now I think I know.

5

I always looked for new ways to play. One day, my initiative resulted in an accident—a large slab of concrete fell on my right toe, damaging it forever. Even today if someone steps on it, I shiver with pain.

I often observed my brother Binbin orchestrating cricket fights. Binbin and his friends raised captured crickets with cabbage leaves and carried them around in perforated boxes. Once they agreed on a battleground, they put a shallow container on a flat surface and picked a few contestants to start the fight. Binbin was the ringleader. Using a straw, he tickled the cricket's feelers and got it to turn against the other. Soon enough, crickets chirped and fluttered their wings, ready to fight. All the boys in the group circled around Binbin, stretching their heads above the container for a better view. During the fights, they held their breath, and whenever a winner was evident, they exploded with cheers and excitement. The winner proudly stood in the middle of the battleground, chirping with triumph. The boys excluded me from their game and ignored my pleas to cut in and take a look. "Go ahead and make your own," Nainai often said when I whined about being excluded from my siblings' activities.

One day, I decided to take Wuzi to catch crickets and start our own games. We could hear them chirping all around us. After some chasing and tumbling, we managed to catch two fine specimens from under a pile of broken tiles. We put them in a tin box and were thrilled when they responded to our tease with vibrating wings. I was proud to start our own games.

Wuzi and I treasured our crickets. We constantly touched them, massaging their soft bellies and smooth wings, but within a couple of hours, we were dismayed to see their bodies go limp in our hands. We decided to put them in a place similar to their natural habitat so they could recuperate. We looked around. We didn't want them to fall prey to the chickens. Soon, a big concrete block caught our attention. It was three inches thick, and two square feet wide. It was a manhole cover for the underground water pipes. The cool air underneath must be good for them, we reasoned. We decided to place the crickets under the slab.

Mrs. Han, Wuzi's mother, was reading a newspaper in the shade of a large date tree in front of our families' duplex apartment building. She tilted her head and looked at us over her reading glasses.

"Listen, there are plenty of crickets out there. Why don't you feed these two to the chickens and go catch fresh ones?" she asked absent-mindedly.

"Sh..." I put a finger to my mouth to silence Wuzi, and he giggled. I was determined to save the crickets. I put the two drooping creatures on the ground and gestured to Wuzi to help me lift the concrete block. It was heavy and probably had not been moved by anyone for ages. After some joint effort on our part, it reluctantly shifted to one side. A gush of cool air chilled our sweat. We were thrilled, full of excitement, full of pride. We got hold of the edge on one end and lifted the slab straight up.

"Wuzi, you hold it. I'll get the crickets," I said. I always bossed Wuzi around.

Just as my hands touched the crickets, Wuzi gave out a cry, and the heavy block slipped from his grasp. He instinctively jumped half a step back. The concrete mass flattened the big toe of my right foot as it slammed to the ground. I screamed in shock. Blood gushed out from under my smashed toenail and covered my green plastic sandal. I cried at the sight. It was not until a few minutes later—when Mrs. Han rushed over and picked me up in her arms—that I felt the sting of sharp pain. My sister Ping rushed me to a nearby clinic on a bicycle.

All through the next month, I had to go to the clinic numerous times for treatment. It hurt terribly when the nurse removed the hardened layer of the bandage and dressed the wound.

Mother shook her head in disapproval as I hopped around and grimaced with pain. She lost no time in lecturing me.

"You see? You weren't behaving like a good child, and you got hurt," she said.

I nodded. No room for argument in this case.

6

The concept of becoming Chairman Mao's good child, however, was vague to me. What I really wanted was to please my mother. I was desperate for her approval. After working as a teacher for a couple of years at the Baicheng Normal College, Mother was transferred to the No. 3 Middle School and promoted to Party Secretary, essentially the head of the school, since the Party represented supreme power. Mother expected us to behave all the time.

"Keep in mind the impact your behavior has on others," she said. I often heard her say this to my older siblings. Both Yan and Ping were students at her school. Mother set a higher standard for us because of the positions she and Father held. When I grew older, I continued to shoulder the burden of becoming a role model for my peers. Mother was a woman of few words. When she spoke, we listened.

I adored and feared my mother at the same time. I wanted her to be tender and loving. After all, she was a beautiful woman. She had large and radiant eyes. Most people had smaller, slanted eyes. We envied her fair, smooth complexion. White skin was much admired among the Chinese. Many women used umbrellas to block the sun in an effort to keep their skin from tanning, or applied powder to make their face look ghostly pale. Mother had naturally pale skin. I loved to watch her brush her shoulder-length permed hair in the morning. It fell naturally into place with the movement of her hairbrush, black and shining. Mother carried herself with an air of confidence and authority. She did not seem to notice her own beauty, or she didn't think much of it. She was a very decisive person, on large or small issues, and she had no tolerance for whining and sentimentality. She rarely showed any emotion. If we did something right, it was merely what was expected of us. There were no compliments, no pats on our backs. If we did something wrong, a brief but serious lecture was sure to follow.

Her straightforward speech and behavior earned her the reputation of thinking and acting like a male administrator, a compliment her colleagues openly gave her. They liked to come to our home to talk to her about their problems, trusting her fairness and prompt follow-ups. I felt proud of her, yet could not stop feeling a void, an insatiable hunger for her attention and love.

I soon discovered I could receive recognition from my mother when I served tea to her visitors. Whenever they came, for courtesy calls or serious discussions, the task of serving tea always fell on us children. My sisters and brother dreaded such occasions. As soon as I could handle the teakettle safely, they trained me to take over the task. They would prepare tea in the kitchen and send me to serve it. Although I resented the unexpected visitors for taking Mother away from us, I did not mind serving them tea. I liked interacting with them. I also knew that each time I would receive a few compliments. At such moments, Mother would throw me a tender, approving look. A hint of smile appeared on her face, indicating, in my eyes, that she agreed with the comment. That always made me happy and proud, although she never openly praised me. Decades later, she told me that she loved us dearly, and that she often came to our rooms when she returned from work, kissing us on our faces while we were fast asleep.

She never did that when we were awake.

7

I was restless by nature. Not long after the toe incident, the big chimney of the Compound furnace caught my attention. It stood above the tallest buildings. Each morning, the embers in the furnace were rekindled, and I loved watching the black smoke spiraling out of the chimney. Metal rungs lined straight up on one side, leading all the way to the top. They looked like gigantic staples punched into a brick wall, like they were hanging in mid-air, but they were out of my reach. Even the lowest rung was too high up for me. I often stopped by the furnace room to warm myself and watch the workers shovel coal into the four openings at the base of the boiler. Fire sizzled each time, as more coal fueled the flames. Two workers raced to feed the voracious appetite of the furnace, their faces often smeared black and glazed with perspiration in the heat of the golden flame. I would laugh as they wiped sweat away with their dirty hands, adding more black stripes to their faces. It was freezing cold outside, but here in the furnace room, they only wore sleeveless tops. They talked loud and drank water by putting their mouths directly against the faucet in the wall. They didn't even bother to button up their cotton-padded jackets when they went outside for more cartloads of coal. I loved to stand in the back and watch them. Sometimes they made faces at me.

The furnace room was sealed in early May after the heating system was shut down. There was a big metal door at the base of the chimney. Each spring, chimneysweeps crawled in and removed the ashes accumulated during the winter. Occasionally, I could see a worker climbing the metal bars to the top. I had no idea what he could possibly be doing up there, but the view he would have from such a high level intrigued me. How exciting it must be to see the entire city below. I would watch the worker climb up the chimney step by step until my neck hurt, dreaming of a world beyond the Compound. I often wondered what it would be like to simply spread my arms and fly. I looked longingly at birds, as they flew above me, admiring their freedom.

One day I noticed a ladder placed right in front of the chimney, connecting to the lowest metal rung. My heart pounded with excitement. Here was my opportunity. Without hesitation, I ran to the ladder and was soon moving up the wall, gripping each metal bar with both hands. I felt free like a bird. The only thought in my mind was to reach the top and find out how far I could see. I marveled at the idea, climbing up as fast as I could. As it turned out, the perspective from the ground was misleading. The distance between each rung was greater than I thought. I was not tall enough to reach each step easily. I fixed my attention on the bar right above my head, holding it tightly with one hand and lifting up one foot on the opposite side. Carefully, I moved up. I stopped only to catch my breath. The metal bars got narrower as I climbed higher. I could see out of the corners of my eye that I was above the tips of the tall poplar trees. When I finally looked around, I saw the roof of the Wan Building below me, and rows of flat apartment buildings spread out outside the Government Compound, and the middle school my sisters attended. It seemed much closer from up here than on the ground. I looked toward the left and saw low, one-story apartment buildings, packed together row after row like matchboxes. Some had red brick sidings and orange rectangular roofs; others had dark gray walls of straw and mud, their roofs almost flat. I wondered what kind of life was out there, beyond the Compound, beyond the city limit.

But when I looked down, my heart jumped to my throat. A group of people had gathered at the bottom. They looked small, strangely out of proportion, and they were all looking up at me. I suddenly felt dizzy, and my legs trembled. My left foot lost its holding and slipped off the rung. Intuitively, I held the metal bar in front of me with all the strength I could muster.

"Don't look down!" I heard a voice shouting.

I raised my head and stared at the red brick right in front of my nose.

"Take it easy. Come down slowly, one step at a time," the same voice shouted again.

I secured my body weight on the bar by wrapping it under my arms and tried to calm down. A quick thought flashed through my mind. "Is Mother going to find out what I did? Will she be mad at me?"

Slowly, I moved a few steps down without looking under my feet. I wished the group of people would disappear so I could sneak away once I reached the ground. I closed my eyes and imagined their presence a mere dream, but when I stole a glance underneath, there they were. As time passed by, the crowd seemed to have gotten larger. I held my breath and decided to descend and face the consequence. The metal bars seemed endless. When I finally planted my feet on the bottom one, a man standing on the top of the ladder scooped me up in one arm as if I were a parcel. He held me so tightly that I could hardly breathe, but I stayed still and did not make a sound. The stares of the people silenced me.

"How dangerous!" a middle-aged woman sighed and shook her head.

"A naughty girl she is, isn't she?" Mr. Wang, Manager of Office Services, mumbled, his voice low but annoyed. He was in charge of the furnace building and would probably be blamed if I had hurt myself or worse, if I had fallen.

I was shocked to see Mother standing in front of the group, and Nainai right by her side. Mother seldom let anything interfere with her work. There were times when I suffered high fevers that reached a dangerous level, but she still left for work after making me take some medicine. No begging or crying could make her miss a day of work. I wondered who was able to persuade her to return to the Compound in the middle of the day. As soon as I touched the ground, Mother rushed forward, but did not say a word. She took me into her arms and held me there, her cheek touching mine. I couldn't remember the last time she held me. Immediately, her embrace made me feel better. Nainai reached over and kept rubbing my hands against hers, tears trailing down her etched face. "Don't you ever do that again!" Mother said with clenched teeth. She grasped my shoulders so hard that it hurt me. "That's definitely the behavior of a bad child," she added. They never put a ladder near that chimney again.

8

Soon after the chimney episode, my parents decided to send me to the kindergarten located in the Compound for training and discipline, a scheme, which soon failed.

The kindergarten had about sixty children ranging from babies to age six. The government staff working in the Compound could send their children there. Nainai had taken me to their playground before in the evenings or Sundays. I loved their sand boxes, slides, and swings. But no children living in the Compound attended the kindergarten. Most of them, like my older siblings, were already in school. And the remaining three or four children of my age all had a grandmother at home to care for them. I was curious about the kindergarten and longed to have more friends. So I did not object to the idea. Father took me there early on a Monday morning. I felt like I was ready to start school.

Mrs. Gao, Director of the kindergarten, met us at the door.

"We are so happy to have Jian," she said to Father, smiling from ear to ear.

Father shook hands with her. For a moment, I was worried he would explain why I was there.

"Jian is full of energy," he said. "Please feel free to contact me if there is any problem."

Gao smiled, revealing two rows of unevenly lined teeth.

"Don't worry," she said. "We'll take good care of her."

Gao was tall and overweight. I had hardly ever seen anyone as large as her. She extended one hand to me, and I obediently placed mine in hers. Father patted me on the shoulder and told me, once again, to be a good girl. I nodded and watched him walk toward his office building half a block away.

It was still early in the morning. I saw other children being dropped off by their parents. They arrived on bicycles, toddlers sitting on baby seats mounted on the front bar between the seat and the handle. The bigger kids sat sideways, either on the front bar or on the back seat. I always loved it when Mother put me on her bicycle to go somewhere. I held the bicycle handle in front of me, leaning my weight forward. The bare metal bar I sat on cut into my thighs and hindered my blood circulation. My legs quickly fell asleep. But it was worth it. Sitting next to Mother, I felt her body warmth and the rhythm of her breathing as she pedaled. I loved it and did not mind limping around until my feet and legs regained their sensation. But those occasions were rare. I wished our home were far away so that one of my parents would have to take me to the kindergarten on a bicycle. Later when I was in school, I was very jealous of other children when I saw their mothers holding their hands to walk them to school or putting lunch boxes into their school bags.

I behaved the first few days at the kindergarten and observed the routine. Fruit and snack distribution in the morning, a two-hour nap after lunch, and another snack in the afternoon. I joined the older children, five- and six-year-olds, in their study sessions in arithmetic and Chinese. Playtime, especially outside on the playground, was limited. The children were quiet and timid. Nobody responded to my requests to stay outside longer to play, or took up my challenges to climb a crabapple tree in the front yard. My restless spirit found no resonance among these well-tamed children.

I ran away after a snack break one morning. The front gate of the playground was fastened with a bolt, but not locked. I gradually edged my way toward the fence. When I thought nobody was looking, I flipped the bolt and took off. It happened in a flash, I thought, but I immediately heard Mrs. Gao calling after me. I picked up speed when I realized she was coming. I charged into the White Building where Father worked. I knew the layout of the three sets of stairs by heart. I ran up from the one next to the kindergarten, raced down the main staircase in the middle of the building, and eventually charged out from the third set of stairs on the far end.

Gao's heavy footsteps faded away. I wandered in the Compound until I felt hungry, and then went home. It was two or three hours after my escape. Nainai made me call Father on the phone and cooked me some string beans and rice, my favorites. It felt so good to be able to do whatever I wanted to do. Father said what I had done was wrong and demanded I apologize to Mrs. Gao. Apparently, Gao had stopped by his office during the day. Reluctantly I returned to the kindergarten again the following day and said I was sorry. I stayed and got extremely bored. I feared the two-hour nap. No one could move or talk during this rest period. I had seldom slept during the day before and lying there motionless was simply torture. By ten o'clock the day after my return, I decided I had to leave. I would beg my parents not to send me back again. During a break, I ran to the gate without hesitation. This time, I dashed toward the Red Office Building. The chase began again, and I soon outran Gao. Father realized I was making too much trouble at the kindergarten and decided to keep me at home with Nainai. Mother agreed, and I was pleasantly surprised. I wondered if Nainai had talked to her. Nainai appeared as happy as I was, now that I was home again. That marked the end of my first exposure to institutional discipline.

Chapter Nine

Heroes of the Compound

1

As the baby of the family, I adored my older siblings. I felt close to them all except Wei, my half-sister, who had left for college by the time I was born. When she came home for a visit, Wei always called me her "pretty little doll," but since she was more than twenty years my senior, I never developed a close bond with her. With my sisters Yan, Ping, and Wen, and my brother Binbin, it was different. I loved to hang around them and be part of their activities. However, because they were six to ten years older than me, they never took me seriously. They ditched me without hesitation whenever they felt like it. Nainai was the only person who welcomed my company. With each passing year, my desire to join my siblings increased. I marked my growth on the frame of my bedroom door, anxious to catch up, but they seemed to grow faster than me.

My sister Ping was the one I admired most. Although she was a year younger than Yan, she was the leader among us. Her almond-shaped large eyes, finely lined dark eyebrows, and perfectly curved jaw made her a beauty. From time to time, strangers stopped her in the street, wanting to take a closer look. "What a pretty girl," they said. Ping was indifferent to their remarks. She was quick-witted and active. Intelligence was more important to her than her looks.

Ping was a tomboy and liked to climb trees and buildings. Once she led Binbin and Min, my friend Wuzi's older sister, to the top of the Wan Building. They wanted to collect bird eggs. Sparrow nests were scattered beneath the arched gray tiles.

Traces of feathers and straw revealed their whereabouts. Ping had a sharp eye and spotted more of them than others. Whenever she lifted a tile and found a few eggs, or sometimes baby sparrows, she would shout with delight: "I've found another one!"

That day, Ping ignored the forecast of strong wind and moved on the steep roof with a small basket in hand. Min and Binbin followed her, bending low and edging up. Normally, adult birds would flutter all around the intruders, frightened and chirping loudly. That afternoon, the wind kept them away. By the time the three daring explorers realized how strong the wind had become, they could no longer descend the roof. It was difficult for them to move. Ping, carrying the basket with two dozen eggs, saw a small chimney nearby. She zigzagged her way behind it, calling out to Binbin and Min to follow her. The howling wind swallowed her voice. When she heard no response from them, she poked her head out. Not far away, she saw Min struggling to maintain her balance. Her shoulder-length hair flew with the wind, covering her face and eyes. Binbin was further away. He curled up his small frame like a rabbit, gripping the shingles in front of him with both hands.

"Crawl on all fours!" Ping shouted at the top of her lung, and they finally heard her.

Min and Binbin lay down and slowly began crawling toward her. The eggs in their pockets broke, and the egg white and yolk seeped through. Their clothes became a sticky mess. Ping ventured out of the sheltered area. She moved on her bottom, using her arms and legs for support. She reached Min and guided her toward the chimney. As soon as Min gained a footing behind the buffer, Ping handed her the basket and cautiously made her way to Binbin. Locking one arm with Binbin, Ping used all her skills and strength to pull him closer. They crawled together, breaking a few shingles along the way as they pushed hard with their feet. After what seemed like an eternity, they reached the area behind the rectangular chimney. They were shaking, and Min was on the verge of crying.

"Sit against the wall!" Ping shouted. She placed herself in the center and flattened her back against the chimney. The narrow structure barely sheltered all three of them.

Ping gripped Min's arm with one hand and wrapped the other around Binbin. "We will be okay," she said, trying to assure herself and her two younger companions.

They huddled together, engulfed by the hurling and howling of the wind. The sky turned yellow. Sand, leaves, and twigs lashed at them. Binbin's face was pale and his body stiff. He didn't say a word. Min leaned against Ping's shoulder and sobbed. They waited. All this time, Ping held the basket between her legs.

An hour later, the wind finally let up. The three adventurers were exhausted. Their legs were numb and weak, and their hair and clothing in disarray. Ping cautiously led the way down, holding the basket in one hand. Only half of the eggs they collected remained intact.

Ping's daring and composure in times of crisis earned her our respect. After this episode, Ping learned to take weather forecasts seriously, but she didn't let the weather slow her down in her other endeavors. Binbin and I, and even the amiable Wen, followed her, climbing trees and buildings whenever we had a chance.

Yan was the exception. She was the oldest among the five of us and the most domestic. Yan had a round face and was a little chubby. She was humorous, often poking fun at her own expense. Yan enjoyed sewing and knitting, and voluntarily did many household chores, including mopping the floors and washing our laundry. She was always busy doing something with her hands.

Nainai had taught her to make shoes from scratch. Following her instructions, Yan mixed flour with water and boiled it to a thick paste to use as glue. She cut our worn-out clothes to pieces. After taking out the seams and patches, she laid the clothing on a flat board. Layer after layer, she pasted them together. When they were dry, she used a paper pattern the size of her shoes and traced five or six pieces out of the hardened board of clothing. By weaving stitches through them with thick hemp strings, especially on the soles and heels, she made a firm bottom. She liked to imitate the latest style in stores. She was always proud to wear her own handmade shoes.

Yan was outspoken. She talked and laughed in a hearty, loud voice. She always regretted that she had a different look than the rest of us. Particularly her eyes. In Chinese culture, eyelids held a place of special importance. There were two kinds: one was "single," the other "double," meaning a person either had one layer of skin over his or her eyelids, or two. "Double" was the desirable form. It made one's eyes seem larger, which was considered more attractive. In our family, we all had double layered eyelids except Yan.

"Mother, are you sure you didn't bring me home by mistake from the hospital?" she asked whenever she became conscious of her looks.

"Nonsense."

Mother always gave her the same answer. Yan laughed at herself.

Yan was handy, but didn't like to pore over books. When she was eight, a second grader in Changchun, she had an accident at her boarding school. It happened as she and a few others were playing jump rope. Yan was waiting her turn, cutting her fingernails with a pair of scissors. When her turn came, she eagerly ran to the rope that two of her classmates were swinging. She jumped, but miscalculated and fell. She landed heavily on her left side. She drove the small scissors into her temple as she hit the ground. For a moment, Yan was dazed and didn't feel any pain. She managed to sit up and pull the scissors out by herself. A piece of flesh stuck to the two sharp ends. As blood gushed out, her classmates screamed. She later claimed that part of her brain came out.

"A chunk of white," she said to me, showing me the size with her fingers.

A teacher heard the commotion and rushed Yan to the school clinic. Yan passed out the moment she stepped into the door. When she regained consciousness, she was in the hospital, with Mother sitting at her bedside. She was hospitalized for fifteen days. She could walk and recognize people, but had no control over her urine and bowel movements. Doctors predicted that she'd never fully recover from her brain damage. Miraculously, she did, although she suffered from chronic headaches for more than five years. Yan attributed her lack of interest in academic studies to this accident, often claiming it made her dumb.

"You are as smart as anybody," Mother kept telling her. "Look at the socks and sweaters you knit, and the embroidery you made. They are beautiful."

"I'm good with my hands, not my brain, Mother," Yan would say, laughing. She strove for excellence in her handiwork, but shrugged when she got Bs, or occasionally Cs, while her younger siblings were all straight A students.

Every day, Yan mopped our wood floor and nagged at us to keep it clean. The burgundy colored paint on the floor chipped away in heavily trodden areas, and the exposed raw wood made cleaning more difficult. "Don't enter the room until the floor is dry," Yan ordered. She often leaned against the long handle of the mop by the door and prevented us from entering a room until the floor was dry. Once in a while, to protest against her regime, Ping would lead us marching through the rooms despite Yan's protests.

"You can't do this!" Yan yelled after us. But one couldn't effectively stop a herd of four. Our dirty footprints left a muddy trail on the freshly mopped floors.

"That is for the little tyrant," Ping declared.

"For the tyrant!" we chanted along.

Yan burst into tears. "Nainai, look what they are doing!"

She appealed to Nainai for help, but before Nainai could carry out justice, we fled from the scene.

One day, Yan cornered Ping alone and threatened her. "If you do it again, I'll slap you so hard that your face will be red for days."

When Father came home that evening, Ping reported the incident to him. He sat down with Yan. "It's good you keep the house clean," he said. "But you don't expect your siblings to walk with their legs over their shoulders, do you?"

Ping was delighted with her triumph.

Yan never seemed to hold any grudge against us. The next time it happened, she chased us out of the room, and wiped the floor again. Ping felt guilty enough to bring her some bird eggs to make up. These eggs were so small that Ping cooked them by rinsing them with hot water. They were delicious.

Binbin was the only son in the family and ran around mostly with his own friends. Although he was not given any privileges over us daughters, our parents were certainly relieved they had a son, the designated person to carry on the family name. In traditional Chinese culture, a son was supposed to live with his parents and take care of them in their old age. But Father's view was more modern.

"Boys and girls are the same to me," he often said as his daughters surrounded him. But every once in a while, he jokingly said: "Girls are like spilled water. Once they are married, they belong to another family." He laughed when we protested. Chairman Mao said: "Women hold half the sky."

Binbin looked very much like Father. With his outgoing character, ready smile, and easy nature, he attracted a group of boys around him and was the monitor of his class at school. Binbin was handsome, and his good looks earned him many compliments. Our parents were a good-looking couple, and our neighbors often referred to us children as "five golden flowers." The term was taken from a film about five beautiful girls. Whenever Binbin heard that, he grimaced, but he merely rolled his eyes and went back to playing with his friends.

Binbin liked to play with caterpillars. His favorite kind had green skin and a smooth body. He often picked one from the bushes to place it on his sleeve. It had a large head, and its tail had a sharp end pointing upwards, like a short antenna in the rear. Its body was cold and always curled up when being touched. Binbin put the caterpillar back on a tree after playing with it, hoping it would turn into a butterfly. However, there was another kind of caterpillar that we all hated. It had gray hair and dark stripes. It looked mean and scary and could grow three inches long. They tended to cluster in groups on tree trunks or large branches. Pines, elms, or poplars, they discriminated against none. For tree climbers, these caterpillars could be dangerous. With one careless move, one could land the palm of his or her hand on top of them. It happened to me once. I was racing to get to an elm branch when I put my right hand into a cluster. Their soft bodies instantly curled up, releasing their toxic hair into my palm. It felt like needles. I screamed and let go. I fell out of the tree, but fortunately, I didn't break any bones. Nainai used a pair of tweezers and a magnifying glass to remove each of the gray hairs from my swollen palm. It took her a full hour. The shock and pain kept me from climbing trees for a long time.

While I avoided these caterpillars, Binbin, ever the brave warrior, continued fighting them. It was not uncommon for Binbin and his friends to get stung by these caterpillars as well. Whenever that happened, they sought revenge. They moved up and down the big trees to scoop up patches of these vicious looking creatures, placing them in a glass jar. They set up a bonfire in an open area and heated a sheet of iron on its top. Binbin took the lead to dump the caterpillars onto it. Then they stood back, watching the caterpillars twist and jump until they dropped dead. Binbin and his soldier friends were proud. They did a more efficient job than the woodpeckers in the trees. The scene made my stomach sick, but I could not pull myself away from the action and excitement.

Wen, who was closest to me in age and had the most amiable temperament, was the sibling I dared to make a fuss with. She was quiet, soft-spoken, and hardly ever said no to anyone. She kept her hair short and always wore hand-me-down clothes from Yan and Ping. If she did nice things at home, such as cleaning up or feeding the chickens we raised, she did them quietly and never asked for credit. We gave Wen a nickname, "Lao Huang Niu," "the old yellow cow." It was a popular term used to describe people who silently bore the burden of hard work, like a cow. She simply smiled, keeping at the tasks she deemed necessary. She was Nainai's right hand.

I often bombarded Wen with my requests. "Please play with me," or "Take me with you." When she had friends over, I would find all kinds of excuses to stay by her side. I liked to cut into their conversations, feeling more grown-up than I was. I wanted to get their attention and refused to admit I was a nuisance. Many times, Wen had to go to Nainai to ask her to usher me away.

One summer day when I was four or five, I insisted that Wen take me along to see her friends. I followed her every step, but I sensed her frustration. She finally threw her arms in the air.

"All right, then," she said. "I'm not going anywhere."

She went back to her room and picked up a book to read.

"Fine," I said to myself. I took Nainai's small stool to the front door. "I'll sit here and wait," I announced loud and clear.

I waited and waited. She didn't emerge from her room. Eventually I went inside and knocked on her door. There was no response. I ran to the backyard. Next to her bedroom was an area that had been fenced off with tree branches. Inside was our chicken coop made of brick and tiles. The golden rooster, always combative, flared up the feathers around his neck as I charged into his territory. I ignored him and pushed my way through the crackling hens and quickly climbed on top of the coop. I pressed my forehead against her window, but I saw no one inside. I realized she must have escaped through the window. I ran to Nainai and cried my heart out.

But I continued to follow her, begging her to take me along.

2

Of all my siblings, Ping influenced me the most. I was always anxious to please her, wishing I could be as intelligent as she was. When I turned five, Ping decided it was time for me to learn how to read and write. She was a patient teacher. She taught me the phonetics first. When I couldn't grasp the components to figure out the correct pronunciation, Ping encouraged me to memorize individual words.

"When you learn enough words, you'll understand the phonetic system," she said.

She started with the simple ones, such as horse, ram, and cow, which had fewer strokes and were easy to remember. She showed me how to write each of them in the order of calligraphy strokes. Ping never seemed to tire of my endless questions and my slow pace, but she had absolutely no tolerance for what she called "lack of effort." She set a goal for me to memorize a few new words each day.

As I made progress, she added more difficult characters. One day, she challenged me to recite and copy two lines of Chairman Mao's most famous statement. "The force at the core leading our cause forward is the Chinese Communist Party. The theoretical basis guiding our thinking is Marxism-Leninism." She sat down with me and repeated the two sentences until I could follow. It didn't take me long to recite it like a parrot, but I had no idea what the words meant.

Ping guided my hand to write the new words and then left me to practice them on my own. The pronunciation was the easiest part. When it came to writing, the challenge seemed insurmountable. Some words had so many strokes that the composing particles danced in front of my eyes like butterflies, shifting positions each time I attempted to capture them. After wrestling with them repeatedly, the idea of playing jump rope with my friend Wuzi became irresistible. I pushed my bedroom door ajar and saw no one in the hallway. I closed the door quietly behind me and left. I reminded myself to repeat the two lines from time to time while playing, making sure I would not fail her test by the end of the day. I sent Wuzi to check the front of my home before I ventured back. I was sweating and happy to have gotten a break from the strenuous effort of copying words. Just as I thought I could step into the apartment unnoticed, the front door swung open. Right in the middle of the doorway stood Ping, her hands on her hips. I stopped two yards away from the door. The grim smile on her face clearly indicated that no excuse would be accepted for such a violation.

"Don't even dream of going anywhere for the rest of the week!"

Ping threw the inevitable punishment at me: Two more paragraphs of Mao's quotations.

"You want to join the Young Pioneer Organization when you start school, don't you?" she asked.

Her voice was harsh, and her words set off an internal alarm. The Young Pioneer Organization was a group for outstanding students in elementary school. Its admission was strictly based on academic performance and political behavior. Members of the Young Pioneers wore a triangular red scarf around their necks, symbolizing a corner of the national five-star flag. All my older siblings became Young Pioneer members soon after they started school. I admired them and certainly didn't want to fall behind.

"Of course I do," I said, feeling ashamed of myself.

How could I become a Young Pioneer if I could not even keep my commitment to a single task? I took on my new assignment, and by the end of the week, I was able to recite and write both paragraphs unfalteringly.

3

There were a few activities we siblings enjoyed together. We loved swimming at Sha Keng, a large man-made pond. The pond was a quarry from the 1940s, supplying sand and gravel for the Baicheng Train Station. It was more than two hundred feet in width and half a mile in length. Toward the center, the water was very deep and cold. Weeds floated beneath the surface in a few areas, making it dangerous for swimmers. Every year, one or two people drowned in there, but that did not prevent children from going.

Government employees at the Compound went to swim at Sha Keng during their two-hour lunch break in the summer. They rode on an open truck, and many older children, including my siblings, invited themselves along. Schools, too, had a long lunch break, and most children went home and took a nap. My siblings preferred to go to Sha Keng.

Every once in a while, on Sundays, Father would go as well, along with one or two other high-ranking officials. They went in a government car. Father would not let any of us children tag along for a ride. But that didn't deter us. We took the truck and joined Father at the pond. Father, having learned how to swim in Mishan, was a good coach. We loved those rare occasions when he spent time with us. I clung to him whenever I had a chance, enjoying a ride on his back.

We were forbidden to go to Sha Keng on our own. "It's too dangerous," Mother warned us. Nevertheless, my older siblings continued to go. They teamed up with a few others in the Compound. It was an open secret among us, but our parents didn't know. We didn't own swimsuits. My older siblings swam in their undershirts and shorts. Drying them on a clothing line wouldn't betray my siblings' whereabouts. In due time, Ping, Binbin, and Wen all became good swimmers. Yan, afraid of deeper water, was the only one who never learned how to swim.

One sunny day in the summer, my siblings took the truck ride to swim in Sha Keng. I tagged along, thrilled to be included. Yan volunteered to keep an eye on me. Ping and Binbin rolled their eyes, but didn't voice any objections.

Yan and I each took a tire inner tube as a lifesaver. As soon as we arrived at Sha Keng, Ping and Binbin disappeared. They were swimming back and forth across the pond. True to her word, Yan took me by the hand and stayed with me in shallow water. When she got bored, she put a tube around her waist, and placed the other one on me. She pushed me slowly away from the shore. When she got distracted, I slipped through the middle. I felt water reach my face and then I was submerged. In my effort to come to the surface, I swallowed mouthfuls of water and choked. I kicked and paddled with my arms as hard as I could, but I kept sinking. Seized with fear, I opened my tightly closed eyes. I saw my tube floating above my head, but couldn't reach it. Yan was idling not far from me, her arms resting on her tube, but I couldn't reach her either. I wanted to shout to get Yan's attention. It didn't work. Instead, I swallowed more water. I felt my lungs were about to burst. I panicked. Fortunately, a woman nearby noticed my struggle and rushed over to my rescue. I threw up over her shoulder as she carried me to the shore. It was my first encounter with a life-threatening experience. I was scared of water afterward and never learned how to swim when I was a child.

4

But I continued to join my siblings in their activities. One that I enjoyed most was raising silkworms. Ping introduced us to the practice. One day, she came home from school with a piece of paper covered with little black dots. "These are silkworm eggs," she said. A girl in Ping's class had given them to her. There must have been two or three hundred eggs, standing out on the white paper.

We immediately surrounded Ping, eager to take a look. We had heard about silkworms and used silk products, but we had not seen a real silkworm. We touched the shell of these eggs and were amazed that they were smaller than grains of millet.

"Silkworms weave until their last threads; Candles weep until their wicks turn to ashes." Binbin quoted one of the best-known poems from Li Shangyin, a poet from the Tang Dynasty. Li always used words in a most subtle and allusive way. He lived late in the Tang Dynasty, when Chinese civilization reached a high point. The two stanzas Binbin quoted were from a love poem, but the image of silkworms spinning until their last breath had become a symbol of giving. We could hardly wait for them to come out.

When spring finally arrived, we kept a close eye on the silkworm eggs. Big Aunt, Father's older sister who often stayed with us after we moved to Baicheng, advised us what to do. She had raised silkworms in her village before. We stared with fascination as a tiny hole cracked on the shell and out came a string-like creature, smaller than the tiniest ant. We ran to the mulberry trees in the Compound and collected the freshly budding leaves. Within a few days, the silkworms shed their first layer of skin and crawled freely. They grew fast. As they shed layers of skin, their bodies turned from black to gray and eventually to ivory white. In a month, they reached their full length of about two and a half inches.

"If a baby were to grow like a silkworm, he would be the size of an elephant as an adult!" Big Aunt said, laughing.

The silkworms ate faster and faster. All we heard was munching. They fascinated us. As soon as we spread a layer of mulberry leaves over them, they crawled to the edges of the leaves and moved their heads up and down in rhythm. Within minutes, they reduced a leaf to its skeleton. As the process continued, picking leaves to feed them became a chore, so we changed our approach. Instead of selecting the finest leaves, we simply stripped an entire branch with a single sweep.

Most of the leaves came from the five mulberry trees behind the Wan Building. They didn't grow tall. Their trunks split into several limbs not far from the ground, and they extended horizontally, like pine trees at an oceanfront. We moved up and down these trees easily. Our rough harvesting broke their branches and damaged many fluffy, tiny flowers in the early spring. Some managed to produce berries. Despite our vow to pick the fruits when they were ripe, we raced to eat them as soon as they changed from green to pink. The pungent, sour flavor made our mouths water and our eyes narrow to slits. By the time the berries turned to a ripened dark purple and were ready to burst with sweet juice, we had to search all over the trees for the remaining few that had escaped our impatient raids.

Unlike the resilient mulberry trees, the silkworms were delicate. When we touched them, they curled up their bodies in retreat. In the mornings the leaves were covered with dew. We had to dry them with towels because the silkworms might drown in just a few drops of water. Once Father accidentally blew a mouthful of cigarette smoke toward them. Those close by immediately jolted up their heads and waved back and forth as if in protest. Amazed by their reaction, we begged him to do it again. He repeated it a few more times. We were astonished to find more than a dozen silkworms dead the following morning.

We took care of the silkworms as if they were our pets. When the silkworms were ready to produce silk, their bodies turned amber. Big Aunt showed us how to collect small branches of trees and tie them together, so that the silkworms could nest in the twigs and weave their cocoons. She also laid down a smooth wooden board and placed a number of silkworms on it.

"This way, they will make a flat sheet of silk," she said.

For three days, the silkworms weaved continuously. While those on the tree branches soon enclosed themselves in their cocoons, the ones on the plank fully exposed their work to our eyes. They moved their heads smoothly in all directions, with a very fine line of silk spilling out like an inexhaustible fine stream of spring water. They spread their silk evenly on the surface as if orchestrated by an invisible hand. They had no possibility to make cocoons, but they kept spinning.

"Each silkworm can produce a thread about a mile long," Big Aunt told us.

We were impressed. It was astonishing to learn that a silk dress would take seventeen hundred cocoons to make. We felt more appreciative of silk products. The following year, we raised more silkworms. Ping moved her bedding to Nainai's room and gave up her bedroom for the silkworms. As we took care of our silkworms, we also learned more about mulberry trees. The ones that made their way to the northeast were the hardiest species. They were self-pollinating, and their leaves, even on the same tree, were different in size and shape. Although they were able to withstand the winter and our abuse, they also had their vulnerabilities. If a large branch was broken off or a big batch of bark was scaled, the wounds would bleed, spreading thick, liquid resin over the cuts. They could die from the wounds.

5

I always looked up to my older siblings as my role models. At a time when patriotic heroism was hailed in movies and books, and was emphasized in school, my sisters and brother waged their own guerrilla wars in the Compound. They were following the example of many heroic revolutionaries who would rather die than surrender to the enemies. We admired these heroes and martyrs for their bravery, their self-sacrifice. Two movies, *The Tunnel Battles* and *The Mine Battles*, featuring guerrilla warfare against the Japanese in the early 1940s, especially fascinated us. To learn from the protagonists, my sisters and brother, together with a few older children in the Compound, posed as infantry soldiers and played war games. Many evenings, they divided their group into two and fought their guerrilla wars in the darkness. I would press my forehead against Nainai's bedroom window, trying hard to get a glimpse of their whereabouts. I admired them, but did not dare to follow them into the night.

The self-proclaimed young warriors made wood spears and each tied a red tassel to the head, just like the images of the young pioneers we saw in the movies. Rifles were carved out of wood, their favorite weapons. During the day, I loved to stand close to them as they drilled and marched with pride. "Charge! Kill!" Their shouting echoed in the air and their weapons collided with force.

A favorite song of the time was called the "Ballad of the Machete," an anti-Japanese song composed in 1937 when Japan invaded China. They put their makeshift weapons on their shoulders and marched on the open area, loudly belting out the song, their voices trembling with rage and indignation.

"Swing the machete at the heads of the foreign devils,
Patriots around the county,
The day to fight the Japanese is here,
The day to fight the Japanese is here.

Our volunteer soldiers march in front,
Our nation's civilians strengthen their back.
Soldiers and civilians unite together,
Forward we march, bravely.
Aim at the enemies,
Wipe them out, wipe them out,
Strike!"

Although I had no idea who the enemy might be at the moment, I knew for sure that, one day, facing the same situation, my siblings would act heroically as well. In my eyes, they already looked like heroes.

Not being able to join them in their fighting games, I begged them to tell me wartime stories. One that particularly touched me was the death of a girl called Liu Hulan. She was only fifteen when captured by the Kuomintang Army in 1947. The Kuomintang asked her to denounce the Communist Party in front of the gathered villagers. Her mother and other family members were standing in the crowd. She refused, with her back straight and her head up high. No threat of death or torture would change her mind. She stood side by side with six other captured men, all of them members of the Communist Party. Their hands were tied behind their backs, and their bodies bruised from beating.

The enemy set up three huge straw choppers, threatening to behead them if they would not cooperate. None of them gave in. One after another, they were executed, their blood spilling all over the ground. Facing her comrades' brutal death, Liu Hulan calmly announced that as a Communist Party member, she was not afraid to die. "I'll serve the cause of the people and the Communist Party until my last breath," she declared, looking at the executioners in contempt. With her voice still echoing in the air, she walked over to a large straw chopper, lay down and placed her head right under the shining blade. Chairman Mao learned of her heroic deed and wrote an inscription to praise her: "A great birth; a glorious death." Liu became a national heroine and household name. Her story was made into a film and numerous picture books. Fortunately, they were all black-and-white. It would have been unbearable to see all that blood in vivid color.

I never tired of listening to her story. However, I felt scared when I closed my eyes and imagined putting my head under a glistening knife. I wondered if I would ever possess the courage to die heroically like Liu. I was appalled that I could not give an honest, straightforward answer. Quietly, I felt ashamed of my cowardice.

I continued to tail my older siblings and was always thrilled when I could be part of their group. Once during a snowball fight, I bundled up and joined them. One group was throwing big snowballs from the second floor of the Wan Pagoda, and the other was attacking them from all directions surrounding the building, calling the "enemy" to surrender. Everyone was hiding behind a tree, sticking his or her head out only to make a quick attack. My snowball could not even reach half way up the staircase. Desperate to be recognized as a brave fighter, I decided to move behind a big tree next to the pagoda. I was certain that from there, my attack would be effective. I jumped out of my hiding place and ran toward the tree, exposing myself in the open. No more than five steps on my way, I felt a hard-pressed snowball hitting my face. I staggered and fell. More snowballs started to fly toward me, landing against my heavily padded coat. I put my arms around my hood in a vain attempt to protect my head. My mittens were wet and my hands numb from the cold. I didn't know how long I could withstand the attack. I felt helpless and stupid. The barrage of snowballs gave me no time to get on my feet and run away.

"Cover me," I heard a shout. Someone ran to me and whisked me away in his arms. Once at a safe distance, he dropped me down and rushed back to the battle without a word. I was terribly embarrassed. Slowly, I turned to look at the "battlefield." Everyone was busy fighting. I could not even tell who the brave soul who rescued me was. To my relief, however, no one seemed to have noticed that I needed saving. It was then I felt my face was burning with pain. I fought back the emerging tears and ran home. Looking at a bruise the size of a ping-pong ball on my face in the mirror, with blood still seeping out, I cried. Nainai came and cleaned the wound with cotton balls. Then she let me sob in her arms. When my sisters and brother came home later, I acted as if the pain and the bruise did not bother me at all.

6

That was nothing compared to what came next. One evening, Wen asked me to join her in taking a bath. I was overjoyed. A bath was a special treat, requiring a team effort. The tub in the bathroom served more as a decoration since there was no hot water. In summertime, Mother and Yan used it to wash our bed sheets. It was too cold to carry out such tasks in the winter. To take a bath in it, we had to boil kettles of water on the single stove-top in the kitchen, as well as fetch additional water from a heating radiator in Binbin's bedroom. In order to fully utilize the result of our joint efforts, two of my sisters usually took a bath together or, if one of them was in good humor, I would be invited.

It took us more than an hour to fill up the tub. I joyfully jumped into the hot water. Wen tolerated the splashes and clamor I made. She kneeled behind me and washed my back and hair. As soon as she was done, I started running the slippery soap up and down my body and marveled how quickly the water became murky.

"That's enough," Wen finally said. Using a ladle, she rinsed my body clean of soap. She helped me out of the tub, and told me to dry myself with a towel and get dressed. She pointed to a small stand at the corner and asked me to sit there and wait for her.

The room was warm and filled with steam. The fresh smell of soap made me feel wonderful. Moisture had condensed on the window, sliding down the glass and leaving strips of curved lines as if earthworms had just crawled over its surface. I dried myself and slipped on a loose shirt. The small stand in the corner was an old fruit crate. The top cover was torn out. The crate, placed upside down, served as a makeshift seat. A piece of burgundy cloth covered the surface. I climbed on its top. The thick fabric felt soft to my bare feet, though the uneven slices of wood boards under the cover pressed against my soles.

I stood on tiptoes and wiped clean the misty layer on the window. A new foggy layer took its place quickly, leaving no trace of the former patterns on the glass. I put my index and middle fingers together and drew a smiling face as I often did on a piece of paper. Wen ignored my creation, seemingly absorbed in her own thoughts.

To get my sister's attention, I turned away from the window and planted myself in the middle of the crate.

"How high do you think I could raise my right foot?" I asked.

I had seen ballerinas lift their legs nearly vertically up or bent backward, reaching the ground with their hands behind their heads. I had practiced with Wuzi.

"Don't be naughty," Wen said. "I'll be out in a minute."

"Look, I bet I can do..." Before I finished my sentence, I felt the crate shift under my foot. I was startled and tried to regain my balance. The crate flipped over in a flash, launching me heavily onto my back. Even with the shock, I felt something sharp pierce through my skin and penetrate my back. The pain struck me like lightning. I let out a scream. Wen jumped out of the bathtub. She reached over to lift me up, but the box came up with me together. The pull from the box made me yelp.

"No, no, no..." was all I could say. Realizing the crate got stuck on my back, Wen put me down. She didn't know what to do.

Yan and Ping ran over from their room and started pounding on the door.

"What happened?"

"Open the door!"

They shook the handle on the door, and the loose metal lock clanged in the socket, but would not release. Their voices became more urgent and desperate with each passing moment. I howled. The sharp pain seemed to spread from my back to my chest, and my crying and shaking only made it worse.

Wen fumbled to throw on her nightgown and the water on her body immediately soaked the thin fabric. Her trembling hands couldn't release the bolt.

"Stop pushing the door!" she yelled. Wen's bursting high pitch silenced the noise in the hallway. No one had ever heard Wen raise her voice.

The door swung open, and Yan and Ping charged in. They rushed toward me.

"Don't move her!" Wen shouted again. "The box stuck to her back!" Wen started crying.

After a moment of confusion, Ping lifted me up slowly while Yan held down the crate. The pull on my back made me let out another howling. I felt the box separate from my body, but instead of relief, the pain was more acute. I screamed at the top of my voice as they carried me out of the bathroom. Through her tears, Wen saw the long, rusty nail on the back of the crate that had been driven into my back.

Ping urged Binbin to call Mother. He ran to the only phone, which had been provided to Father for official uses. He asked an operator to connect him to the No. 3 Middle School. As always, Mother was working late, and Father was out of town, but no one answered the phone on the other side. It was 9 o'clock in the evening. The switch board at the school had long since closed for the night.

The commotion woke up Nainai. She charged over as fast as her bound feet permitted. Nainai, who never dealt with the outside world in the city, resorted to her folk remedy. She burned a few cotton balls and applied the ashes to the wound to stop the bleeding. She paced back and forth by the front door, anxiously expecting Mother's return. I was crying and shivering uncontrollably. My sisters and brother put me on our parents' large bed and surrounded me.

"I don't think tears can ease the pain, Jian," Ping said after a while, taking command of the situation. She wiped my face tenderly with a handkerchief. Her softness and attention touched me like a warm current. I tried to control my hysterical crying, and the result was a muted sobbing.

"Let me tell you the story of our hero Wang Cheng," Ping said.

We all knew Wang Cheng's story. It was one of the few feature films shown in 1964, and we had all seen it several times. Wang Cheng was a hero during the Korean War in the early

1950s. He was in the People's Volunteer Army of China, fighting against the US in Korea. At the fierce Battle of Sukchon-Sunchon, he was a radio operator. When his fellow soldiers were all killed by the bombing and attacks of the US Army, he lined up the rest of the ammunition along the sandbag barriers and fired at the enemy climbing up the hill until he could no longer fend them off. "Comrades, fire the cannons at me!" he shouted one last time into the two-way radio connected to the headquarters and threw away the headphone. He ignited the fuse of an explosive tube and jumped on top of the barrier. The American soldiers were struck with horror. They dropped their weapons and tried in vain to retreat. Wang Cheng jumped off the barrier and landed in the middle of the approaching troops. A giant explosion ripped the air. Scores of enemy soldiers were killed instantly. The survivors ran down the hill, a human avalanche.

"Wang Cheng was not afraid, not even of death. I'm sure you won't surrender to the pain." Ping squeezed my right hand and looked at me, encouragingly. I bit my lower lip and stopped sobbing, but my body continued to shake, like a kite caught in a tree, shivering in the wind, struggling in vain to get free.

At 9:30, Mother got home. The moment she parked her bicycle, Nainai and my siblings surrounded her. Everyone started speaking at the same time.

"Calm down, let Nainai speak first," Mother said. She realized something terrible must have happened.

"It's Jian. She got hurt. She is in your bedroom," Nainai said.

Mother raced to my bedside, followed by Yan, Ping, and Binbin. Wen was the only one who didn't move from my side. "Oh, Jian, I'm so sorry," she kept saying.

My pale face must have startled Mother. "Why didn't you call for a car and send her to the hospital?" she asked. The garage, where all the government vehicles were kept, was less than half a block away. Father had always emphasized that none of us should use the cars for personal purposes. It did not occur to any of my siblings, Ping included, to break the rule. Mother placed the call, and within three minutes, a car was at the door.

I was lucky that the nail had stopped short of penetrating my lung, but the subsequent pain of disinfecting the wound sent chills down my spine. Two nurses held me down, and another poked alcohol-soaked cotton tips into the wound. I felt like a dull sword was stabbing me again and again. I bit the vinyl cover of the examination table in the emergency room and sank my fingernails into my arms. Ping stood dutifully by my side, giving me encouragement.

"You are so brave, Jian!" she murmured into my ears, her face bent close to mine.

Mother put a hand on my head, but looked the other way. My body quivered with the twisting of the nurse's hand, but I did not cry this time. I wanted to prove myself to Ping and Mother, and wanted them to be proud of me. The nurse gasped in surprise, saying she had never treated a girl so brave. I felt proud. The more I endured the pain, the more heroic I could be when I would confront a real ordeal set up by our enemies.

Although I could not visualize the future enemy, the very thought was enough to make me behave like a heroine. The strong smell of disinfectant in the hospital added a heightened sense of tragedy to my imagination. This was a battle I had to win.

I heard the scream of a little boy in the next room. That was not heroic, I thought, and deliberately let go of my bite on the cover. I wanted to show I had the courage and will to face my pain.

A month later, the bandages were removed. A scar the size of a thumb formed on my back. It always feels itchy on rainy days and reminds me of an age that was innocent and pure. This innocence, however, would soon be destroyed with the start of the Cultural Revolution.

Chapter Ten

Hit by the Storm

1

I was six at the start of the Cultural Revolution. This unprecedented political movement was officially announced as a campaign to eliminate bourgeois elements and continue the class struggle. It was Mao's initiative to topple his rivals. The Central Government, or what was left of it, called the movement "a great revolution that touches people to their very souls." It certainly spared no one. In a short period of time, China was turned upside down. Many top-level officials were purged from office. Among them, Liu Shaoqi, Chairman of the nation, and Deng Xiaoping, General Secretary of the Communist Party. They were condemned as China's "biggest capitalist roaders," a term used to refer to those who attempted to develop capitalism under the pretense of upholding socialism. With their fall, millions more were persecuted.

In August 1966, as I just started elementary school, the world around me turned red. Red flags, red armbands, and Mao's little red books. People beat drums and shouted revolutionary slogans everywhere. Old street signs were taken down to be replaced with revolutionary names. And old shop signs were smashed. In their place, new names with words such as "red" or "revolution" appeared.

Most prominent of all was the appearance of the Red Guard, a newly formed student organization. Members wore red bands on their arms and marched all over the city streets, carrying Chairman Mao's little red books, a collection of his quotations. Workers, institution staff, and government employees also formed their own "rebel groups." They were responding to Mao's call to carry out the Great Proletarian Cultural Revolution.

As if infected with a fever, the Red Guards and the rebels crushed the "four olds" without reservation—old ideas, old culture, old customs, and old habits. Our life fell into chaos.

Chairman Mao fully supported the Red Guards, calling them "young revolutionary generals." Within a few months of their organization's establishment, Mao granted them eight audiences at the Tiananmen Square in Beijing. Mao waved to them from the top of the Tiananmen Gate or in a convertible cruising through the Changanjie, the main street between Tiananmen Gate and the Square. Prominently displayed on his right arm was a Red Guard armband. Millions of Red Guards from all over the country were "blessed" by Mao. They traveled free of charge across the country because they were spreading the revolution—paralyzing the nation's railroad system. Their subsequent action of "Duo Quan," "taking over power," threw the country into anarchy.

And Chairman Mao cheered them on. At an interview Mao gave to the Red Guards, a young girl presented him with an armband. Mao asked: "What is your name?"

"Song Binbin," she said, a small, thin girl, dressed in a washed-out army uniform with the insignia removed. "Binbin" means "refined and courteous." But Mao said to her: "Yaowu would be better." Yaowu meant to "wish for violence."

Song not only changed her name immediately, but also advocated that her school change its name to Yaowu.

To my brother's embarrassment, his given name was spelled exactly the same as that of Song Binbin. He quickly changed his name to Yaowu as well, but at home, he was always Binbin. "Yaowu" sounded awkward.

The fever of the Cultural Revolution spread through the country like an epidemic, infecting the old and the young, turning each and every one into either predator or prey. The revolution was devouring its children.

2

I didn't know what was going on around us, but I could feel the change in the atmosphere. As the outside world was charged with a dark passion and excitement, inside our home, my parents seemed increasingly concerned. And despite Binbin's change of name, my older siblings' reaction toward the movement was less than lukewarm.

Before the start of the Cultural Revolution, my sister Yan had been accepted by a two-year medical school; and Ping had left home to study at a special aviation training center. Earlier that year, Ping had gone through a highly selective process, both physically and academically. Among more than one thousand applicants, only four girls and twenty-six boys passed the rigorous tests. It was her first step toward realizing her cherished dream of becoming a pilot. Ping soon established herself as a top student and was the first one among her peers to take a large glider into the sky. "I'm flying! I'm up in the air!" she shouted. All her classmates were on the ground looking up at her. But her dream was short-lived. The center was shut down at the start of the Cultural Revolution.

At the time, Mother was Party Secretary at the No. 3 Middle School. Since the Red Guards were at the forefront of the Cultural Revolution, the education system was among the first to be scrutinized. Consequently, Mother fell at the beginning of the movement. She, Mr. He, the Principal, and Mr. Jiang, the Deputy Principal, were accused of following a "revisionist line of education" and Mother was forced to subject herself to "self-criticism."

Mother took it very hard. She couldn't understand how all these years of hard work were condemned as wrong. Faced with repeated requests for self-criticism, she admitted in general terms that she might have made mistakes in her work, but she denied the accusation that she had deliberately carried out a revisionist line. "I faithfully followed the orders of the Party and the Education Bureau," she said. Mother had always been a straightforward person, and she didn't hesitate to defend herself.

As Party Secretary, she was in charge of the key to the drawers where all the Party members' files were kept. The Red Guards demanded she give them the key.

"I'll only turn over the key to a Party representative," she said. "Not any of you."

The Red Guards were furious, but they couldn't make her obey. In the end, they sealed the door to the file room.

Mr. He and Jiang were not so courageous. Mr. He came from a family of landlords, and Jiang from a rich peasant family. An entire system was in place to classify family backgrounds. Five categories were regarded as "class enemies." Landlords and rich peasants were among them. This classification was important to everyone. Starting from elementary school, every one had to fill in a form and state his or her family background. A person's future depended on it. The classifications were set up in the late 1940s, when the Communists first took over the country. Each family was placed into a category according to its financial situation. The classifications could not be changed. They became a family's stigma. Children born after the liberation, meaning after 1949, carried the burden of their ancestors. Even when people chose their spouses, they had to take the family background into consideration. Marrying a person with a bad classification would not only impact the spouse, it would also negatively impact their children.

Because of their problematic family backgrounds, He and Jiang didn't dare voice any objections. They were condemned as snakes that had sneaked into the revolution by hiding their true nature. The Red Guards—all students at this school—smeared black ink on their hands and arms and forced their former principals to stand on top of a bench. They placed paper dunce hats on their heads and wrote on the hats in large characters: "Dark Hands Sneaked into the Revolution."

"Down with He and Jiang!"

"Down with the Black Hands!"

"Long live Chairman Mao!" they shouted.

They beat He and Jiang and paraded them in circles around the campus. They were overthrowing their own teachers.

Since Mother came from a family of hired laborers, and Father, at the beginning of the Cultural Revolution, was still a leading official, the Red Guards didn't beat her. They confined her in the school's furnace room and requested she confess her crimes. Mother insisted she was innocent and expressed her devotion to the Party. Enraged by her behavior, the Red Guards organized a large rally meeting against her. Such meetings were called "struggle meetings." Mother was placed in the center of the rally.

"Our policy is lenient to those who confess and severe to those who do not. You know that, don't you?" they shouted at her. That was a familiar phrase. During the land reform movement in the late 1940s, Mother had used the same phrase against the landlords.

Her head was throbbing. "I didn't commit any crime," Mother said. "I did my best to follow the Party."

"How dare you!" A Red Guard shouted at her. "You are against Chairman Mao and Mao Zedong Thoughts," another chanted.

"I am not. Without Chairman Mao and the Communist Party, I would not be alive today," she shot back.

The Red Guards pounded on the desks and told her to shut up. They closed in on her. Mother was surrounded. The Red Guards were waving their fists in her face. She felt blood surging to her head. She had difficulties breathing. Mother had gone through many political movements before, but had never been accused of opposing Mao. Tears came to her eyes. This was a matter of principle, and she couldn't accept the charges. She argued with the Red Guards, putting her safety aside.

As the pushing and shouting went on, Mother's voice was buried in the noise. She felt nauseated. Sweat dripped from her forehead and soaked her blouse. Eventually, her legs buckled, and she collapsed in the middle of a sentence.

Mother didn't know how long she had passed out. When she came to, her limbs felt weak and her throat dry. She couldn't move or talk. She heard a Red Guard next to her say she was faking it, and another suggested they send this "stubborn granite head" to the school's clinic to find out if she was playing tricks on them. A few hands reached down to her and lifted her up by her limbs. She felt like a corpse.

They dropped her on the dirt floor at the clinic. The doctor, who was also being criticized, didn't dare treat her.

"She is dehydrated," the doctor said. "Let her have some water and rest. She should be fine." The Red Guards dragged her away. Mother passed out again.

The Red Guards, enraged by Mother's refusal to cooperate, detained her in school. They made her write self-criticism day and night. When she dozed off at her desk, they poked her awake. Mother had been suffering from insomnia for years. Her situation deteriorated quickly. She started smoking. Like Father, she found it calming in her isolation. She wrote pages and pages of self-criticism, but the Red Guards were not satisfied.

"You are downplaying your crimes," they said to her. "Dig deeper. You should go beyond the daily administrative issues."

Mother underwent serious self-reflection. She wrote about her inadequacy in dealing with certain personnel matters, about her blindly following municipal directives, and about her unwillingness to accept criticism, a bad attitude, as the students pointed out to her.

The Red Guards kept her confined in school for nearly three months. They watched her every move. During the day, they held struggle meetings against her or made her stand on the street in front of the school, with a placard around her neck denouncing her as a capitalist roader. At night, they forced her to write more self-criticism or, as they called it, "confessions." They would not let her alone. Even when she went to the outhouse, they had one or two female Red Guards following her: suicides were common. Mother told them there was no need for them to keep an eye on her. "I won't run away, nor will I ever commit suicide," she said. The Red Guards started calling her "granite head."

Since the Red Guards weren't able to pinpoint any counterrevolutionary activities at school, they sent representatives to Mother's hometown to investigate her past. When they found her history immaculate—her parents extremely poor and fully supportive of the Communist Army and the Central Government—they let Mother go home. They started the process to "rehabilitate" her. By then, Revolution Committees were set up at all levels of the government agencies and institutions. They consisted of rebels, representatives of factory workers, the voice of the proletarians, and in some cases, former administrators or officials who were trustworthy enough to be incorporated. They were in charge of the development of the revolution and managed the daily administration. They considered allowing Mother to be a member.

It was at this time that Father fell from grace. He was accused of treason and denounced in the entire Baicheng Prefecture. Mother was dragged down for the second time.

3

At the beginning of the Cultural Revolution, Father was conscripted into the Revolution Committee. He was concerned that the movement might spin out of control. He tried hard to guide the rebellious young, and protect the other officials. But with each passing day, he found it more difficult to perform his duties. In 1967, as the Cultural Revolution moved forward with more vigor, Chairman Mao decided to receive local government representatives in Beijing. He wanted to provide them with more support. Father went to Beijing. Shortly before Mao's reception, however, word came that anyone with "historical problems" would not be granted an audience. Father's capture by the Japanese, despite his exoneration by the army in 1941, was considered "problematic." He was sent back to Baicheng under escort.

News of Father's rejection reached Baicheng before his arrival. It immediately put him on the other side of the revolution. By then, the Red Guards in the city had divided into several factions, with the "Baicheng Commune" and the "Baicheng Rebels" as the two major forces. They got wind of Father's return and went to the train station to intercept him. Posters with big hand-written Chinese characters were pasted all over the walls of the station and the Government Compound, denouncing him as a "Big Traitor" and a "Capitalist Roader." The night of Father's arrival, he didn't make it home. We waited in vain. Hours passed, and in the encroaching darkness, our hopes grew dim. That night, we went to bed not knowing where Father was.

The following day, there was a knock at the door. We received a small bundle of his belongings, but we weren't told where he was or what had happened to him. That same day, a loudspeaker was set up in a tall poplar tree in front of our building. It blasted angry words against Father, accusing him of betraying the country at the hands of the Japanese. "Other comrades captured by the Japanese died. How could you survive the brutality of the Japanese and come back alive?"

For three days, my sisters Yan and Ping looked for him. They didn't dare make direct inquiries. They were afraid of being criticized as not "cutting a clear line of demarcation" from Father, a class enemy. They discreetly wandered around the headquarters of the Red Guards, keeping their eyes and ears open. Their search produced no results. We didn't know if Father was alive or dead. Mother had never appeared so worried and restless. Nainai, who could not understand any of the political jargon blasted in the air, sensed something was wrong.

"What are they talking about?" she asked. "Why do they keep calling my son?"

We didn't know what to tell her. Mother came to our rescue. "There is a Cultural Revolution going on," Mother said, as if that could explain everything. Seeing Nainai's puzzled look,

Mother added: "Your son is fine. He is out of town." Mother lied and told Nainai that she misunderstood the name. "They are talking about a man named Hu Kai, not Hou Kai."

We looked at each other in bewilderment. Mother had always told us to be honest and straightforward, no matter what. In her effort to protect Nainai, she was breaking her principles.

One day, Father appeared at a large struggle meeting organized by the Red Guards. He had been kept by one of the Red Guard groups. A number of other former officials were at this struggle meeting as well. Governor Yuan, Deputy Governor Chen, Xia, and Duan were all labeled the biggest capitalist roaders in Baicheng. Their hands were tied behind their backs, and their heads covered with paper dunce hats. In front of their chests, wood placards hung from their necks. Their names were written in black, with two red lines crossing over it in the shape of "X," as if they were criminals on the way to their execution. My sister Ping hid herself behind a tree and watched the process. Governor Yuan was badly beaten and had to be carried away. He suffered multiple head injuries, and three of his ribs were broken.

In the commotion, Ping was surprised to see Mr. Fang among the persecuted. Fang was a former Deputy Governor, who had been banished to the countryside nearly two years before. He stood side by side with the other top officials. In addition to a wooden board, a string of worn-out shoes hung from his neck. His head was bent so low that Ping didn't recognize him at first.

Fang was in his early forties and used to be one of the most talented and handsome deputy governors at the Baicheng Prefecture. Besides tending government affairs, he also enjoyed writing. He had one novel published to moderate success. With his royalty payment from the book, he had generously lent money to our family, helping us relieve a financial crisis we faced that year.

Fang spent long hours after work in his office to work on his writing. A typist, a young woman in her late twenties, readily extended her help to type the manuscript for him. She was impressed by his talent and fell in love with him. No one knew when they started a love affair. One day, his wife found a note from the young woman in his pocket when she washed his clothing. The young woman poured out her admiration for him. His wife was infuriated. She cried, yelled, and had endless fights with him. No apology could soothe her wounded heart.

In her rage, she turned in the letter to the Organization Department of the Baicheng Prefecture. She wanted the Party to give him a disciplinary warning, which, she hoped, would teach him a lesson and prevent him from having any extramarital affairs in the future. She didn't consider that affairs were strictly forbidden, and that anyone, not to mention a prominent official, who had committed such indecency, would face the end of his or her career. Sexual scandals were dealt with in a most severe measure. The Party took the matter seriously. Fang was fired from his position and sent to the countryside. His wife and five children ended up going with him.

The term "Po Xie," worn-out shoe, was often used for promiscuous women. At the rally meetings, dirty shoes were dangling in front of his chest. The heavy blow devastated him. Later, it was reported that he went blind. No one ever saw him or his family members again.

That day, looking at the worn-out shoes, Ping's thought turned to Shu, the oldest daughter of Deputy Governor Zhao. She was nineteen when a love affair ruined her life. It happened the year before the start of the Cultural Revolution. She had just graduated from high school, a tall and pretty young woman. She fell in love with a married man and became pregnant. They couldn't marry—that would be an endorsement for an illegitimate relationship. Abortion for an unmarried girl, especially a Governor's daughter, would create a scandal. The Zhao family quietly made a hasty arrangement and married her off to a low-level government staff member. When the baby was born and the husband realized it could not possibly be his, he abandoned her, leaving her in a more devastating situation. Shu had to raise the child on her own. She lived at her parents' house, rarely taking her child out, proof of her sin. People avoided her, as if association would contaminate them. She was called "Po Xie." After the Cultural Revolution started, it was not unusual to see worn-out shoes thrown at her door.

The shouting of revolutionary slogans brought Ping back to reality. She felt disgusted that Mr. Fang was put under the spotlight and humiliated again, as if the punishment he had received was not enough.

Then she saw Father standing close to the center on the platform. The Red Guards attacked him. They took turns hitting him. His nose, which had been broken by the Japanese, bled without stopping. That didn't stop them. Two Red Guards forced him to bend so low that the fountain pen in his pocket broke, adding dark blue ink to his blood stained shirt.

Ping couldn't bear to watch any longer. She ran home weeping, and locked herself in her room.

After the beating at this struggle meeting, the local army units retained Father and a few other high-ranking officials. The Red Guards could sign them out for rally meetings or to parade them in the streets, essentially "borrowing" people to abuse, but they had to send them back to the army by the end of the day. There, beatings were discouraged.

In 1968, when the country was plunged into further chaos, the Central Government called upon the army to take control of local affairs and maintain order. Groups of army representatives were sent to all local institutions. They supported the Cultural Revolution and the Red Guards and were supposed to keep the chaotic situation under control. Their involvement in local affairs, however, also made things complicated. In many cases, the army let groups of Red Guards gain access to guns and ammunition to help maintain control, paving the road for more violence. For the time being, their interference saved Father and a few other top officials from being beaten to death. In a way, the military retention, bad as it was, served as a buffer from the more excessive abuse by the Red Guards. But we were not allowed to see Father. If he needed anything, from clothing to his life-saving tobacco leaves, we had to leave it with the guard at the place of his detention.

Later, Father was made to stand in front of the Government Compound for an hour in the morning, sometimes with another official. He had to carry the "Big Traitor" placard in front of him and face the ridicule and humiliation of passers-by. We avoided going through the main gate. We couldn't bear to see him like this.

4

We were torn between our loyalty to Mao and our parents. We had been brought up to be the successors of the revolution. Now, a revolution was in full swing, but our parents had become targets. We were requested to expose them and criticize them. The phrase "cutting a clear line of demarcation" was repeated to us every day.

Yan was the first one to criticize Mother at a school meeting. Mother was made to stand on the platform. Yan read a paper on the podium. She avoided looking at Mother.

"I'm determined to follow Chairman Mao and the Party," she said. She was asked to expose Mother's counterrevolutionary activities. Failing to come up with any, she listed Mother's refusal to let us swim in Sha Keng as an offence. "Our beloved leader Chairman Mao called upon us to experience the storms of the world, but she wouldn't even allow us to swim in a pond," Yan said, pointing her finger at Mother. The Red Guards applauded her. It was a crime to hinder education. Apparently, education now included frolicking in a pond. Mother was hurt and disappointed by Yan's behavior, but she said nothing. Her eyes were cast downward. The uneasy tension between mother and daughter was palpable. Every sound seemed amplified. Yang cleared her throat. The paper in her hand was rustling slightly, her fingers trembling. She looked at her tormentors.

The Red Guards seemed satisfied, at least for now.

Ping played a double role. When she was first sent back from the training school, she was readily accepted into the Red Guard. As a class monitor, Ping had been well respected by her peers before. She was required to denounce Mother as well. Just like Yan, she followed instructions. In this political frenzy, no one was in a position to say no. After all, Chairman Mao promoted violence and thoroughness, but none of us could view Mother as a class enemy. Ping became restless. She browsed the big character posters on campus and eventually copied a few lines to read in her denunciation speech. "My mother followed the revisionist education line. She placed teachers with strong academic credentials into important positions, neglecting to consider their problematic family background." But in her heart, Ping didn't believe that was wrong. She was a top student. She always respected those teachers.

After many sleepless nights, Ping eventually concluded that both Father and Mother were wrongly accused by the radicals. She found the address of the Central Revolution Committee in Beijing from a newspaper and wrote to them. She listed our parents' background and former positions and stated their devotion to the Party and Chairman Mao. She asked the

Committee to help rectify the wrong accusations made against them and to clear their name.

We admired her courage, but dared not breathe a word. We had been taught to follow Mao and the Party without question. Any deviation from this path was cause for concern and could trigger self-criticism. Although Ping didn't question Mao or the Party, we felt nervous and afraid. Ping was cautious. She was worried that if her letters were intercepted, they would endanger our parents and ourselves. She went out of the way to drop each letter in a different mailbox outside of the Compound. Ping never received a response. She was disheartened. The frequency of her letters changed from once a week to once every other week. Three months later, she stopped writing.

Yan tried hard to join the Red Guards, but was never accepted. "You are not worthy of the honor," her Red Guard classmates told her. When Father was labeled as the biggest traitor in Baicheng, Ping was asked to give up her membership. She was reluctant. The red armband not only marked a person as a revolutionary, but also served as a safeguard against suspicion and abuse on the street. One day, Ping was summoned to school. She was concerned. Walking into her classroom, Ping clenched her hands and composed herself. She was conscious of the hostile stares of her classmates. Many of them were busy writing big character posters in the back of the room. They were all Red Guards. When Ping stepped in, they stopped writing.

"Gou Zai Zi," one murmured. The term, meaning "shitty dog," was newly created to name the children of the fallen officials.

"Take off your armband," another demanded. "You bring shame to our organization!" Ping stood in front of the classroom. She was silent. As the Red Guards started moving toward her, she ripped the armband from her arm and quickly threw it on the ground.

"As you wish," she said as calmly as she could manage. Then she turned and walked out of the door. Once she got home, Ping burst into tears.

To avoid further humiliation, Yan and Ping decided to stay at home. All the schools had been shut down to allow the students to participate in the Cultural Revolution. Since the school teachers were being criticized, made to study Mao's work, and conduct self-criticism every day, the students were left on their own. Ping and Yan wandered around the big character posters in the Compound, trying to figure out what dirt the rebels were putting on our parents and the other officials.

Binbin graduated from elementary school in 1967 and was assigned to the No. 3 Middle School. Since there were no classes, he was left to fend for himself. As the children of the Big Traitor and the Capitalist Roader, we were openly cursed and attacked in the streets. They called us names and threw stones at us. My sisters and I avoided confrontation and stayed in the Compound most of the time. But staying in was harder for Binbin. He and two other boys formed a small group for self protection, and their close friendship continued to sustain them later in difficult situations. Yongbing was the son of the Deputy President of the Party Institute in Baicheng, where local Party members once received their training. Yongbing was chubby and quiet, but his penetrating eyes revealed intelligence and strong will. When he smiled, his sweet, toothy expression made him look like a small boy. And Dongsheng, son of a government employee, was tall and strong. He was sympathetic to Binbin and Yongbing and was ready to get into a fight when he felt injustice was done to his friends. Dongsheng had a booming voice. When he started shouting, he could be heard from a distance. The three of them stayed together like brothers.

Wen, meanwhile, took a more passive position. When school was closed, she first stayed at home, and later went to visit our First Uncle Wensheng, Mother's younger brother, in Harbin. Laolao, our maternal grandmother, lived with First Uncle. Wen stayed with them and First Uncle's three children for four months, during the most turbulent time.

I was at a loss. I had once enjoyed the attention and praise from the government staff in the Compound. I was talkative and outgoing, eager to greet anyone coming my way with a big grin. They used to be all smiles in response and called me a "butterfly," "pretty," "cute," or "polite." They were generous with their compliments, especially when Father was around. After Father's fall, they turned away from me. My greeting "Ni Hao" fell on deaf ears. They treated me as if I were invisible. I choked back tears of humiliation. I learned quickly to retreat into silence. In an effort to keep my dignity, I went out of the way to avoid people. As the Cultural Revolution raged on, my siblings and I felt like green leaves being ripped from a large tree in a storm, torn and swirled without a place to settle.

5

With the encouragement of Mao and the Central Revolution Committee, the Red Guards in Baicheng, like their counterparts in the rest of the country, took matters of revolution into their own hands. They outperformed one another in attacking counterrevolutionaries and ransacking their homes. Several families in the Compound were raided. Mother prepared us for a possible house raid as well.

To avoid being accused of pursuing a bourgeois lifestyle, Mother threw away her two pairs of earrings and a ring, and tore her dresses into pieces. When she saw the Red Guards set up stands at street corners and cut off women's high heels, she chopped the heels on her dress shoes to a third of their length. She also burned Father's collection of classic Chinese literature and had her shoulder-length permed hair cut short. Even a set of hand-carved ivory Mahjong tiles, which she and Father had cherished, were thrown into the fire.

"They caught on fire," she exclaimed. She was worried they would not burn. Nainai was her accomplice. They blocked the small window in the kitchen with a blanket and, at night, fed all the "bourgeois" items to the flames. Mother and Nainai combed through everything. They exchanged few words and kept their actions from us, working in conspiratorial silence. Piece by piece, Mother and Nainai burnt our belongings, and the pieces of their hearts. Each time, they carefully removed the ashes from the stove and flushed them down the toilet.

Despite our anticipation, we still felt shocked and shaken when the first raid came in the spring of 1967. A group of Red Guards swung open our door early one morning. It was raining. Dark clouds loomed low and sent a sporadic downpour, as if in anguish over the man-made disaster on earth. Young revolutionaries charged into our apartment, kicking over all obstacles in their way. They held Mao's little red book in their hands and wore the Red Guard armbands. These two items placed their holders above the law, granting them the right to create new rules at will. That included ransacking the homes of "capitalist roaders," confiscating their property, and humiliating their family members.

They acted in the name of revolution. For months, I had observed the Red Guards from a distance. Their faces burned with feverish excitement as they beat the accused, pounding the victims with their fists, which they called "the revolutionary iron fists," or swinging their belts with metal buckles, "the revolutionary whips." They accompanied these beatings with thunderous shouts of slogans and denunciations. "Defend Chairman Mao Till Our Death!" That was one of their favorite slogans. They tied their belts around their waists like soldiers, and dressed in worn army uniforms without the insignia. They proudly declared their action to be "the red terror."

Those who raided our home that day were teenage boys and girls, a year or two older than Yan and Ping. They were restless and indignant, as if we had done something to enrage them. They rushed in and out of each room, leaving a trail of dirty water and mud from their rain-soaked shoes on our wood floor. They were looking for evidence of the "four olds" or any counterrevolutionary materials that they could use against my parents.

Nainai held me tightly by her side. Our bedroom was the simplest of all. A large Kang bed filled two-thirds of the space. A built-in cabinet contained most of our clothing, and underneath, two large drawers kept the eggs from the chickens we raised. There were no books or decorative items in this room. The Red Guards rudely pushed open the doors of the cabinets and ripped away the covers of the two wood plank boxes on the far end of the Kang. Our simple attire did not interest them, and they ignored Nainai and me. Their behavior was not so moderate in the other rooms. They emptied drawers and tossed clothes around. Even the bed covers were lifted, leaving the straw mattresses exposed and ripped apart.

"Where have you hidden your stuff?" one Red Guard asked impatiently.

Mother and my older siblings stood in the hallway and remained silent.

"Are you deaf?" another shouted.

"Everything we have is right in front of you," Mother answered.

There was no point in reasoning or explaining. Those who had become the targets of the revolution had no right to speak for themselves. Their only choice was to confess their crimes. Any attempt of self-defense would be viewed as the wrong attitude and would bring on harsher retaliation. Mother revealed no emotion, and my sisters and brother followed her example, as if the fiasco unfolding in front of their eyes did not involve them. This was a self-protective mechanism we all acquired.

We did not have any valuable items. Despite my parents' positions, we were never well off financially. We didn't even have a radio. The two things of value were a "Flying Pigeon" sewing machine that Mother used to make clothes for us, and her "Everlast" bicycle. The government provided other basic items such as our wood plank beds and built-in cabinets. Our few pieces of furniture included a dining table, several chairs, a wooden coat rack, and two large wood boxes that contained quilts and out-of-season clothing. Our parents took pride in living the simple life of the ordinary citizen. After all, the Party had always glorified the nobility of self-sacrifice. Being a member of the proletarian class had always been honorable. We had no means to acquire material things, and since none of us had been exposed to any, we didn't feel any need for them.

The Red Guards, however, would not leave empty-handed. They hauled away our dining table and the coat rack. Piles of furniture confiscated from the homes of the persecuted were eventually stored in a warehouse in the Compound, where they collected dust for many years. Some pieces, if they had withstood the abuse, were returned to their owners years later, while most were discarded as garbage. I could not understand why the Red Guards had to take our things away, but gathered from their conversation that these items signified a bourgeois lifestyle, and the action taken was intended to teach us a lesson. It was at this time that the accusation of "bourgeois lifestyle" started setting off threatening alarms in my mind. The concept of bourgeois lifestyle was broad, and the accusation was terrifying and real.

I was scared and nervous as the Red Guards rummaged through our apartment, leaving no corner unturned. Nainai held my hand the whole time. We watched as they hauled away the large items. Then they scooped up a few small things they deemed useful into a gunnysack and took them. Among them were Father's working journals that Mother did not have the heart to destroy. When the head of the Red Guards waved his hand and called upon the rest to leave, our apartment looked as if it had been looted.

"Even bandits in the old days didn't do this to us," Nainai said as she helped to clean up the mess. Mother and my older siblings all looked pale, but none of them said a word. No one wanted to reveal the fear, anger, and indignation that were boiling inside. We each took it in silently, learning from Mother and Nainai the strength of forbearance, an important lesson to keep our feelings to ourselves. Hard as it was, we learned to regard unloading one's own pain to others as selfish. To shoulder it all in silence, however, was terribly heavy, and I often found it suffocating, but that day, I observed firsthand Mother's composure and Nainai's calmness. I admired them. I squeezed Nainai's hand, feeling suddenly grown up. We were one family, and we had each other, I thought.

"They are young and don't know what they are doing," Mother finally said, referring to the Red Guards. After a pause, she added, "We should keep our faith in the Party and trust that the truth will prevail." She reiterated the official line. She might well have believed in it. She held the radicals and Red Guards responsible for the violence and abuse, and she believed the Party had temporarily lost control in the chaos. She directed her anger toward the members of the Revolution Committee. Mother possessed a single-minded trust in the Communist Party, and nothing seemed to be able to change her mind.

In her personal life, Mother maintained a similar dedication. At a time when many people denounced their spouses and family members to protect themselves, Mother never wavered. She would protect her family at all costs.

The chief military representative at the school took the lead in pushing her for a divorce. It started in late 1967. One day, two Red Guards escorted Mother into his office at the No. 3 Middle School. She had met with this officer before. Standing in front of him, Mother noticed how young he looked in his uniform. His complexion was dark, and he didn't show any emotion. He ignored Mother and directed the two Red Guards to stand outside. After he walked to his desk and settled in his chair, he motioned Mother to take a seat across from him.

Mother sat down and looked at him. The red star on his hat glistened under the light, and the two red stripes on his collars stood out. He returned Mother's gaze, his eyes cold and penetrating.

"You are from a poor family," he said to Mother. "You should stand on the side of the revolution and stay clear of the Big Traitor."

Mother listened, wondering what would come next. "The Big Traitor" had become an epithet for Father.

"The best action you can take is to divorce the Big Traitor." He raised his voice. He stared at Mother, as if he wanted to crush her with his look.

Mother felt a chill running down her spine. This was not the first time she had heard such a request. She had read it on the big character posters on campus and had dismissed the words as another folly of the young rebels, but when the request came directly from a military representative, she had to take it seriously. Mother was worried. To resist would further jeopardize her situation.

"Hou Kai's problem has not been officially settled," Mother said, making careful choice of her words. "I'd rather wait until an official verdict is reached."

"There is no need to wait any longer," the military representative cut in impatiently. "Your problem can be resolved once you cut the line of demarcation from the Big Traitor," he continued.

He was irritated when Mother gave no response.

He cleared his throat. "Chairman Mao said 'A revolution is not a dinner party, or writing an essay, or painting a picture, or doing embroidery.'" He pointed at a Mao's little red book on his desk. "Why don't you finish Chairman Mao's quotation?" he asked.

"Revolution cannot be so refined, so leisurely and so temperate, courteous, and restrained," Mother continued obediently where he left off. The popular quotation was repeated daily at the struggle meetings, or over the loudspeakers all over the places. Everyone could recite it.

"Go on," he urged.

"A revolution is an insurrection, an act of violence, by which one class overthrows another," Mother finished the quotation.

"We are not asking you to take any violent revolutionary action," said the military representative. "All you need to do is to sign a divorce paper."

"Hou Kai is the father of my children," Mother said slowly. She felt anger rising inside her. "I've known him for nearly twenty years. He is not a counterrevolutionary." Mother's voice was low, but firm. She tried hard to conceal her emotion.

The military representative's face changed color. "How dare you defend a traitor?"

Mother remained silent.

The military representative took out a pad of paper and a pen from his drawer. He threw them across the desk and asked Mother to write her divorce request.

Mother pushed the paper to the side. "I'm not going to divorce the father of my children," she said, her voice trembling.

Enraged, the military representative slammed his fist on the desk. "The Revolution Committee demands you to divorce the Big Traitor. I don't give a damn who he is!"

"But I do," Mother said. She was ready to burst with rage. Her life had already been intruded upon and thrown into havoc. She knew she was not going to get a divorce no matter what.

"I have six children," she said in a controlled voice. "I'm not going to make them fatherless."

The military representative sprang up from his chair and charged toward the door. The two Red Guards rushed in as soon as he swung the door open.

"Take the granite head to a struggle meeting," the military representative yelled. "Make sure she listens and yields!"

When Mother passed him on her way out, he waved his fist at her, like a madman. He shouted at the Red Guards to start a denunciation campaign.

The next day, when Mother arrived at school, she saw large characters painted in white and black all over the school walls. One said: "No Divorce, No Way Out!" Another read: "Shame on You, Big Traitor's Stinky Wife!" She stopped at the school entrance and scanned her surroundings. "Break the Granite Head!" "Down with the Stubborn Capitalist Roader!" The slogans on the walls went on and on.

As she walked to the furnace room where she was made to spend most of her time writing self-criticism, she noticed a newly pasted big character poster by the door. The title was written in thick brush and the black ink was still wet: "You Are Headed toward Disaster!"

When the campaign at school didn't make her bend, the Red Guards painted similar slogans on the walls of the Government Compound, and on the surface of the streets that led her to school. Residents in the Compound and the government employees could all see them on their way in and out. But Mother did not change her stand. She endured the humiliation and steadfastly maintained her position.

But she was concerned about the impact on us.

When Nainai was doing dishes in the kitchen one evening, Mother said to us: "You may have seen all the slogans." She looked at each of us, observing our reaction. We remained silent and waited.

"I'm not going to apply for a divorce," she said after a pause. "Our family will remain intact as a whole no matter what." She gave us her assurance. It was inconceivable for us to entertain the idea of our parents getting a divorce. Nevertheless, it was reassuring to hear Mother say it loud and clear.

Twice more our home was raided by the Red Guards and the rebels among the government staff. Since there was nothing left that could possibly incriminate us further, we were less worried. We kept our silence as they searched one room after another; and after they left, we cleaned up the mess. Sometimes Nainai shed tears. She was increasingly worried about her son.

Then, the suicide of the parents of a former official shocked us. Mr. Xia, a Deputy Governor who was labeled as one of the four top capitalist roaders in Baicheng, came from a landlord family. Despite the fact Xia had rebelled against his family and joined the Communist Army, his parents, former landlords, were bombarded with accusations. It was the custom in China that a son should support his aging parents and take care of their needs. Xia's parents had moved in with him when he settled in Baicheng. The Red Guards pasted large character posters on their door, demanding they move out. Xia had no choice but to arrange for them to live somewhere else. He rented a small mud hut outside of the Compound and moved them there. The move gave the Red Guards free access to them. They threatened the old couple and wanted to parade them in the street. Not wanting to suffer further humiliation and subjecting their son to more persecution, they hanged themselves inside their small hut. They died facing each other. News of their death passed from one person to another in hushed voices. Suicide was regarded as a betrayal to the Party and the revolutionary masses. It was openly denounced. Consequently, the parents' death only aggravated their son's situation. The Xia family was soon evacuated from the Compound to the countryside for reeducation.

The older couple's suicide, however, suddenly compelled me to contemplate death, a subject that had not crossed my mind before. I was terrified. Suddenly life seemed fragile. I was particularly worried about Nainai. Secretly I watched Nainai, trying to read her mind. I insisted on holding her hand while going to sleep at night.

The violent storm of the Cultural Revolution swept us off the ground. We didn't know what to expect next.

Me in the Compound

Chapter Eleven

Little Heroine

1

While Mother was confined at school and Father was away in Beijing, Nainai became the sole adult at home. During the day, when we were around her, she appeared perfectly calm. She continued to tend the chickens we raised, care for the garden, and put three meals on the table, but at night, she tossed and turned. Lying next to her, I could hear her sigh and sometimes sob in the darkness.

One day, Nainai said she was going to visit Mother at the No. 3 Middle School. We were all astonished. Ever since we settled in the Compound, Nainai had never set foot out of the enclosed area. Her age and her bound feet prevented her from going far. Even though there were still many women of her generation whose feet had been bound, they were seldom seen in the streets. Foot binding was associated with the feudal society and backwardness. The era of the "golden lotuses" was long gone. Older women were very conscious of their crippled appearance and were reluctant to be seen in public. As for Nainai, in addition to worrying about the physical limitations imposed by her feet, we worried about her safety. A visit to Mother was obviously a demonstration of support. It could be seen as a counter-revolutionary act. Would Nainai be able to stand on her feet should some Red Guard push her? Could she move out of the way quickly enough?

"What can they do to an old woman like me? Keep me, too?" Nainai said, undeterred.

The two-mile distance from our home to school was a long journey for Nainai.

"The walk is going to be very hard on your feet," Ping said. She encouraged my other siblings to speak up.

"The Red Guards can be violent," Yan chimed in. "Even if you could safely reach the school, the Red Guards may not allow you to see Mother."

My sisters and brother tried to talk her out of it. They had all been pressured to denounce Mother at school. A visit to her from anyone in the family could be viewed as defiance and support.

Nainai seemed to understand my siblings' concerns, but she wouldn't change her mind. To avoid causing them any trouble, she did not ask any of them to go with her. Instead, she turned to me, her youngest grandchild.

"Jian can show me the way," she said, putting a hand on my shoulder. "Can't you?"

I was a first grader. The impact on me, Nainai figured, would be inconsequential.

I looked at Nainai. Her back hunched forward, and her eyes were red from lack of sleep and crying. It was a big step for her. Nainai must have thought it over thoroughly. I had never said no to Nainai, and couldn't do so at this time. I nodded yes.

"If anyone questions you," Nainai said, "Tell him Nainai has threatened to beat you with her walking stick."

That sounded outrageous. Nainai had never laid a finger on any of us, and I had always been her little darling, but I dutifully agreed. I knew Nainai could not make the trip by herself. Despite my mounting fears, I wanted to accompany her. I had never seen my soft-spoken, good-tempered Nainai so determined. Besides, the possibility of seeing Mother, however remote, was very tempting. I had only attended school for a few months. I didn't understand the political pressures.

We set out on a warm day in the early fall. Nainai put on her traditional light gray blouse, a pair of baggy black pants, and her small black shoes—all made herself. The day before our visit, she killed a chicken. She simmered it in a clay pot with green onion and ginger over low heat for a couple of hours. Supposedly, chicken prepared this way was very nourishing to the body. Nainai put half the chicken and the broth in a large jar, and together with a few steamed flour buns, put them carefully in a basket. I watched as she covered them with a headscarf. My mouth watered, but I didn't ask for any. We started our journey early in the morning. Nainai was eighty-four, and I was seven. Holding her with one hand, I assured Nainai I could find the way.

Since all the schools were closed, students were everywhere. The Red Guards used military trucks to spread revolutionary messages. Some trucks raced to their destinations, leaving behind echoes of revolutionary songs blasted from loud-speakers. Swirls of dust trailed behind them. Others crawled through the streets, with Red Guards beating drums and announcing Mao's latest instructions. Their high-pitched voices sounded like sirens. Most of the vehicles in the streets, however, were horse-pulled carts. Peasants, sitting on the front edge of the flat, wooden frames, shouted at the horses. From time to time, they whipped their animals, hoping to speed them up. They delivered produce to retailers in the city, or hauled human manure scooped from the outhouses back to the countryside to be used as fertilizer.

Nainai and I walked slowly on the dirt sidewalk. She held her walking stick with one hand and grasped my hand, or my shoulder, with the other. The curious stares of passers-by and their murmuring made me nervous. I looked at Nainai. She seemed to be focused only on the road in front of her. I tried to follow her example.

We stopped frequently for Nainai to catch her breath. Each time we took a rest, she stood still, putting both hands on the walking stick for support. She needed to give her feet some relief from her weight. She couldn't sit down on the side of the street. She knew I was not strong enough to pull her up. I didn't mind the rest. I needed to get a break from the heavy basket hanging on my arm as well.

By the time we arrived at the No. 3 Middle School, it was almost noon. Mrs. Yu and Mrs. Chen, two schoolteachers who used to come to our house to visit Mother, ran into us at the entrance.

"Little Jian, oh, Grandma, what do you think you are doing here?" Mrs. Yu was shocked to see us.

"I need to see Gu Wenxiu," Nainai said. "Can you tell us where she is?"

Mrs. Yu threw a glance over her shoulder. Seeing no Red Guards nearby, she pointed to a low building. "She is in there," she said quickly.

"Jian, you should take Nainai home as soon as you can," said Mrs. Chen in a hushed voice, grabbing my shoulder.

Then they rushed away.

We walked slowly toward the building. As we drew closer, I saw two teenage girls wearing Red Guard armbands sitting behind a desk at the door. They looked at us with curiosity.

"Who are you?" one girl asked.

"What do you want?" the other added before I could answer.

"Young ladies," Nainai said with difficulty. She was trying hard to catch her breath. "I'm here to see Gu Wenxiu, my daughter-in-law," she continued. Her voice was soft, but firm.

"Visitors are not allowed." The girl who was taller stood up and extended an arm to stop us.

"We've come a long way," Nainai said, slowly. "We are not going to leave without seeing Jian's mother."

The other girl, who wore a washed-out arm uniform and had two ponytails above her shoulders, moved forward as well. She stared at us, but said nothing. The mere sight of Nainai and me must have taken them by surprise.

They exchanged a few words in a low voice, and the girl with the ponytails took off.

I watched the tall girl in front of me carefully, thinking she must be in the same grade as Yan or Ping.

Nainai was exhausted. She moved toward the small desk and leaned against it. The desk shifted with Nainai's weight. I gave out a cry and clutched her right arm. The chicken jar in my hand spilled some soup.

"I'll have to sit for a moment," Nainai said. With considerable effort, she supported herself on the back of the girl's chair and slowly settled herself on the seat.

"You can't do that," the tall girl yelled.

I put the chicken jar under the desk and stood by Nainai. I didn't know how to stop her, should she try to chase Nainai out of the chair. She was much bigger than me. But I knew I would not let her touch Nainai.

As we stared at each other, the other girl came back, with a man trailing her. The man also wore a Red Guard armband. He was slim and tall. His expression was more amazement than anger when he saw Nainai and me.

Nainai wiped the sweat off her forehead with the back of her hand. She looked tired, and her blouse and pants were covered with dust.

The young man came closer. He examined Nainai up and down, his two thick eyebrows furrowed into a knot. He said nothing.

I bit my lower lip and looked at him nervously. The moment he turned to face me, I cast my eyes to the ground, my heart pounding with anxiety.

"Young man," Nainai said. "I need to see my daughter-in-law. I won't be long."

I admired Nainai for being so calm and composed. She was not begging, nor was she reproaching the young man or the two girls. She was totally herself, an old reasonable woman asking permission to see her detained daughter-in-law. She was humble, but not without dignity.

"I'm not going to leave before I see her," Nainai added quietly, returning the man's gaze with her usual grandmotherly look.

"You are not supposed to be here," the young man said. He paused for a moment. "But today is your lucky day," he continued when Nainai said nothing. "I'll give you thirty minutes."

It was our turn to be surprised. I helped Nainai to her feet. Through the corners of my eye, I saw the young man whispering to the two girls. Then he left without saying another word.

The tall girl unlocked the door. She threw an angry look at us. Nainai and I slowly walked in. There, standing right at the doorway was Mother. She must have heard all the commotion outside and had been waiting at the door.

She stepped forward and took Nainai's hands in hers.

"Niang, I'm sorry I had you worried," she said gently to Nainai, tears welling up in her eyes. Mother rarely used the term Niang, a Shandong dialect for mother.

Mother and Nainai had always had a good relationship. I remembered once Nainai was sick. For two days, she hardly touched any food. Each of the grandchildren took turns to beg her to eat, bringing a cup of soup or a few mung bean biscuits to her side. She simply shook her head and closed her eyes. We were very concerned. Normally a cold or a minor discomfort would not even slow her down. When Mother arrived home in the evening on the second day, she rolled up her sleeves and went straight into the kitchen. She beat two eggs and steamed them to a soft custard, with a touch of salt, green onion, and sesame oil. The aroma of the oil and fresh egg permeated the room. Only on special occasions did we enjoy a treat of eggs, whether hard-boiled, stir-fried, or steamed. Preparing steamed eggs required considerable skill. Too long would make them hard; too short and they would not solidify, but when cooked just right, steamed eggs melted in your mouth. They were one of my favorite treats.

"Niang," Mother called out to Nainai. "Please have some egg."

She took the perfectly prepared egg custard to Nainai's side. Mother propped up two pillows against the wall and helped Nainai to sit up. She intended to feed Nainai, but her position was awkward. I watched Mother from behind, trying to offer my assistance. Without another word, Mother took off her shoes and climbed on top of the Kang. She kneeled in front of Nainai and fed her the soft egg one spoonful after another. Nainai opened her mouth each time the spoon touched her lower lip. She did not say a word, but slowly, one mouthful after another, she managed to swallow everything Mother fed her. That image of Mother on her knees tending Nainai was carved into my mind.

Seeing them stand face to face after the separation, I was not sure what was going to happen. The two Red Guards were close by, watching our every move. I was worried Nainai would shed tears and say something inappropriate for the Red Guards to hear. But she did not. They just stood by the door, staring into each other's eyes as if all they had to say was revealed in them.

Mother's hair was long and messy, and she had dark circles under her eyes. I hid behind Nainai, trying to keep a distance despite my eagerness to get close. It had been more than a month since I had last seen her. She looked so different. After what seemed a long time, Mother led Nainai to one of the chairs by the only desk in the room. Papers and Mao's books were scattered on its surface. A pack of cigarettes lay open by a notepad.

"You started smoking?" Nainai asked.

"Only at night. It helps me to stay awake," Mother answered lightheartedly.

As far as I knew, Mother was always looking for ways to get more sleep. Trying to stay awake by smoking? That did not make sense to me. Yet, many things these days did not make sense.

Mother pulled me to her side when she sat down. The room was dark compared to the bright sunshine outside. The two windows, one in the front, and the other in the back, were covered with newspapers. A flimsy bed with a straw mattress was behind the desk. A few pieces of clothing were folded up as a pillow, and the thin bedding did not cover the loose straw at the edge of the mattress. A big poster of Mao was pasted on the wall, waving one hand over his head toward the ocean of Red Guards on Tiananmen Square.

Nainai could not read, but she understood Mother was going through a difficult time. She could not make sense of the political movement, but she knew her daughter-in-law was a person of integrity. She trusted her and loved her, as she did her own son. The political turmoil had no impact on that. If anything, it only pushed her to visibly reveal her love and support, not so much with words, but through action. In our family, as in most traditional Chinese families, there had never been much verbal communication. Children obeyed and listened—they were supposed to be seen, not heard. We learned from our parents about dedication and resilience by observing them, and we loved Nainai for her kindness. But words were rare, especially when it came to feelings and emotions. Our parents lived in harmony. If they had any conflicts, they were never revealed to us. They always appeared strong and in control, solving whatever problems came their way. That, to us children, was a manifestation of strength. To succumb to emotion was to surrender to bourgeois sentimentality. The difficult life in the countryside had strengthened Nainai and trained her to face hardship without complaining; and the revolutionary cause Mother and Father took up had molded their temperaments. Even at this highly intense moment, Nainai and Mother remained calm.

Nainai removed the jar of chicken carefully from the basket and urged Mother to taste it. There was not much soup left. During our journey, I had shifted the basket from one arm to the other so many times that much of the liquid had spilled.

"I have to know for sure you are all right," Nainai said, looking at Mother. Nainai's cataracts were getting worse, and I wondered if she could see Mother clearly in the dim light. Tears filled Mother's eyes. She quickly fought them back.

"I'm quite all right," she said. Her voice was controlled.

I became nervous and stole a glance at the two Red Guards.

"You need to take care of yourself," Mother turned the focus of their conversation to Nainai.

Nainai held Mother's hands in hers most of the time, veins visible on the back of her hands like blue earthworms. They did not speak much under the scrutinizing eyes of the two Red Guards. I moved restlessly between Mother and Nainai. I wanted to cheer up Mother, but I didn't know what to do. A song I had practiced to sing for her did not seem appropriate. I had many questions I wanted to ask. When would she be coming home? When would school start again? Why was she the only woman in the Compound who was detained? But I didn't dare speak. My senses told me I was walking in a minefield. The wrong step could trigger an explosion. With two pairs of watchful eyes not far away, I feared I would bring more trouble to Mother if I opened my mouth. After a moment or two, I decided to direct my energy to feel her presence. I leaned against Mother's shoulder, feeling the movement of her hands as she carefully tugged my blouse under my pants.

"I've seen many kinds of bad weather in the countryside," Nainai said slowly. "Eventually, it all passed."

Mother nodded. She had already gone through several political movements, although none had gone this far. She changed the subject and insisted we share the chicken and steamed buns with her. She begged Nainai not to come all the way to school again.

"I don't know what's going on in this world," Nainai said before our departure. "But I will live to see you and my son both home safe and sound."

Mother walked us to the door and told me to be good and take care of Nainai.

"I will," I promised solemnly. I wanted to urge her to come home soon. Instead, I simply said goodbye. I wondered when I would see her again. Nainai picked up her walking stick and stepped out of the room, without lingering, as if we were at home and she could come and go as she pleased.

With the basket empty, the trip home was much easier for me. Somehow, I felt strangely elated. Our mission was accomplished. Nainai and I had seen Mother, and I had sat on her lap. Maybe Mother might return home soon.

But Nainai looked very tired. She walked more slowly and rested longer. Every step seemed a great effort, but I knew, under her fragile appearance, Nainai was fearless and strong-willed. I put one hand into hers and felt proud to be by her side.

"Mother will be okay," I said to Nainai, trying to cheer her up.

Nainai squeezed my hand in response and continued to walk in silence. By the time we finally reached home, the last ray of the reddish sunset was disappearing in the west. Before going to bed that night, Nainai gently touched my face. "You did well today," she said. "You are a little heroine." I gave her my biggest smile.

Years later, Mrs. Yu told me she had to rush away that day, otherwise she would have burst into tears—showing feelings for us would have been a crime. Mother told the story of our visit repeatedly to many people—it must have meant so much to her.

One month later, Mother was allowed to come home at night. She spoke even less to us, but dutifully rode her bike to school each morning to face her daily ordeal. She never mentioned the details of her day, and none of us children asked. We each tried to maintain a calm appearance.

2

The chaos created by the Cultural Revolution continued. With each passing day, we felt Father's absence more strongly. Since we all shied away from struggle meetings, we saw less of him. We all missed him. Mother, as always, kept her composure. She didn't talk to us about Father, but Nainai was more verbal about her concerns. Could we attempt to visit him? We thought about it. Father was kept at the Military Compound, which was right in town. The distance was not an issue, but could we cross the line? Mother was being pressured to divorce him, to "cut a line of demarcation" from him. Apparently, she couldn't go. My older siblings looked at one another. What would happen to them if they were to make the attempt? Mother was worried. They were old enough to be held responsible for their actions. Mother suggested we stay put and wait a little longer. This madness couldn't possibly be going on for too long. She didn't want us to take more risks.

Seeing how concerned everyone was about Father, and how agonized they were about the consequence, I told Mother and Nainai I would give it a try.

"You?" Mother was surprised by my offer.

"Yes," I said. "I know where the Military Compound is. I'll go and tell them I want to see Father."

Mother hesitated. She put a hand on my shoulder and looked me in the eye.

"If they say no, I'll come back," I said. "I promise I won't get anyone in trouble."

"I think it's worth a try," Nainai said to Mother. "What could they do to a child?"

Mother remained silent. After a while, she said she would think about it.

The following day, when Mother left for school, I decided to act on my idea. Mother didn't give me her permission, but she didn't say no either. I didn't feel there was any danger. I was more worried about being ridiculed and turned back.

I walked over to the Military Compound that afternoon. I watched the gate from a distance. A soldier with a rifle on his side stood guard. Behind him was a reception room. People visiting the Military Compound had to first step up to the guard, and then proceed to the reception room for registration. The gate faced a large street. On the far north side, I could see the Baicheng Train Station. A group of Red Guards were pasting new big character posters on the brick wall of the station. On the street, pedestrians, horse-pulled carts, and army trucks passed by. I moved closer to the gate. I prepared what I needed to say and stepped forward.

"Uncle Soldier," I said politely. "I'm here to see my father."

The guard in uniform looked puzzled. "Who is your father?" he asked.

"Hou Kai. He is kept in here. I know." I added quickly. My heart pounded.

"Get out of here," he waved his free hand at me, as if to brush away a fly.

"Please," I pled. "My grandma sent me."

He ignored me, resuming his posture. His head lifted and he stared straight ahead.

I stepped back. I was not expecting miracles, but I was afraid I'd make him angry if I kept begging him. I took out my shuttlecock from my pocket and kicked it on the side street to pass time. The guard threw a glance in my direction from time to time. I waited. Finally, there was a change of shift and a new guard took position. I approached the stand again, making the same request. For three weeks, I was there every day. I spent a lot of time kicking the shuttlecock or doing jump rope. Sometimes, I wandered off to the train station and watched the heavy-duty steam engines puff black smoke, pulling the trains in and out of the station.

I kept returning to the guards. If I found a sympathetic soldier willing to listen, I'd tell him my eighty-four-year-old grandma insisted on my coming. The guards changed shift by the hour, and soon they all knew me. They were all young soldiers recruited from the countryside. They followed orders, but were not without sympathy.

One day, a guard signaled me to go to the reception office. I was stunned.

"Me?" I pointed a finger at my nose.

He nodded. I detected a grin on his face.

I was so thrilled that I immediately ran to the office. Only later did I realize I forgot to say thank you. I charged in.

"So, you are the little girl who comes here every day," an officer behind a desk said to me. He asked for my name and age and jotted it down on a piece of paper. Then he stood up and pointed to a red brick building, further in the back of the compound.

"Go over there," he said. "Don't stay for long."

I ran to the building where Father was kept. It had been more than six months since we waved goodbye to him for that Beijing trip. I had to catch my breath before knocking on the door. There was no answer. I pushed it open timidly and poked my head in. The creaking of the door drew the attention of the men inside. My bewildered look met with four pairs of eyes. They seemed just as astonished as I was, if not more. They were all former top officials accused of being capitalist roaders. Their hair was long, and their faces unshaven. No one uttered a word. I recognized my father sitting in a far corner on a horsehair mattress. He opened his mouth, but no sound came out.

"Little Jian, is that you?" The question came from Mr. Chen, former Deputy Governor and Wuzi's father. His voice was hushed, as if he was afraid he would scare me away.

"Yes, Uncle Chen," I responded eagerly. I put a hand against my mouth when I realized my blunder. I looked around and was relieved to see no one was within earshot. Calling him "Uncle," a common term used by children to address adults, was certainly not an act of "cutting a line of demarcation."

I had never seen Father spring up from a bed so quickly. He stood still for a moment, as if to make sure I was not an illusion. Then he rushed toward me. He knelt down on one knee to bring himself to my level and cupped my face in his hands. I lost my words.

"Jian, it is you. Oh, my little Jian. You are my heroine," he said. He tucked a strand of loose hair behind my ear and examined me from head to toe. Nainai had said that to me as well, I thought.

"Nainai sent me," I blurted out, as my thought turned to her.

Father hushed me. He took me by the hand and led me to his bed. How was Nainai? How was Mother? How was each of my siblings? Father had more questions for me than I had for him. I answered his questions, but couldn't bring up the ones I had for him. "Are you a traitor? Are you a capitalist roader?"

I didn't stay for long. I didn't want to jeopardize my opportunity for the next visit. Father didn't try to keep me for long either. He walked me to the door and asked me to be careful. "I'll tell Wuzi I saw you," I said to Mr. Chen before closing the door behind me. Chen only nodded at me.

I became the family's ambassador to Father. I managed to see him from time to time. I brought him food, clothing, and tobacco leaves. Father was confined in the room all the time when he was not being "struggled" against. He felt cut off from the outside world. He asked for a radio. Ping and Yan ran around town and purchased a radio, the first in our family. It was the size of two shoe boxes. It could be plugged in a socket or use eight large batteries. The radio was too large for me to take to Father. Wen volunteered to come along. We wrapped the radio in a blanket and put it in a fabric bag. We were relieved when the guard didn't ask us to open it. Father was very pleased to have the radio.

Another time, unbeknownst to me, Mother hid a poem she wrote for Father in a bunch of tobacco leaves. When Mother told me about it years later, it was well after the Cultural Revolution, but she could still recite it word for word:

Happily reunited we will be, one day;
I laugh at the burning flames of the battlefield.
My thoughts, like gently flowing water, are with you;
You are my hero, made of unbending steel.

3

When school reopened, I returned to my former class. Mrs. Liu, our former homeroom teacher, resumed her position. I always liked Mrs. Liu. She was in her early thirties, hardly five feet tall. She had two thick ponytails, which made her look like one of the students, especially from behind. She was kind and soft-spoken. When we had first entered school nearly a year before, she organized a five-member student committee to assist her in managing the large class. She had appointed me as one of the committee members. I had worked with enthusiasm, collecting students' homework on her behalf and leading my peers to keep our classroom clean.

One day, soon after we resumed our classes, Mrs. Liu asked me to stay behind after her class. There was something she would like to talk with me about, she said. I was nervous. I felt like a different person returning to school. Most of the children in the Compound, like my older siblings, were much older. Only two other girls of my age were in my school. Their mothers held cleric jobs and were not persecuted, and their fathers were pushed to the sideline, but not singled out like my father. The majority of the children at school were from families of ordinary civilians, and they belonged to the revolutionary mass. I was conscious of being the daughter of the former Deputy Governor, currently condemned as the Big Traitor and Capitalist Roader.

Liu sat me down at a desk. "I know it must be hard on you," she said. "But you are doing well." She continued without giving me a chance to speak. I sat straight, trying hard to suppress the tears that came to my eyes.

"I heard a boy shouting 'Down with Hou Kai' at you a moment ago," she continued. "You must learn to take a revolutionary stand."

I lowered my head and nodded.

"Our school will hold a struggle meeting," she said after a pause. "It's a good opportunity for you to step forward."

My heart sank. I knew what it meant. My sisters and brother had all been asked to criticize our parents at such meetings. My turn had come. My thought turned to Father.

Mrs. Liu had been nice and protective to me. She didn't allow anyone in her class to curse me or attack me. "Jian is young," she said to the entire class one day. "She should be treated differently from her parents." I was appreciative, but embarrassed. I didn't want anyone to single me out. I could feel the stares from my classmates.

That day, when Mrs. Liu asked me to criticize my parents, I didn't say no. I didn't even ask if I had any other options. Mrs. Liu gave me a list of names my parents were openly being accused of: a traitor, a capitalist roader, and a revisionist, along with a newspaper clipping that criticized my father. "This should help you get a start," she said, handing them to me. "It doesn't have to be long," she added, as if it were an afterthought. "You know you should be on the side of the revolution."

I said yes.

As the day progressed, I became more nervous. What could I possibly say about my parents? Besides, I barely acquired enough vocabulary to write a statement of criticism. I went home with a heavy heart and asked Ping for help. I didn't know if Mrs. Liu was trying to protect me by having me speak out, or if she was requested to do so.

Ping didn't ask me any questions. She threw a glance at the list I brought to her and tossed it aside. "I'll help you with it," she said. She sat down with me, and quickly wrote a page and a half in script. I copied it, wanting to show it in my own handwriting. Ping helped me with the pronunciation of a few unfamiliar words. Most of the sentences she wrote were slogan-like phrases we heard every day on the radio. "The Proletarian Cultural Revolution is an unprecedented and magnificent political movement." "Our beloved leader Chairman Mao initiated this soul-touching revolution and we should all participate in it." "I will devote myself to this great revolution!" The only personal statement appeared toward the end, declaring loud and clear that I would "cut a clear line of demarcation" from that big traitor Hou Kai. I didn't explicitly say Hou Kai was my father, but everyone knew the relationship. I didn't know how to cut the line of demarcation within a family. I felt confused and torn.

The struggle meeting was long and students were enthusiastic. After each student delivered his or her speech, slogans such as "Down with Anti-Revolutionaries!" and "Long Live Chairman Mao!" echoed in the air. When my name was called, I went to the platform slowly. Mrs. Liu had approved my paper. I could see her nodding at me encouragingly as I passed by her. I stood at the podium and cleared my throat. I was very nervous. With so many pairs of eyes focusing on me, I felt like I was giving a performance on stage. I exerted more effort to ensure I'd pronounce the words correctly. I read line by line, and my voice sounded mechanical and stiff. When it was over, I noticed Mrs. Liu smiling at me. "Long Live Chairman Mao," I joined the group in their shouting. "Down with Hou Kai!" I chanted along, as if Hou Kai were not related to me.

Ping met me at the door when I got home. She took the paper out of my school bag and ripped it to pieces. "Forget about it," she said, turning me by the shoulder to face her. I nodded.

Ping gave me a couple of "White Rabbit" candies, as if to reward me. I looked into her eyes. I felt grateful for her protection and comfort, but felt guilty. I couldn't bring myself to face Father. For three weeks, I didn't visit him. Eventually I decided to go and make my confession.

I told him what I did. In addition, I also told him children on the street cursed me and shouted slogans at me. Some even threw stones at me.

Father listened to me patiently, holding my hands in his the entire time. He paused for a moment after I finished. Then, to my surprise, he told me I had done the right thing. He said I should continue to do so. He even suggested that I join them in their shouting.

"Down with Hou Kai!" he imitated the Red Guards, raising his fist above his head, his voice almost lighthearted. "You see. Just like that. It's not difficult. Join them. Be a little revolutionary. That will stop them from throwing stones at you," Father continued. He took a deep draw off his hand-rolled cigarette and slowly let the smoke out. Together, we stared at the rising haze. Neither of us said another word.

A Neighborhood Boy, Binbin, Wen and Me

Chapter Twelve

The Family Warrior

1

The Government Compound became a world of big character posters and a forum for debate and denunciations. When the big character posters filled the walls of the office buildings, wires were set up between wooden poles, or even trees, and large bulletin boards were placed in the open. They were soon covered with layer after layer of new posters. Like neglected laundry hanging in the sun, the big character posters fluttered in the wind until they fell apart. Then, another wave of posters would come to replace them.

Inside our home, it was quiet. Mother was silent most of the time. We tiptoed around her, speaking in hushed voices and quietly closing the doors behind us. With the world outside turning chaotic, the stillness at home seemed more important than ever. My siblings and I looked up to Mother, and, each in our own way, tried hard to follow her example. We wanted to keep our dignity.

Mother made no complaints about our situation nor did she prevent us from speaking up at the struggle meetings at school. The only explicit instruction she gave us was to stay out of trouble, especially when confronted with verbal abuse or physical attacks.

"Don't talk back," she said. "Don't get into any fights."

She always looked at Binbin when she emphasized this point.

My brother Binbin was more prone to lose his temper than the rest of us. Many times he returned home with a torn sleeve and a black and blue face. His big, sparkling eyes, a feature that once received so many compliments, sank into their sockets. He often looked at Mother nervously. His usual wide, brilliant smile disappeared, and in its place was a concerned, anguished expression, as if he had changed from a boy to an old man within a matter of days. He never explained what had happened to him, and Mother didn't ask for details. She only demanded he walk away from trouble.

"You must learn to endure, Binbin," Mother said sternly each time Binbin came home with evidence of a fight. "For your own safety and for your father's sake."

Binbin never talked back to Mother. Although he was just a teenager, he felt it was his responsibility to protect his sisters, especially Wen and me, who were younger than he was. In front of Mother, he always behaved obediently. Each time, when Mother finished speaking, he nodded and retreated to his room, but we knew it was common for him to lose control and get into a fight.

It's hard not to when somebody spits in our faces.

One day, Binbin burst into our apartment. His nose was bleeding, and one of his eyes was swollen so badly that it was nearly closed. A large bruise on his forehead oozed blood, and two black and blue marks darkened his face. Even his shirt was smeared with mud and blood. He charged directly into the kitchen. He grabbed a big chopping knife from the counter and headed toward the door.

"Those bastards," he shouted. "I'm going to kill them." He was oblivious to our astonished looks.

We were having dinner at a makeshift table by the entry door. Two large wooden boxes piled on top of each other served as our dining table. We had to sit sideways, since there was no room for our legs. Mother leaped to the door before Binbin could reach it.

I was horrified as I watched Mother block the door like a statue. She stared at Binbin, her face distorted.

"You can't go out with that knife in your hand," Mother said. Her voice was harsh and shrill. She stretched her arms and planted her hands firmly on each side of the wooden doorframe.

"I'm not going to take this anymore," Binbin yelled.

Mother didn't move.

"You'll have to kill me first to get through this door," she said.

"Let me go." Binbin's rage seemed to have blinded him.

I held Nainai's arm with both hands. I was afraid Binbin would threaten Mother with the knife.

"If you hurt someone, you may never make it home alive! You know that, don't you?" Mother raised her voice even louder.

"I don't care if I die!"

Mother fixed her eyes on Binbin, while he shifted left and right in front of her like a wounded animal, trying to figure out a way to get out.

"Listen," Mother said. "I was criticized at a meeting all day today. But I'm here. I want to be here when your father comes home, with you beside me. If you have to go out to fight, you will have to go over my dead body," she continued. She stood firm like a rock.

The look on Binbin's face was hard and cold. He was mesmerized with rage. His mind was on those who had beaten him. For a moment, he seemed to be ready to force his way through. My heart pounded. I started to cry.

"Don't, please don't!" I wanted to beg him, but didn't dare utter a sound.

"Nainai, do something. Please!" I pulled at Nainai's sleeve and murmured into her ear. Nainai gave a slight sigh, but said nothing. She put an arm around my waist.

At that moment, two streams of tears ran down Mother's face, and her body started shaking. Binbin was taken aback. Mother had never lost her composure in front of us before. Her tears must have shocked him. He suddenly stood still and stared at Mother. Slowly, his head began to drop, like a balloon losing air. He lowered the knife, its blade reflecting the dim light. Nainai quietly walked over. She put one hand on Binbin's shoulder and gently took the knife with the other. Binbin remained there for a moment as if an invisible power had glued him to the ground. Then he screamed. A long, mournful howling, like the sound of a wounded bull. It made my hair stand on end. He suddenly turned and stormed off toward his room. The heavy wooden door slammed shut behind him. We could hear him kicking the bed frame and yelling incomprehensibly.

Mother sat down at the table. Her tears continued to flow. It was the first time I had ever seen her cry.

She understood how hard it was to swallow those unprovoked insults and how humiliating it felt, tumbling from the top of the world all the way down to the bottom. Yet there was nothing she could do to protect us.

Mother soon regained her composure. She warned us never to lose our self-restraint. After a while, she knocked on Binbin's door. Binbin called out that he wanted to be left alone. Mother retreated to her room and didn't come out for the rest of the evening.

Mother continued to go to her school each morning and came home late in the evening, as if she were still doing her job. In reality, her time was spent writing self-criticisms, being criticized, or sweeping the schoolyard. We longed for Mother to tell us what was going on and what we should do. Mother, however, didn't give us any direction. If she ever said anything, it was more or less in line with the official statement.

"An unprecedented revolution is going on. We should support it," she said. When we pressed on, she would say: "We should believe in the Party and Chairman Mao. The truth will eventually prevail."

Only after the Cultural Revolution did I come to understand her cautious approach. If she had given us advice that was different from the official line, we could all end up facing more persecution. It was quite common for family members to turn against each other, proof of their dedication to the revolution.

2

At school, we spent most of our time unsupervised, since our teachers had to attend endless political or self-criticism meetings. Because we were absent from school most of the time in our first year, we repeated the first grade. They called us the "old first graders."

I used to walk to school with Aimin and Xiaohong, two girls of my age from the Compound. Aimin was tall and athletic. We enjoyed racing each other on the outdoor track field, with Xiaohong serving as our referee. Aimin was in my grade, but was in a different class. Xiaohong was chubby and quiet. She followed me everywhere like a little sister. We all used to be good friends. We walked to school together, did our homework together, or played in the Compound after school, but after Father was detained, they stayed away from me. When our paths crossed, they treated me like a stranger. I no longer had any friends.

To make matters worse, I faced more assaults when I stepped out of the Compound. School children cursed me when I passed by, and many shouted slogans at me as if they were at a struggle meeting. "Down with Hou Kai!" "Leniency for Confession, Punishment for Defiance!" Except for a few familiar faces from my class, I didn't know any of them. Sometimes, stones were thrown at me, as if falling out of the sky. But what hurt me the most was to hear Father's name shouted. My ears were most sensitive to these two syllables: Hou Kai. His permission to treat it lightly couldn't lessen the pain. Long after the verbal insults, I still felt the echo of the sound and the suffocating pain in my heart. There were times I wanted to yell, cry, or fight, but I couldn't. In addition to Mother urging us to stay out of trouble, I was fully aware that I was alone. Whenever one of the stones hit me, laughter erupted from all sides.

I soon realized that the twenty-minute walk from the Compound to school and back was the greatest trial of the day. To escape the flying stones and loud curses in the streets, I started running the moment I was out of the Compound, tucking my schoolbag under my arm. As soon as school was over, I raced back without stopping. Only when I crossed the gate of the Compound did I finally feel safe. Sometimes, one of my sisters or my brother Binbin would wait for me at the school entrance and walk me home. I felt much safer with them around.

A heavy, fat-faced boy from my class was particularly vicious. He spat at me and shouted "Down with the Shitty Dog!" every time he ran into me. I hated him. Sometimes, after enduring his ridicule and humiliation, I imagined scratching his big face with my fingernails and leaving him with scars. These were only consoling thoughts, however, since I knew the Revolution Committee would make Mother responsible for any unruly behavior on my part.

All I could do was run.

I tried hard to emulate Mother, to draw strength from her composure. One day I heard her talking with Nainai about her refusal to break down in front of the Red Guards.

"I won't give them the satisfaction," she said.

My heart skipped a beat, lightened with a new awareness. I couldn't fight back, but I could hold on to my pride. I had to ignore the insults and the bullying. For a moment, I felt strong, but keeping my pride was much harder than I thought. Insults and bullying still made me feel angry, confused, and vulnerable.

One day, the fat-faced boy approached me on my way home. I had a cold and the constant coughing prevented me from running. As he got closer, I crossed the street to walk on the other side, but he followed me, making faces at me along the way. A few children walking with him giggled. Suddenly, without warning, he snatched my schoolbag from my shoulder and threw it into the open sewer on the side of the street. A loud cheer followed. I was shocked. I had not encountered direct and personal physical attack. Even the stones were thrown from the safety of an anonymous crowd. But this? Anger and fear engulfed me at the same time. I threw a glance at my schoolbag. It lay flat at the edge of the smelly ditch, my pencil box and notebook sticking out and the strap of the bag dipping into the dirty water. Immediately, I moved to retrieve my bag. The fat-faced boy stepped over and blocked my way. More cheering.

As if possessed by a demon, I was overtaken by rage. I lowered my head and charged into him like a bull. He was taken aback and staggered. I was surprised by my own action, but it felt good, at least for the moment. He quickly regained his balance and charged toward me. All of a sudden, I sneezed on him. "Yuck!" he paused, wiping his eyes and nose with his sleeve. Then he grabbed me. We wrestled. He was bigger and stronger than I was. I pounded at him and pulled his shirt on his back, trying to get him away from me. In the chaos, I felt him pushing on my shoulder and reaching for my hair. Then he got hold of my pigtails and yanked. I gasped with pain. The chanting of the crowd disheartened me. I was losing ground, but kept on fighting. I didn't know what would happen next, but I couldn't stop. As I was about to be toppled to the ground, I heard my brother Binbin's voice from a distance.

"Stop it!" he yelled. Through my tears, I could see him charging at full speed toward me. "I mean you!" he halted beside the fat boy and me, our arms entangled together. Binbin reached out and dragged him off me by the collar. The boy let go. I was free. I coughed and gasped for air, my face burning. Binbin's sudden appearance and fearless attitude shocked all the school children.

"Don't you dare bully her!" Binbin shouted at the boy.

Binbin stood in front of me, facing the crowd. His eyes darted around, measuring the situation. As he was doing that, he loosened a bicycle chain tied around his waist. The metal chain glistened under the sun.

"The chain is stronger than a whip," he said, twisting the chain in his hands like a snake. He fixed his gaze on the fat-faced boy. His voice was full of rage, and his big eyes blazed with hatred.

I fetched my schoolbag and tugged him by his sleeve to leave. I was relieved and grateful that he had come to my rescue, but I was also shocked that my handsome and good-humored brother had been transformed into a reckless, furious fighter. We both knew, however, that the situation might escalate, and that we would be on the receiving end of it. We had no right to resist the revolutionary mass. Binbin took me by my hand and quickly led me out of the crowd. For a moment, there was only silence. I had to jog to keep pace with Binbin. We didn't look back. Binbin, fourteen at the time, took it upon himself to protect me whenever he could.

Binbin was not like this before. He used to be fun and curious. He spent much of his time collecting radio components and welding them together onto a printed circuit board to build his own radio. He grinned with pride when he received a station on the radio, despite the poor quality. He was also interested in film projectors. There was a large auditorium in the Compound where two film projectors took turns showing 16 millimeter films every Saturday evening. Binbin and his friends would do everything in their power to sneak into the auditorium for the show. During the week, fascinated by the mechanism of the projectors, they returned to take them apart and study how they worked. The manager of the auditorium was at his wit's end trying to keep the officials' children away from the equipment. Binbin laughed and dodged the manager, but somehow always assembled the projectors in time for the next show.

But the wide, toothy smile on Binbin's face was long gone.

3

One day, Mother came home with a gloomy face. She asked Binbin if he was involved in any fight. Binbin lowered his head, but didn't respond. I had noticed a large bruise on his right arm earlier that day. His pants were dusty, and his shirt was missing two buttons, but I didn't ask any questions. His darkened expression kept me at a distance. When Mother came back, he had changed into a different shirt with long sleeves.

"The worker representative of the Revolution Committee yelled at me today," Mother said. "Is there anything you should tell me?"

Binbin didn't respond. He shifted his weight from one foot to another, casting his eyes on the ground.

"Were you involved in a big fight?" Mother asked.

Binbin remained silent.

"What happened?" Mother pressed on. "Tell me." She raised her voice.

"There was a fight..." Binbin mumbled. "It was in self defense."

"A Red Guard reported it to the Revolution Committee. Did anyone get hurt?"

"Not seriously," Binbin shook his head.

His friend Dongsheng had started the fight. Binbin, Dongsheng, and Yongbing were on their way to Dongsheng's home. They ran into a group of Red Guards from their school. Two of them immediately started ridiculing Dongsheng for hanging around with the "shitty dogs."

"What's wrong with this idiot?" one said.

"Must be blind or retarded," the other chanted, laughing.

Yongbing urged them to move faster and get out of harm's way, but the Red Guards persisted. They followed them, making insulting remarks. Then someone threw a rock at Dongsheng. He lost his temper.

"You are picking on the wrong guy!" Dongsheng yelled and turned to face the Red Guards, but the two Red Guards trailing closely behind didn't hesitate to jump on him. "Who do you think you are?" they shouted.

Once the fight started, Yongbing and Binbin had no choice but to join in. They pushed the two off Dongsheng and the three of them formed a circle, with their backs against one another.

All hell broke loose and soon the group of Red Guards surrounded them. First came shouts, then came the first kicks and punches. Dongsheng, nearly a head taller than everyone else, took advantage of his height and threw a Red Guard to the ground. Binbin, bottled up with rage, kicked his attackers and swung his fists as if his life depended on it. But they were outnumbered. Soon each of them was wrestling with two or three people at the same time.

Frustrated, Dongsheng aimed at a Red Guard and punched him hard on his face, sending him swinging backward. His nose started bleeding and a fist-size black and blue bruise appeared on the right side of his face. "My nose!" he cried out in pain.

As the Red Guards got distracted by his cries and tended his bleeding, the three fighters fled the scene. Dongsheng's home was not far away. They disappeared into the alley. The incident was immediately reported to school.

"The worker representative requested you turn yourself in tomorrow." Mother sounded worried. She looked at Binbin from head to toe.

"How many times have I asked you not to fight?" Mother sighed.

Binbin lowered his head. I could see he was working hard to fight back his tears. His face turned pale.

Mother didn't press further. Binbin went to his room.

The following day, Mother left before seven o'clock. She asked Nainai to remind Binbin to report to school.

Binbin, however, stayed in bed. Nainai sent me to wake him up. I opened his door carefully and peeped in. He was lying in his twin bed, his bedding covering his head. Only part of his disarrayed black hair was visible. There was no sign of movement. I tiptoed toward him.

"Leave me alone," he said, startling me. I stopped in my tracks.

"Mother said..." I was about to repeat what Nainai told me to say.

"I said, leave me alone!" He raised his voice. Suddenly he flipped his bedding to the side and bolted up in his bed. He looked at me angrily. His eyes were puffy and red. He had been crying.

I stepped back and ran away.

When Binbin eventually came out of his room, Nainai urged him to have his breakfast first. A bowl of millet porridge, a piece of steamed corn bread, and some leftover dish from the night before were put aside for him. I noticed Nainai also cooked him a boiled egg. A special treat for him alone? I looked at Nainai, and my mouth watered.

"You can have it," Binbin said, pushing the egg toward me.

"You eat it," Nainai said. "I'll get something for Jian later."

I shook my head slowly and stepped behind Nainai.

"I'm not going anywhere today," he said to Nainai. "If they want to arrest me and put me in jail, they'll have to come and get me."

Binbin finished his porridge, but left the corn bread and egg untouched. He returned to his room. When he emerged again, his eyes were red. He went straight to the shed where we kept our garden tools and chicken feed. He took down the big ax hanging on a side wall, which he used to chop firewood for cooking. The edge of the ax still looked sharp, but the sidings were covered with rust. He had not touched it for a while. The wood handle was more than two feet long. It was stained with sweat, particularly at the end and middle where Binbin grasped it. He touched the edge with his thumb and set a grindstone on a bench. He dripped a spoonful of water on the grindstone and started sharpening the ax, moving it back and forth. He appeared totally absorbed in the task. When he was done, the blade shone in his hands. The rust was all gone. He took the ax to his bedroom and placed it carefully under his bed. When Nainai noticed it and said the ax should be kept in the shed, Binbin told her not to worry. "I won't be the first one to use force," he said.

Binbin was restless. He moved in and out of his room numerous times, but said very little. He was so preoccupied that he didn't seem to notice our concern, or for that matter, even our existence. He waited, anxiously.

There were so many political campaigns and rally meetings going on at school. Would they send people over to get Binbin if he didn't turn himself in? Would they throw him in jail? Would they beat him? But each of us kept our worries and questions to ourselves, as if to utter them would make them come true.

Nainai kept an eye on Binbin. She couldn't tell what was going on in her grandson's mind, but she knew he was scared and desperate.

Ping tried to take the ax away. She played innocent and pretended she needed to use the ax in the yard. Binbin stopped her. "The ax stays with me today," he said. There was no room for negotiation in his tone.

By noon, no one came. Binbin joined us for lunch, but he barely touched his food. Nainai sighed and put everything away.

Only years later he told us the ordeal he went through that day.

Not wanting to face charges and be sent to jail, he had decided to commit suicide. After Mother told him to report to school, he slept little through the night. He was in despair. Ever since he entered the No. 3 Middle School, life had been nothing but humiliation. He used to be the president of the Young Pioneer League at elementary school and a top student, but in middle school, he had become an outcast. His sense of pride and belonging was destroyed. Father had been kept away for a year, and there was no prospect of his return. Mother seemed to live solely on forbearance and blind belief. What was right or wrong? There was no right or wrong. The words of the Revolution Committee were the law, and the Red Guards could do whatever they liked. There was no rule to keep them in check. He had put up a brave face. He had had his fights, but they brought no relief. If anything, he felt worse. Our family's situation deteriorated by the day. Lying in total darkness under his covers, he sobbed, miserably. He bit the thin towel covering his pillow to prevent himself from letting out a sound. He didn't want anyone to see he was collapsing.

But how to commit suicide? The pale face of the young man who hanged himself in the park was still fresh in his mind. He didn't want to be a "hanging ghost." Then what? Drowning, perhaps? No, the prolonged process of suffocating seemed too painful. Or jumping off a tall building? The image of such a death flashed in his mind. He shivered. Even death was not an easy option. He hardly slept through the night. He didn't want to die, but living with dignity seemed to have become impossible.

He heard Mother get up and, an hour or so later, leave for school. He bid her farewell, silently. More tears came. He had exerted so much self-control since Father's fall that he never cried. He let himself go. His tears flowed.

He considered writing a letter to Mother, to let her know he couldn't take this anymore. He needed to clear her name—the taking of his life was his own decision. His alone. Then he dismissed the idea. What would that achieve? If the Revolution Committee found the note and realized it was a suicide, Mother, and possibly Father, would be blamed for it anyway. Suicide had always been regarded as an act of betrayal. It was openly condemned as "self-alienation," an act "against the people and the Party." In death, he might be condemned as counterrevolutionary. He thought of Mother, and her sunken eyes and haunted look hurt him. His stomach twisted in pain.

He was disgusted by his own weakness. "Damn it!" He said to himself. "If I have to die," he decided, he would fight to death. "I'll take a couple of them with me," he thought. That was when he pushed himself out of bed and sharpened the ax, the only tool he could effectively use as a weapon.

All he could think of that day was death. He was scared of killing others, and scared of being killed. He couldn't stop the tears. He was fourteen. He could not bring himself to say goodbye to anyone, not even silently in his mind.

To this day, Binbin remembers every single moment of that day. He calls it the darkest day of his life, a day of total despair.

He kept all these feelings to himself. Only years later did he relate the incident and his turmoil to me. And he mentioned it only once. He didn't want to revisit that painful past. "It makes me angry. And it hurts," he said. Even today, when my sisters cautiously talk with me about their experiences and feelings during the Cultural Revolution, Binbin clams up. "Focus on something positive taking place today," he says. "Don't go back to the past."

That day in 1967, as Binbin cried his heart out and prepared to fight to his death, the Revolution Committee at the No. 3 Middle School had other, more important issues to deal with. They never sent anyone.

After the incident, Dongsheng's parents sent their son to a relative's home for a while, to let the issue settle and pass. With the key person out of sight, the case was not brought up again. But Binbin was never the same. He armed himself with a pocket knife or wrapped the bicycle chain around his waist, ready to fight like a warrior.

He never shed tears again.

Chapter Thirteen

Moving

1

Our life passed as episodes of a recurring nightmare. Each day, the loudspeaker set up in a tree next to our apartment woke us up, denouncing Father and other former officials as capitalist roaders. Each night, we went to bed fearful of what the next day might bring. Prisoners in our own home, we moved quietly through the darkened rooms. We followed Mother's example. We didn't talk about our deteriorating circumstances. We were terrified but powerless to break free.

Within a year of its inception, the Cultural Revolution had plunged the nation into chaos. Most of the former officials were purged from office. The railway system was paralyzed with millions of Red Guards traveling free of charge around the country to spread the revolution—the government called it the "Big Connection." Colleges were shut down, and most factories— with the exception of steel and iron manufacturers—were operating at minimum capacity, if they were in operation at all. Newly formed Revolution Committees at various levels were running the daily administration. What they really focused on was political persecution.

The Red Guards and the so-called "rebels" in Baicheng and elsewhere in the nation formed into paramilitary units to combat "revisionist" authorities and officials. Mao was using them to regain his grip of the Communist Party, which had been slipping, but he had unleashed a wave of violence throughout the country. In their extraordinary zeal, the groups soon split into different factions. In 1967, they began to confront one another not only with verbal attacks, but also with real ammunition. In

Baicheng, ten people were killed and scores more were injured, all within a matter of three months. The Central Government soon directed the Army to take over local authorities and maintain order.

To regain control, Chairman Mao launched a new initiative. He exiled the students from the cities to the villages. "The educated youth should go to the countryside and receive re-education from the peasants. It is necessary."

Chairman Mao's newest "supreme directive" was spread via loudspeakers throughout the city. His call sparked a mass youth exodus. Some left with enthusiasm, some with reluctance, and some because they had no choice. Some students, with the support of their parents, faked illness to remain in the city. A common excuse was "night blindness," a physical defect that couldn't be easily disputed by medical tests. Another was bed-wetting. But their future wasn't too bright either. Staying behind meant their parents would have to continue to support them.

In late 1968, students from the No. 3 Middle School were getting ready to leave. They were divided into small groups based on their grades and classes, and each group was sent to one of the many "collective youth centers" that had been hastily built in the villages to accommodate them. In the northeast, these so-called youth centers were nothing more than three-room, single-story mud houses. One room was for males, another for females, with one or two Kangs for them to sleep on. The third room in the middle served as a kitchen. There were two or four stoves set up in this room, depending on how many Kangs were in the bedrooms. Smoke from cooking in each of the stoves was the sole source of heat for the Kang, which in turn, warmed up the room. However, this never generated enough heat, and the rooms were all ice cold.

Yan was supposed to graduate that year, but she, like the rest of the students in her grade, had not had a chance to learn anything in the previous two years. Mother encouraged her to go. It was the call of Chairman Mao and the Central Government. With Father still in detention, staying behind was not an option. The Municipal Government set up a special administrative office to arrange for student groups to settle in different communes and villages.

Yan faced a major challenge. None of the student groups in her class wanted to be with her. She cried with humiliation. In the end, her homeroom teacher put her into a mixed group that consisted mostly of students from a lower grade.

Ping was only a junior in 1968, but the students of her grade were asked to go to the countryside as well. Her group was assigned to a poorer village even further away from Baicheng.

In November 1968, for several days in a row, a total of nearly six thousand middle school students in Baicheng were sent to the countryside. They were all supposed to leave with a large red paper bow pinned to their chests, but the city had soon exhausted its supply of red paper and most of them left without the glorious decoration.

Yan and Ping were among the first to leave. They packed their bedding in large bundles and tied them together with ropes. A thin canvas bag was stuffed with their clothing, and a string bag was filled with a metal round basin, a thin metal mug, a couple of face towels, and a few bars of soap. Some also packed large insulated bottles for hot water. We helped Yan and Ping carry their belongings to the school campus. It was a very cold day.

Everyone's string bags and basins were nearly identical. Shops had offered wooden boxes as suitcases, and some students brought them along. The front of the box was adorned with Mao's latest directives, in bold, red ink. Considering our financial difficulties, Yan and Ping decided not to purchase the box.

We heard distant drums, as well as praises for the departing students coming from loudspeakers. We passed numerous military trucks on our way, with students standing in the open cargo areas. They were beating drums and waving the national red flags. Some were singing revolutionary songs. At the No. 3 Middle School, a line of military trucks was waiting for the students to get on board.

Mother, Binbin, Wen, and I all went to see Yan and Ping off. Villagers from nearby sent their horse-drawn carts to pick up the students who were assigned to them. The students who were sent further away were transported with military trucks. Some parents also squeezed themselves in, wanting to help their children during their journey. Mother, too, had obtained a permit to go. A mixture of revolutionary enthusiasm and passive sadness permeated the air.

Since Ping was a year younger than Yan, and her group was going further away, Mother chose to accompany her to her village. Binbin, Wen and I, together with Mother and Ping, first walked Yan to her group. Two horse-pulled carts were waiting to take them away. We bid a tearful farewell to her. Then we tracked down Ping's group and their vehicle. As we had expected, they had a military truck. While the students jumped up onto the open truck with ease, Mother had difficulties getting herself up on the loading area. She stood on the step that led to the driver's cab and climbed over the waist-high rail from there. She took Ping's belongings, which we handed up to her, and then stood back. Ping soon joined her. They urged us to go home. My hands and feet were hurting from the cold, but I didn't want to leave. I looked at Mother and Ping. They stood side by side, all bundled up. Their faces didn't show any emotion. Ping didn't have a red bow.

When we first arrived at school, I was excited by all the commotion. I even felt jealous of Yan and Ping. They were breaking away from our endless nightmare, I thought. At least they didn't have to listen to the denouncements anymore. But with Yan gone, and Ping's truck starting to move, I was struck with a sense of loss. We followed the truck out of the campus, waving goodbye to Ping. When it finally picked up speed and headed toward the road leading to the countryside, I found tears running down my face. Wen was crying as well.

"I've got to go," Binbin suddenly said. He turned quickly and disappeared in the crowd. He didn't want anyone to see his tears.

I saw two women standing next to us wipe their eyes. Then I heard Wen urge me to go home.

Nainai was waiting for us.

"Are they both gone?" she asked as we stepped in.

"Yes, Nainai," Wen answered.

Nainai sighed, as if she was expecting us to give her a different answer. I walked into the room Yan and Ping used to share. A few pages of loose paper were scattered on the desk between their twin beds. With their bedding gone, the room seemed utterly empty. I closed the door behind me, not wanting to dwell on their absence.

Later that night, Mother returned. We were already in bed by the time she got home. The following day, we asked what the youth center was like, and how large the village was. Mother, as usual, said little. It took some prodding for her to tell us.

The conditions at the youth center were appalling. The rooms were so cold that the students had to wear their scarves and mittens all the time. Except for the two Kangs in each bedroom and a bench, there was nothing else in the house. Mother had helped Ping spread her bedding between two girls on the cold Kang. She couldn't imagine how they were going to cope with the situation. Their grain allocations were stacked in a kitchen corner, but there were no vegetables. It was the dead of winter. Worse, there was no fuel for cooking and heating. The "center" used to be a tool shed, next to the stables. All day they heard the horses neigh, and smelled the dung. There was a well that provided water for the horses, but it wasn't very deep and the water was murky. They had to use the dirty water for drinking, cooking, and washing. Each village was called a "production unit," and several villages formed a "commune." A man named Zhao was the leader of Ping's village. He was a man in his fifties. He was all bundled up with dark cotton-padded pants and jacket and looked at these young men and women without emotion. He told them he would have some red sorghum stalks dropped off for fuel later.

"Tomorrow, you'll have to go to the meadows to gather grass for cooking and heating," he told them. He held a long pipe in his hand. From time to time, he took a deep draw and blew out irritating tobacco smoke. He didn't show any kindness to these city teenagers. He was at a loss and didn't know what to do with them. The winter in the northeast was long and cold. There was not much work to do. And here he was, suddenly entrusted with twenty young men and women who didn't know a thing about country life. He already had enough on his mind. As the village leader, he was responsible for a hundred or so households.

Mother climbed back onto the open truck with a heavy heart. The wind in the open country seemed to blow more fiercely. She saw low, one-story mud buildings scattered around the village. There were hardly any people out on the narrow dirt roads. A few children ran over to look at the newcomers, but by the time the truck was ready to take off again, they had all gone home.

Mother, along with a school teacher and two other parents, tightened her scarves, mittens and her face mask. Everyone was quiet. There was no more excitement. The stark conditions shocked the students, and made the departing adults even more worried. Mother let out a long, silent sigh. She knew that Ping and the others had embarked on a long and hard journey.

2

January 1969 arrived with a cold front from Siberia. The temperature dropped to 20 degrees below zero Fahrenheit. People wore masks, or wrapped their faces with scarves to keep warm. The moisture that seeped through these protective layers turned men's mustaches into small icicles and frosted women's eyelashes and eyebrows. A few years earlier, despite the cold, the children in the Compound might have played with snowballs and built snowmen in the yard, but the Cultural Revolution had put an end to that. Most of the older children had been sent to the countryside for reeducation. The ones who were left behind were in no mood to play, as their fathers were either in detention or being denounced. Besides, it was not safe to play outside, even in the Compound. Different rebel groups were fighting each other, and it was not unusual to hear stray bullets hissing through the air.

In our apartment, it was even quieter without Yan and Ping.

The only sound that broke the stillness of the cold morning was the loudspeakers, repeatedly bellowing out Mao's orders, or singing revolutionary songs.

Sailing the high seas requires a helmsman,
Life on earth depends on the sun.
Plants grow vigorously with rain and dew,
Revolution is directed by Mao Zedong Thought.

Fish can't leave the water,
Nor melons leave the vine.
The revolutionary masses can't do without the Communist Party,
Mao Zedong Thought is the sun that forever shines.

The song was blasted so many time that it became nothing more than background noise, despite its high volume.

On one of these cold days, a week before the Chinese New Year, Mother came home from work. She had a serious expression.

She told us we were moving.

"We'll pack up all our belongings and move out of here before the New Year," she said. Seeing the tension and fear on our faces, she added: "The new apartment is not far away."

Mother didn't look any of us in the eye, nor did she display any emotion. She seemed preoccupied. As usual, she gave no explanation. The only thing she mentioned was that our next door neighbor, Wuzi's family, was also moving. As if that was consolation. We had been living in the Compound for eight years. It was the only place I called my home. The news sent chills down my spine, a sensation I had been experiencing more frequently these days. I bit my lip and restrained myself from asking questions.

Mother had lost a lot of weight. The dark circles under her eyes had become permanent. Although she still walked with her back straight and her head high, her self-confident demeanor had given way to sadness. She had not seen Father for over a year, and was single-handedly holding the family together. I was eight that year, and had long before learned not to ask questions. We had to face what we were dealt with. Through the corner of my eye, I stole a glance at Binbin and Wen. They looked pale and scared, but remained silent. Only Nainai clenched her fists and said she would not move. Grief and anxiety seemed to have aged her. To make matter worse, she had almost lost her eyesight to cataracts. Mother had invited Big Aunt, Father's older sister, to stay with us permanently to help take care of Nainai.

"I'm not going anywhere," Nainai said. She had turned eighty-five, and the deterioration of her eyesight had made it nearly impossible for her to walk around on her own.

Nainai's voice was soft but firm. We all knew how strong and persistent she could be.

"Let them come and get me out of my home by force!" she said.

"The Red Guards can hurt you," Mother said patiently. "Besides, we should move out of here with dignity."

Big Aunt cursed. "This world is going to the dogs!" she exclaimed, waving her arms. Big Aunt looked like Nainai. The same height, same bound feet, and the same hair style—tied back in a bun. But she had a totally different personality. She was short-tempered and loud. She didn't like anyone being picky about the food she prepared. When she was unhappy, she didn't hesitate for a second to let others know.

Mother put one hand on Big Aunt's shoulder. "This isn't up for discussion," she said. "We have no choice, and we should save our strength for the move."

Mother's words settled the issue. She started putting our things together. Then she asked Binbin to help her take down the fence of our vegetable garden. I watched them as they hauled the pieces of wood away in a large two-wheel cart they had borrowed. One load after another. I had never seen our garden so bare. I felt it was not the fence that was being dismantled, but our life. I asked Mother to take me to see the new place.

"I'll take you there when it's ready," she said. She sounded dismissive and didn't even look at me.

Three days before the Chinese New Year, Mother spent her first night at the new place by herself. Then, another night. Each morning she returned home, looking gloomier than the day before, but she said nothing. I watched her every move when she was home.

I had secretly wished the Chinese New Year would bring the family together—Father returning home and my two sisters coming back for a reunion. After all, this was the most important festival of the year, a time for family gatherings. I was particularly looking forward to the loud bang of firecrackers on New Year's Eve. They were supposed to drive away evil spirits and bring good luck. I wanted to see our whole family make dumplings together, and enjoy the traditional food at midnight on New Year's Eve, accompanied by candlelit lanterns. Except for the last two years, we had always observed this tradition and had a wonderful time. I wanted this to happen more than anything else.

Binbin and Wen quietly helped Mother prepare for the move. Our belongings were minimal. The cabinets and bookshelves were built into the walls, and our plank beds were the property of the government and could not be removed. Only a few books remained on the built-in shelves after the raid by the Red Guard: *Selections of Mao Zedong's Works* and translations of writings by Marx, Engels, Lenin, and Stalin. The items that needed to be packed were mostly pots and pans and bulky cotton padded bedding and clothes.

We moved on New Year's Eve.

3

There was no sense of festivity on this New Year's Eve. We all got up early for the move. Mother, together with Binbin and Wen, swiftly walked in and out of the front door, piling our utensils and parcels of small household items onto the two-wheel cart. I watched them from behind a window. Mr. Zhang, a family friend, showed up late in the morning. Zhang was a stout man. His face was always red as if whipped by the cold wind, and his nose, the shape of garlic, stood out as a most prominent feature. He was good-natured and laughed readily. He was a low-level clerk in the government hierarchy. I don't know how Father befriended him. He visited us frequently, stopping by to say hello without notice, as was the custom. When my parents were not home, he simply hung around, checking to see if there was any handy job that needed to be done around the apartment. Sometimes he'd play with me. He often expressed his gratitude to Father for treating him with respect.

"Your papa never puts on airs like other high-ranking officials," he used to tell me.

After Father's fall, visitors and friends from the government offices disappeared. But Zhang continued to come. He would show up at odd hours to see if we needed anything. Once he pushed a two-wheel cart and delivered to us our ration of coal from the supply center. Another time, he bought tobacco leaves for Father, a commodity he had to go to the countryside to acquire. Grateful as Mother was for his help, she asked him to stay away.

"You shouldn't have any association with us," Mother said to him. "It could get you into trouble if someone reported you."

Zhang shrugged his shoulders. "I don't have much to lose," he said.

He continued to come, but he was cautious. Instead of the front entrance, he climbed over the Compound wall behind our apartment and visited us at night. I would learn years later that his wife, who had a sharp tongue and a loud voice, fought with him many times over those visits.

"Hou Kai is not your father," she'd yell. "Nowadays, even family members sever their relationships. Think about the future of our children."

I could imagine how his wife, a head taller than Zhang, would block his way and give him a hard time, but it didn't stop him from coming out to help us move. His family lived right behind the mud building we were moving into. He must have seen Mother and her two children with the cart. He came over and insisted in giving a hand. Mother was touched and grateful.

Zhang pulled the cart, while Mother, Binbin, and Wen pushed from the side and behind. The snow-covered ground was slippery, and the overloaded cart jerked along the bumpy road. I waited inside our apartment. It seemed to take them forever to come back for another load. Nainai sat on her usual spot on the Kang, all bundled up. She said nothing the whole morning, her lips pursed as if to prevent an outburst of protest, and her wrinkled face appeared tired from lack of sleep. Big Aunt had gone to the new place earlier in the day. I zoomed in and out of the five empty bedrooms, listening to the hollow echoes of my own footsteps on the wooden floor. The three large windows facing south, one in each bedroom, had been mostly bricked up, allowing only a narrow beam of sunlight to shine high on the walls. It hadn't always been like this.

On an August afternoon, when Yan and Ping were still at home, factions of the Red Guards were shooting at each other with rifles. A stray bullet cracked a window in Binbin's bedroom, ripping a deep groove along the wall right above his bed before hitting the floor. Binbin had left the room only minutes before. Early that morning, we had heard gunshots and screams from the front yard of the Communist Party Institute, which was located next to the Government Compound. It was separated from our living quarters by two walls and a two-way street. Big Aunt urged us to stay inside. When the noise quieted down, Ping ventured out. She climbed an elm tree by our building to see what was going on. What she saw shocked her. A wounded Red Guard was on a stretcher and four young men were carrying him onto a military truck. A white first-aid box with a red cross was placed next to the truck, and a pool of blood covered the ground. Ping slipped off the tree and ran inside.

"Binbin," she yelled. "Come out. Quick! Someone was shot and they are taking him to the hospital!" Binbin jumped off from his bed and ran out. "Hurry up!" Ping gestured to him. Binbin followed Ping and they raced to a high branch on the elm tree.

There were two major factions among the Red Guards: the Radicals who were determined to topple the former regime and condemn the old officials, and the Moderates who intended to defend some of these overthrown officials. Ping and Binbin held their breath. More people were coming out of the Institute's building, accompanying another wounded man, his arm wrapped in bandage. A Red Guard noticed them.

"You," he raised his gun and waved. "Get away! Now!" Ping and Binbin immediately slipped down from the tree. They ran inside, only to find the bullet on the floor of Binbin's bedroom and the deep mark on the wall.

Binbin's narrow escape scared Mother. She decided not to take any chances. The following Sunday, she sealed all the large windows with bricks, leaving a foot on the upper level to allow light to come through. We were lucky that nobody was hurt. We had seen the body of a teenage boy in front of the Compound entrance. He had been shot in the head. Parts of his scalp and hair had been blown to the electrical wire twelve feet above the street and were hanging there for days—a horrifying sight.

All these images flashed in my mind as I walked from one room to another in the semidarkness. The empty rooms felt like a deserted castle, creating a sense of danger rather than safety. Even the echo of my own footsteps sounded creepy. I felt overwhelmed by this vast emptiness and ran to Nainai for comfort.

Finally, Mother returned for Nainai and me. She put two layers of cotton-padded quilts on the cart and propped another against the back. She walked Nainai slowly to the front door. As Binbin and Wen held the cart handles, Mother and Zhang lifted Nainai onto the cart. No one said a word. I looked at Binbin. Strips of frost were hanging from the edge of his hat, and the scarf over his face was icy with the moisture from his breath. His eyes, sunk behind all these protective covers, were fixed on the handle as if the cart would flip over if he didn't concentrate. Wen looked away when I tried to meet her eyes.

Nainai didn't put up a fight. She sat still and allowed Mother to cover her legs with more bedding and wrap her bound feet with a blanket. Mother put me in the cart beside her. Before I could react, she threw a heavy blanket on top of us, covering us from head to toe. Then she tucked the edge of the blanket under Nainai and me.

Despite the quilt, the blanket, and the overcoat I was wearing, the cold air pierced my body right away. My feet soon became numb. I heard Nainai's subdued sobbing and moved closer to her. I could see vague spots of light through the worn areas of the blanket. The road was bumpy, and the cart rocked us left and right.

"Are we there yet?" I shouted after what seemed an eternity.

There was no answer. The only sound I heard was the muffled squeaking of the wheels in the snow.

When Zhang and Binbin stopped to shift positions, I poked my head out and begged Mother to let me down so I could run and warm up my feet. She reluctantly agreed.

I saw we were already outside the Compound. The entire street was covered with different colors of snow: some of it clear and fresh, some of it turned as hard as a rock by the many footsteps of the passers-by. There were segmented trails dug out beside the one-story apartment buildings next to the street, but the snow on the main road would take its natural course, compressed into hardened ice, melting only with the arrival of spring. To avoid falling, I jumped up and down on the same spot.

Two of Wen's classmates saw us from across the street. They called her name and ran over to see what was going on. They stretched out their arms to keep balance as if they were skating on ice.

"What are you doing, Wen?" one asked.

"What's that?" the other cut in before Wen could answer. She was referring to the pointed bundle on the cart.

"We are moving," Wen said, her usual soft voice barely audible now. "That's my grandma."

The two teenage girls giggled in disbelief and raced to lift the blanket.

There sat Nainai. She leaned back on the quilt, her eyes closed. She didn't respond to the sudden intrusion of light and cold air. Mother rushed over and rearranged the blanket over her.

The two girls were taken aback and watched quietly as we moved away. Wen tightened her grip on the cart handle and pushed it forward with all her strength, making a barely noticeable parting nod to her classmates.

We turned slowly into an alley. I could still see the high brick wall of the Compound. The familiar sight felt reassuring. Halfway into the alley, I gained a better view of our new neighborhood. On one side of the road stood rows of one-story red brick buildings, each one housing four apartment units. And on the other side were flat single-story mud buildings. They were lower than the brick buildings, and each row contained five apartments. We passed a public toilet in the middle of the alley. A glance at the structure sent a wave of nausea through me. It was the same as the outhouse at school. I had always been afraid to use it. Once, when I first started school, I had fallen into one of those rectangular holes. As my right foot slipped and fell into the hole, my left leg and arms intuitively spread out, holding my torso above the planks. Luckily, the pit was deep, so my dangling leg didn't sink into the feces. A school teacher and two other students who were waiting in line came to my rescue and pulled me out. I was covered in urine and dirt. I rushed away, feeling too embarrassed to look at my rescuers or thank them for their help. Ever since that incident, I always tried to return home to use the bathroom. Many times, I had to exert my utmost control against nature's call and often had bad cramps, but I'd rather endure the discomfort than risk the danger of falling in. Not to mention the sight and smell of the open pit.

I froze on the spot. It dawned on me that I would no longer have an alternative. Then, Mother called me. I ran to catch up with the rest of the family.

We came to an open area. A one-meter elevated platform with a water pipe stood in the middle. Ribbons of ice stretched from the base, which looked like an octopus sculpted on the ground. A large mound of frozen garbage was piled next to the platform. I observed with amazement as a teenage girl filled two large pails with water and walked away, balancing the two pails on either end of a long pole securely planted across her shoulders. Soon, I would learn to fetch pails of water just like her.

We stopped in front of a low building. It was built with adobe, a mixture of straw and mud. A smooth layer of mud was smeared on the outer surface, covering the uneven edges. The rooms underneath the low ceilings seemed to be completely dark. Mother pointed to the unit in the middle, saying that was our new home. A pile of chopped wood occupied a corner of the small yard. As I was about to run inside to take a look, Mother asked me to take a few pieces of wood with me. I realized our garden fence had been turned into heating materials.

It took me a while to get used to the dim light inside. The apartment was small. The entrance area also served as a kitchen. There was a small window by the door. The glass was broken, so it was blocked with a layer of plastic, reinforced with a blanket. No light came through the window, making the room darker. The entrance area opened to two adjacent bedrooms. A large stove was located next to the main entrance. A deep cooking wok was mounted permanently on its top. Big Aunt was there, keeping the fire burning. In the larger bedroom, a small cast-iron stove was set up temporarily in the middle. The rusty metal pipe that served as a chimney reached toward the low ceiling, made a 90 degree turn in mid-air and extended all the way to the back. The pipe poked through a hole in the rear wall, releasing smoke into the open air. The uneven dirt floor was as hard as a rock. The walls in both bedrooms were coated with patches of frost and ice, as if someone had decorated them with snow sculptures. Each bedroom had a Kang. It took a third of the space in each room. The second bedroom was so small that besides the Kang, there was hardly any space to move around.

The Kang in the large bedroom had nothing on it. Only half of the surface next to the stove was dry, while the other half had scattered wet spots that looked like a poorly drawn map. Apparently, nobody had lived in this apartment before.

Mother entered the room and put a piece of cotton-padded bedding in the dry area on the Kang. As Nainai settled on it, Mother stirred the fire in the iron stove and threw in a few pieces of wood. The crackling of burning wood and coal echoed in the air. Flames immediately jumped up, giving off badly needed heat.

"The mud house was built in the winter. The walls, the Kang, and the roof were all frozen," Mother explained to Nainai apologetically as if it were her fault. "It will take some time to dry them completely."

So this was our new home: no running water, no radiators, and no indoor toilet.

We kept the fire burning. All our belongings were piled up in the middle of the large bedroom and the entrance area. We spent the rest of the day sorting things out and finding places to store them.

New Year's Eve quietly came to its end. No midnight firecrackers lit up our door. There were no dumplings for celebration. Mother arranged for us to settle in the larger bedroom. She had Nainai sleep next to the stove, with me by her side, and Binbin on the far end by the cold wall. She took the small room in the back. The tiny window on the rear wall only brought in a narrow beam of natural light. Other than a few occasional words of instruction from Mother and brief acknowledgments from Binbin and Wen, the apartment was quiet. I clung to Nainai, trying hard to let reality sink in. I couldn't imagine how we would live in this icebox and wondered if I could still go back to the Compound to play. I tried to dismiss the worries and confusions in my mind. At least we were all together during the three-day New Year holiday.

We went to bed with our clothes, scarves, and mittens on. When we woke up in the morning, we found everything was wet—the adobe blocks under the surface of the Kang gave out moisture. When the fire went out in the middle of the night, the moisture turned icy. We lit up the stove, heated water to wash our faces, and prepared breakfast.

On New Year's Day, Mother went out and bought a pound of pork, the entire family's ration for the month. She and Big Aunt made a traditional northeastern dish—pickled cabbage with mung bean noodles and thinly sliced pork. It was a great treat. We set up our miniature dining table on top of the Kang, with Nainai sitting lotus-style in the center, Big Aunt on her left side, and the three of us grandchildren on her right side. Mother sat on the edge, moving back and forth to the cooking pot on the stove to refill our bowls. We didn't have any rice. Mother cooked red sorghum as a substitute. Red sorghum and corn were local produce and made up most of our monthly ration of grain. We didn't like their rough texture. But that day, none of us complained. The atmosphere in the apartment was heavy and sad, and no one had the heart to make it worse. Besides, as usual, we were hungry.

Mother picked out slices of pork from her bowl and put them in Nainai's and mine. Half way through dinner, the electricity went out. There was not enough power, and it was common that blocks of residential areas had their electricity cut without notice. Mother lit a candle and put it in the middle of the table. The flicker of the candlelight cast our own shadows on the walls, creating an eerie feeling. Noticing our unease, Mother took out several thin, small candlesticks, lit and placed them throughout the room. Normally, in an effort to make our candle supply last longer, we only lit one candle in each room. Mother made an exception that day. We had our first family dinner together in the mud house. This Chinese New Year marked the beginning of a very different life for us.

Nainai and Me in front of Mud House

Chapter Fourteen

A Different World

1

We soon realized that surviving in the mud house required much more than dealing with frozen walls and Kangs. When we finished burning the garden fence for heating and cooking, the powder-like coal hardly kept the fire going. We learned to mix the coal with water to make briquettes, which was messy. The resulting small black dots on the dirt floor near the entrance wouldn't go away, even after we removed the briquettes and cleaned up. The briquettes prevented the coal powder from falling through the grate, but despite our puffing the bellows to fan the fire, they barely gave enough heat for cooking. The apartment was freezing. We cut newspapers into two inch wide strips to seal the windows.

Then, there was the problem of getting water.

Mother bought a pair of large pails, a long wooden pole, and a glazed earthen vat in the shape of a barrel. The pail was made of thin iron sheet, and the vat was three feet tall and two feet in diameter. None of us knew how to balance the long pole across our shoulders to fetch water. At first, Mother used a single pail, swinging the half-filled container left and right to get water home. The closest public water pipe was half a block away. To spare Mother the burden, Binbin and Wen volunteered to do the job. Sliding the pole through the handle of the pail, each of them held one end. It worked, but the children in the neighborhood laughed at them. Binbin and Wen were embarrassed. Binbin tried to put the pole on his shoulders, and the result was worse. The pails swung up and down. Binbin couldn't keep his balance and walk with the load at the same time. To avoid the prospect of

Binbin getting into fights, Wen tried to fill the vat on her own before he got home. One of her classmates across the alley in one of the red brick buildings had running water at home. At first, her classmate allowed Wen to come and get water from their pipe. Not only did it cut the distance to about half, but it also gave her the luxury of staying warm while waiting to fill the pails. As soon as her classmate's parents found out, they put an end to the practice. They didn't want to have anything to do with us.

I wanted to help. When only Nainai and I were around, I practiced using the pole. There was a metal chain at each end of the pole to hook up the pails. The pole, when upright, was a head taller than me. I placed the two pails apart. They were too tall for me to lift above the ground. I wrapped the metal chain at each end of the pole around the pail handle and fastened the hook to the pole. I was proud of my creativity. I ventured out to the platform where the public water pipe was set up. A curved thick pipe extended to the front of the platform, releasing water into the containers placed underneath. It was operated by a T-shaped metal key. To avoid attracting attention, I held the wood pole in one hand and the handles of the two pails in the other. The pails clicked as I walked, but at least they didn't dance up and down, out of balance. I hoped that once they were half full with water, they wouldn't jump like a chained animal struggling to get away.

Spilled water created an icy slope around the platform, making it difficult to place the pails. The lock on the pipe was tight and I couldn't get it to turn. I took off my mittens to get a better grip. When, with a sudden jolt, it turned, the gushing water immediately knocked over my pail. I shut off the water to retrieve the pail. The handle was wet and my fingers instantly stuck to it. I grimaced with pain. When I freed my hand from the handle, a layer of skin stuck on it. I quickly put on my mittens and started all over again.

Eventually, I got the two pails half full and successfully dragged them to the side. I had to pull them toward me with both hands. The pole refused to balance on my shoulders. When I succeeded in lifting one pail, I lost control of the other. Even though the pails were half full, they splashed cold water all over me. First, one pail, then the other, hit the ground. I had witnessed this happening to Binbin. If he was able to handle it after a few rounds, I told myself, so could I. I struggled on. A few adults passed me and looked the other way. But the children were merciless. A small group soon gathered around me.

"Where did this idiot come from?" one remarked.

"A shitty dog," another added. "The cold water will do her good. It will take care of her bourgeois idleness."

I spilled most of the water out of the pails and rushed home, dragging the pails on the ground. I was angry. Not just at the children who ridiculed me, but also with myself. I was determined to handle the task. Once inside, I scooped water out of the vat and filled the pails half full again. I practiced in the narrow room until my shoulders hurt. When I returned home from school the following day, I practiced again. A week later, I was able to carry water home, with the pails half full. There was no rejoicing, though. The hostile attitude of the children in the new neighborhood made me feel nervous and isolated.

Our two immediate neighbors were not much different. The Wang family to our left had built such a tall wall and high gate that we were not able to tell how many members of their family lived there. The Yangs to our right simply avoided us, as if we had a contagious disease, but the brick wall around their yard was low, and I could see each of their family members going in and out of their apartment. Mother was grateful that they didn't go out of their way to make our life more miserable.

I was forced to adapt to the outhouse. Each morning, I stood in line in the biting cold, waiting my turn, taking extra care not to slip into the hole in the middle of the planks. Since no apartment had any indoor facilities, there was always a line in the morning. The women chatted with one another, and fortunately for me, the children were always quiet at this hour. I couldn't tell if it was because they were still half asleep or because there were adults around. In any event, they left me alone.

Nainai stayed inside all the time. She used a chamber pot. My sister Wen and I emptied the pot each time Nainai used it.

We could hardly wait for the arrival of spring and the relief it would bring with warmer weather.

2

As the weather finally turned warm, however, it brought us more astonishment than relief. As the ground began to thaw, the narrow streets and alleys turned into a wetland. Between the puddles of dirty water stood islands of hardened dirt. People laid out bricks, rocks, and wood planks, building an improvised footpath. It took some skill to move about without sinking into the mud. Children leapt from island to island, while adults negotiated their way with bicycles by their sides, or sometimes even balanced over their shoulders. Then the spring rain came, giving us another surprise.

It turned out that the roof of our building was not properly sealed. As the rainwater seeped through the straw and mud ceiling, we set out the laundry basin, washbowls, and even the cooking pots and food containers to catch the drips. We watched in astonishment as the rainfall intensified and the dripping became a shower. Even when the rain outside stopped, the dripping inside continued at a steady pace.

Eventually, Mother hung a big sheet of plastic above the Kang and moved Nainai and her bedding underneath. This proved effective, so Mother went out and bought more plastic sheets. Soon several bedding size plastic sheets were suspended against the ceiling, protecting important areas of the apartment. One was hung over the stove so the cooking could be done without the involuntary addition of raindrops to every dish. We had another sheet over the boxes that contained most of our clothes, and one above a twin bed on which we piled all our bedding. Each plastic sheet was a different color: green, burgundy, blue. Our apartment seemed to be a camp ground for kites. From time to time, Mother used a bamboo stick to tilt the suspended sheets and empty the accumulated water into a bucket. It poured down like a waterfall and splashed all over as it hit the container.

As if to test our survival skills, the spring of 1969 brought plenty of rain. Before we could get our roof fixed, we found our front yard flooded with muddy water. There was no sewage system in the alley. Accumulated water flowed toward lower areas, and our front yard became a pond. Despite our attempt to dam the entrance to the apartment with bricks and mud, the water came through, slowly at first. Then it broke through the barrier like a monstrous, powerful flood.

The dirt floor inside was half a foot lower than the yard. Mother put on her rubber boots and raincoat and began scooping the muddy water off the floor, first into a container and then, as the water built up, bailing it directly out of the door with a pail. Wen and I rolled up our sleeves and pants and joined Mother in her attempt to keep the water out. Binbin worked in the yard, trying to build a buffer under the fence and the gate to block out the water from the alley. Many people raised chickens, ducks, geese, and pigs in the neighborhood. Their waste floated in the water, making the task of building a dam more desperate.

We couldn't wear our ponchos working inside, for they covered our hands and made our efforts less effective. So we put on straw hats to protect our hair, while our bodies became soaking wet. We worked side by side with Mother and did the best we could to salvage the apartment. Garbage and animal manure smeared our arms and legs, and filled our noses with a rank smell. Big Aunt was furious. Her bound feet rendered her useless in this situation. Sitting by Nainai, she waved her fists and cursed.

Big Aunt had spent all her life in her home village in Shandong. After her husband died, she moved in with her son's family. When life in the village became too difficult, the whole family went to the northeast and settled in the Red Star Village in Jilin Province, a two-hour train ride from Baicheng. Big Aunt cooked and cared for Nainai, providing the help we desperately needed, but in the face of this crisis, all she seemed capable of doing was shaking her fists.

Nainai, on the other hand, never lost her temper, not even under these conditions. She sucked in her lips and endured it all in silence.

It was impossible to keep the water out. In the end, Mother sealed the front door. We jumped in and out of the apartment through the bedroom window until the water receded three weeks later.

As we learned to cope with the situation, I kept an eye on my new neighborhood, observing the children and eagerly looking for opportunities to make friends. After all, most of the working people, including the clerks of the government agencies, lived in these simple brick or mud apartment buildings. The condition of their apartments might be better, but the facilities and the layouts were basically the same. As we lived among them, I wanted very much to make a few friends with children of my age.

I ventured timidly out of our small front yard. The Yangs had moved out. Another family, the Lins, had moved into their apartment. I soon figured out the family consisted of an ancient-looking grandmother, the parents, and four children, one girl and three boys. Mr. and Mrs. Lin both worked for the Security Bureau in the Government Compound. As newcomers on the block, they appeared to be friendlier than longstanding residents. Sometimes they politely nodded to us when our paths crossed, but they didn't speak to us.

Mr. Lin was tall and shy. He retreated swiftly inside their apartment whenever one of us stepped into our yard. I could see all the activities on their side, even inside their apartment through the windows—I often craned my neck over the wall when no one was watching. On the few occasions when Mr. Lin ran into us in the narrow alley, his face turned red as if he felt guilty for our disgrace. Mrs. Lin was chubby and short. I could hear her yelling at her children from time to time, but her round face was always kind when our eyes happened to meet. The two older children were teenagers, and their presence painfully reminded me of my sisters Yan and Ping. Their third child, a son by the name of Kun, was my age, and the youngest son, Lu, was a couple of years younger than me. I chose Lu as the first person to approach, thinking he would be easier than anyone else to win over as a friend.

Lu always winked at me or gave me a naughty smile when we met. He had a long face, a shape we referred to as a "sunflower seed," and uneven teeth. He giggled a lot and his large black eyes always seemed to have a slightly mocking look to them. I read his expression as friendly. At least he showed some response, I thought, unlike the stony faces I encountered every day.

One day, I gathered enough courage to talk to him.

"Hey, I'm Jian," I said, trying to appear as carefree I could. "I know your name is Lu," I continued when he didn't respond. He simply giggled and ran into his house as if I had said something funny. I was encouraged.

Several days later, I stopped him again at the gate to his yard. Blocking his way, I introduced myself again. He stared at me with a smile on his face.

"Do you want to play with me?" I asked.

He said nothing. Instead, he raised his left hand slowly, formed a circle with his thumb and index finger as if getting ready to play a game, then he put his right index finger through the hole. I gave him a puzzled look. He started to laugh.

He suddenly thrust his head close to mine. "You idiot!" he hissed, throwing the two words at me before running away in triumph.

I was taken aback. Later, imitating his gesture with my own hands, I still couldn't figure out what it meant.

"What do you think you are doing?" Mother's voice was upset when she caught me imitating the gesture.

"Lu did this when I asked him to play with me," I said. I looked at her, hoping for an explanation.

Mother's eyebrows furrowed and her face turned red. "Don't ever make gestures with your hands like that," she said harshly. I felt hurt and lowered my head.

"You should spend more time with Nainai and Big Aunt at home," she continued.

"But Mom, I wanted to..." Mother waved her hand before I could finish my sentence. No "but," no talking back.

Unable to ignore my inquiring look, however, Mother said, after a pause, "It's a dirty curse. Don't ever do that again."

The warmer weather brought more children outside. Across the alley, in one of the red brick buildings, lived a girl named Jun. She was two years older than me, but not much taller. She lived with her mother, whose left side was paralyzed from a stroke. I knew her father had passed away, but never dared to ask her when and how. Jun didn't speak much. When she was offended, she never hesitated to yell and fight back, even if the other person was her mother. After school, she spent most of her time doing household chores. She hunched forward and walked with her head lowered by the burden of responsibility at such a tender age. One afternoon, as Jun was hanging her laundry in her yard, the clothesline suddenly snapped. I stepped over to help her pick up all the clothes on the ground and hang the line. She became my first friend. She didn't mind walking with me to school, a major benefit to me since her presence stopped other children from bothering me.

We wanted to spend more time together after school, but her apartment was filled with the smell of disinfectant. Her mother's squawking voice, which always sounded impatient and demanding, made it suffocating to be there. Jun couldn't leave her mother, and I couldn't stand to be inside her apartment for long. Even though she sometimes snapped at her mother and complained, she carried out her duties. She was kind to me, which encouraged me to make more friends.

When the rain eventually turned our alley into a galaxy of puddles, truckloads of industrial waste were brought in and dumped in piles to fill the potholes. The waste was a mixture of scrap iron, coal cinder, shards of melted glass, and chunks of wet clay. The children in the neighborhood, along with a few adults, treated each newly arrived load as a treasure chest. A small crowd formed soon after a truck drove off, each person carrying a basket and a garden fork. Unburned charcoal was gathered for much-needed fuel, and the scrap iron and tiny pieces of glass could be sold at a recycling station for a few pennies per pound. By the end of the day, there was nothing unturned in the piles.

One day, I decided to seize this recurrent opportunity to ingratiate myself with the neighborhood children. I tied a scarf over my head to keep my hair clean, put on a sweatshirt handed down from Wen, and a pair of old shoes. I felt if I could have a chance to talk or play with them, I should be able to make one or two friends.

It was a cloudy day, and the humidity was high for early spring. With a small basket and a garden tool in my hands, I edged my way into the crowd, crossing my fingers that nobody would notice me before I settled down on a spot. Out of the corner of my eye I tried to observe what goodies people were picking, so I could follow suit. I had a tough time differentiating a piece of unburned coal from a black rock. As soon as I mistakenly threw a rock into my basket, I heard giggles around me. I froze. I was painfully aware of my ignorance. Instead of leaving, however, I held my place on the junk pile. "Please, give me a chance!" I silently pleaded. I pretended to concentrate on turning over items from the waste pile around me. I didn't care what I put into the basket anyway, I kept telling myself. All I wanted was to strike up a conversation with someone and make a friend.

Suddenly I felt the basket in my hand jerk as a heavy object landed in it. Without turning my head, I could see it was a big chunk of clay. I struggled to keep calm.

"You kids, don't be so naughty," I heard a man's voice. Some of the children started laughing. There were a dozen children around. Instead of retreating, I stubbornly hung on. I pretended I didn't notice the incident, but my silence betrayed me. My non-reaction was viewed as vulnerability. A black rock soon found its way into my basket, triggering more laughter. I shifted the basket to my left side, hoping that would stop further mischief. A moment later, a clay figure in the shape of a man jumped into my basket. Its lumpy, soft body was distorted upon landing. It lay lifelessly next to the big rock, as if both of them were giving me a warning. The laughing and giggling grew louder. I felt my face burning, and I feared that I might burst into tears. The last thing I wanted was a quarrel or fight. Besides, I didn't know who had thrown the objects. I knew I could not afford to cry. I stayed as calm as I could manage. I proceeded with my aimless yet vigorous digging, but found it harder to find anything useful. The man who had tried to stop the children's mischief earlier said to me in a soft voice: "You'd better go home."

I wished Wen would appear from the alley and call me home. Our apartment building was only twenty yards away, but at that moment, that seemed an insurmountable distance to travel. I turned to the man, but he didn't stop his digging nor did he look at me. Sensing my gaze, however, he added after a pause: "You can always come back some other time."

I saw no other option but to take his advice and withdraw. As I slowly moved toward the edge, taking my time to pick up something along the way to cover my retreat, the weight of the basket on my arm increased rapidly. I cast a look toward the group as I finally reached the edge of the waste pile. These children, with their shabby clothes and dirty faces, considered me trashy, a "shitty dog" who deserved no dignity or friendship. I looked at their cracked hands and blackened fingernails. My sense of self-worth and pride faltered. A hole opened in my heart. I felt cold, lonely, and belittled. I realized it didn't matter how hard I tried. I dumped everything out of my basket and looked at the crowd again. They were all busy searching and digging. If it weren't for the junk dumped from my basket at my feet, I might have been able to convince myself that the ridicule had been merely a figment of my imagination.

I went home, but didn't tell anyone about this experience. I learned to withdraw further from the outside world and to become more self-reliant and resourceful. More importantly, I learned to keep unpleasant encounters to myself, a habit that would stay with me throughout my life, like an unhealthy addiction. I acquired the ability to show a high degree of composure in public—calm, pleasant, and peaceful, regardless of the turmoil going on underneath. I regarded this ability as a measure of strength, and patted myself on the back each time I managed a difficult situation on my own. Only decades later did I realize how much this ironclad self-control had adversely affected my relationships with family and friends, and how difficult it was to unlearn it.

After this failed attempt to reach out to the neighborhood children, I sought comfort in playing with Nainai in our apartment. I also spent hours playing tricks with Kitty, my pet, a pretty female cat with white and yellow fur. Kitty seemed thrilled with my undivided attention. Big Aunt was the only one who encouraged me to go out and fight back. She was illiterate and cared nothing about politics. She was in her late fifties. Years of village life had turned her face dark brown. She radiated strength. Only her deformed, bound feet slowed her down. Big Aunt didn't take any nonsense from others. She didn't give a damn about the humiliating circumstances our family had been forced into. She had made her living with hard, honest labor and that was sufficient to live with dignity and pride.

I watched in awe as Big Aunt quickly and easily found camaraderie with a group of elderly ladies who spent long afternoons sitting under the shade of an apartment building in the alley. They chatted leisurely, busying themselves with knitting and sewing. Like Big Aunt, none of them could read, and they cared little about what was going on outside their immediate circle. Nobody bothered this group of older women.

Whenever Big Aunt returned from a visit to her son's family, she would bring millet, peanuts, or other homegrown produce. In the summer of 1969, she brought us a special gift: a large gray-feathered goose. She intended to treat Nainai and the rest of the family to a good meal. The goose, however, seemed intent on avoiding a destiny as dinner. She befriended us by laying eggs, day after day. Every time Big Aunt proposed to kill and eat the goose, Nainai was the first to protest.

"I don't need goose meat," Nainai said. "I need to see my son."

We all joined in to support her.

"I won't take a single bite," Wen added.

"Neither would I," I chimed in.

Big Aunt shook her head. "Look at you," she pointed her finger at each of us. "You are all getting so skinny. You need to eat meat to gain some weight."

"The goose eggs will be just fine," Nainai said.

We put straw in a corner next to the small chicken coop to make a nest. The goose settled in and dutifully made her contribution to our diet—enormous eggs, each bigger than three chicken eggs combined. Soon, she started following Big Aunt into the street, joining several other geese and ducks raised by other families in the neighborhood. She often splashed her huge wings against the muddy puddles of water and made squawking noises. The other geese and ducks readily joined in, making an orchestra of sound, loud and low, long and short. Occasionally, roosters and hens joined in.

I liked to sit by Big Aunt after school and watch them. I was amazed that they could waggle their way out of the dirty water and still manage to keep their bodies clean by grooming their feathers with their beaks. Our large gray goose soon became my companion. She took food from my hand, and occasionally even let me touch her. The feathers on her chest felt like soft cotton, and the ones on her long wings were a bit rougher, with their shafts as strong as a strip of metal. She followed me when I left for school in the morning, taking her time waddling behind, but she wouldn't venture much further than the water supply platform, as if she knew the dangers of the larger world. When I came back from school in the afternoon, she recognized me from a distance like a smart dog. She came to me, squawking along the way, as if to tell me she had been waiting for me. I took it as a sign of welcome and I enjoyed her companionship. She faithfully followed me home, expecting to be rewarded with food for escorting me home safely.

Coming home one day, I didn't see the elderly ladies at their usual gathering place. I didn't think much of it. What surprised me was my goose. I could see her all right. But something was wrong. The other geese in the alley were making noises and splashing their wings in the dirty puddle. My gray friend didn't move, nor did she make any sound. I ran toward her. She twisted her neck back and forth and flapped her wings, but she was not moving.

Tears ran out of my eyes as I saw what had happened: Her feet were nailed to the ground, and her beak was forced open with a stick in her mouth.

"For heaven's sake!" I threw down my school bag and kneeled by her side. I didn't know how I could remove the nails without hurting her. I was desperate. She struggled in pain. As soon as I managed to pull out the stick from her mouth, she let out a loud, frightening howl that sounded almost human to me.

"Oh, poor thing. I'm sorry. I'm so sorry..." I mumbled.

I had to steady her body between my legs as I removed four long nails, two through the bones of each foot. Blood seeped out of the broken bones between her webs. She immediately got away from me. She must have been in terrible pain, for she spread her wings for support on the journey home. From the bloodstain on the ground I could tell she must have been nailed there for a long time. I wanted to carry her, but she wouldn't let me get close. For days she stayed in our yard and moved only to the feeding pan to eat. She must have had internal injuries as well, for yellow egg yolk spilled out of her womb every day, for a whole week.

She survived the ordeal, but she never let anyone touch her again.

My cat Kitty, however, was not so lucky. We had always been careful not to let her out of the apartment. In the winter, she was cooperative, but when spring arrived, she mewed by the door and seized every chance to run out. One morning, she didn't return before I left for school. When I got home in the afternoon, and there was still no sight of her, I started to worry. Wen and I searched the neighborhood—waste piles, dirty ditches, and even in the open sewage. We feared the worst for her. The following day, we widened the search, but to no avail. At a time when human beings were treated with no dignity, animals, especially those from the condemned families, suffered even worse treatment. It was not uncommon to see dead dogs or cats in the streets, abused beyond recognition.

Three days later we were surprised to find Kitty lying in our front yard as we opened the door in the morning. She mewed weakly and raised herself up with her front legs, while her hindquarters lay lifeless on the ground as if her legs weren't attached to her. Wen ran over to her, with me trailing closely. Kitty's mew turned into a sharp cry when Wen picked her up. We were startled. Both of her rear legs had been broken. She had an open wound, swarming with crawling maggots. We couldn't imagine how she managed to drag herself home. Wen carefully carried her inside. Despite waves of nausea, I held Kitty tightly with both hands and Wen used a tweezers to remove the maggots, one after another. Kitty mewed and struggled. Wen silently shed tears as she applied a disinfectant solution to the wounds and tied wood splints to Kitty's broken legs. We nurtured her with great care. Even Nainai joined in, saving Kitty a mouthful of milk from her daily twelve-ounce ration.

Amazingly, Kitty's mischievous nature returned as she got better. She was lying on her back, playing with whatever object I dangled over her head. Occasionally, she jumped up to catch it, only to be weighed down by her splinted legs.

Kitty recovered quickly enough, and didn't confine herself to the apartment for long. Two months later, another search for her ended when we found her body floating in a dirty pond, next to a cluster of trash. She was too far away for us to fetch. I began to sob. Wen bit her lip and put one arm around my shoulder to comfort me. We couldn't even retrieve her body and bury her. For years, whenever I walked by the pond, the image of her body floating among garbage appeared in my mind, pinching my heart with pain.

4

Wuzi's family had been driven out of the Compound soon after our departure. They settled in a brick building that used to be a clinic. There was running water inside, a luxury for the condemned. Wuzi's two older brothers and an older sister had also been sent to the countryside. His father was still in detention. The household now consisted only of his mother, his sister Min, his grandmother, and him. Their apartment was half a block from ours, but we no longer had any dealings with each other. There were watchful eyes all over the place, and we didn't want to be accused of building alliances.

One day, in the dead of winter, a desperate pounding on our door woke us up. It was Min, Wuzi's sister. When Mother opened the door, she was shivering and crying in the dark.

"Please help us," she cried.

The water pipe in their apartment was frozen, and in the middle of the night it burst. They couldn't turn off the main faucet. A foot of water had accumulated in their apartment, and it continued to rise. Binbin rushed over with Min, taking a large pair of pliers with him. Two hours later, when he returned, his cotton-padded shoes and pants had become icicles and his teeth were chattering. He had managed to shut off the water supply then helped Min and her mother remove much of the water. As daylight broke, he returned home. He didn't want others to see that the two families were helping one another in a time of crisis.

We continued to face financial difficulties. Mother's monthly salary was low and Father's had been reduced to half. We struggled to make ends meet. Mother used to give me change to buy a few stuffed buns for lunch for Nainai. That happened less and less frequently. Without our garden, we had to buy vegetables. We had to count every penny.

One afternoon, a young worker from the electricity company came to collect bills, as all the utility companies did on a monthly basis. Wen, Nainai, and I were at home. Mother wouldn't get her pay for three days. Wen opened the drawer where Mother kept the money. There was only two yuan wrapped in a handkerchief, and we needed that money for food. Wen held the money in her hands, not knowing what to do. Tears ran down her face. Slowly she turned to the young man.

"This is all we have," she said. "Take anything you think is of some value from our apartment," she continued, casting her eyes on the ground.

The young man's face turned crimson. "I... I was sent..." he stammered and couldn't finish his sentence.

He awkwardly shifted his bag, which was filled with small notes and coins collected from other families. He didn't press Wen. He must have been sympathetic to us, a rare trait in people in those days. I sat beside Nainai, watching the young man's every move with anxiety. I was relieved when he left without insisting we pay, or worse, humiliating us.

We lived in that mud house for three years. The Red Guards never bothered us in there, and we learned how to take care of our roof by applying a layer of mud mixed with straw early each spring to prevent leaking. We also laid bricks on the dirt floor and mounted a permanent barrier at the main entrance to stop the yard water from running into the apartment. I balanced the long pole on my shoulders, carrying water or delivering horse dung fertilizer to school. I swung the two pails or baskets up and down without spilling anything. The Lin family was very friendly to us once the worst of the Cultural Revolution was over early in the 1970s. It was no longer dangerous to associate with us. Lu and Kun became my friends, and I was free to jump over the low brick wall and wander into their apartment. There was even a picture of Qi, Lu's older sister, and me, smiling into the camera.

Somehow, we managed to adapt to our life in the mud house, to this different world.

Chapter Fifteen

The Vast Countryside

1

While our family learned to adapt to the harsh conditions in the mud house, my sisters Ping and Yan had their share of hardship in the countryside.

From the day of her arrival in the village, Ping was determined to face the hardships and be tough. She was seventeen, a year younger than Yan, but more resilient. Ever since she started elementary school, she had been a student leader. The Cultural Revolution put an end to her status, but it couldn't destroy her resolve. She didn't mind going to the countryside. Anything was better than facing the accusations hurled at Mother and Father every day.

Ping knew her life in the countryside would be hard, but nothing could prepare her for the extreme conditions she and her peers faced. In the dead of winter, with the temperature plunging to 20 degrees below zero Fahrenheit, the youth center where they were housed had no heating. The dirt floor was frozen, and the outhouse was nothing but an open pit encircled by a waist-high wall. The well at a nearby stable wasn't deep enough to provide clean water, but it was all they had. Cold wind swirled through and around the single-paned, wood-framed windows, making the interior of the building nearly as cold as the outside. The two Kangs in each of the bedrooms—one for the boys and one for the girls—were the only source of warmth. They had no fuel for cooking or heating. Ping realized the one crucial lesson they all had to learn: Survival.

On their first day, the village leader did them a favor and had a stack of red sorghum stalks delivered to the center from the stored piles used as fuel for the winter. But the stalks alone were not sufficient. The peasants also gathered dried grass from the meadows as additional material for burning. Mr. Zhao, the leader, had made it clear upon their arrival that they must gather grass on their own. They had no idea what he meant, but were eager to start working.

On their second day, eight of the newly arrived "educated youth" joined a group of peasants on their grass-gathering mission. Young and energetic, Ping and another girl volunteered to go with the men. Two horse-drawn carts took them to the meadow. The peasants were bundled in sheepskin coats and hats, while the city teenagers' cotton-padded jackets and pants were poor protection from the cold. From time to time, they jumped off the cart to jog, in an attempt to warm their frozen feet and bodies. The dirt road was bumpy and deserted, and the fields on both sides were flat. All they could see were stubs of corn, sorghum, and soy beans left over from the harvest. The peasants sat on the carts, smoking their pipes, and occasionally chatting among themselves. They were oblivious to their surroundings and ignored the newcomers.

The horses trotted for two hours before they reached the vast, seemingly endless meadow. Grass and other native plants lay flat on the ground. There were no trees nearby to provide shelter, and the strong wind bit into their faces. Zhao showed the eight young people how to use the wide and awkward rake. A long handle attached to the middle of the rake had a hook on the end. Zhao put the hook on his shoulder and demonstrated how to gather grass.

Ping picked up a rake and followed instructions. The hook felt like a rock against her right shoulder as she tried to gather the grass. She tightened her scarf around her face and tried to imitate the movements of the peasants, who had begun working. This tool was harder to use than it appeared. If she didn't press down hard enough on the rake, she couldn't pick up much grass, but if she applied too much pressure, she couldn't move because the rake stuck to the roots and the woody weeds. After walking back and forth for an hour, Ping didn't collect a third of what a peasant had piled up. Her male counterparts didn't do much better. By the time they stopped for lunch, the eight of them were exhausted. The peasants observed them out of the corner of their eyes, but didn't offer any help or sympathy.

Ping took out the cornbread and gave a piece to each of the students in her group. Despite wrapping the food in layers of towels, they found the cornbread frozen. Ping reached for the insulated hot water bottle and filled her mug. The steam evaporated so quickly that when she put the thin metal mug to her lips, the water was already cold. To her surprise, the metal stuck to her lips. A sharp pain shot through her lip as she pulled the mug from her mouth. She was shocked to see that a layer of her skin had been peeled off.

"Don't drink from your mugs!" Ping warned the others. Each of them had a similar mug. She carefully wiped the blood off her lips.

By the end of the day, as they loaded bales of grass into the carts, Ping's muscles were terribly sore, and her limbs heavy. She could tell the others in her group felt the same. They all dragged their bodies, completely exhausted, but they were happy to have their first load of grass to heat their center.

Zhao had one load dropped off at their door and divided the other between two families. A day's work was usually sufficient for three or four families.

Everyone at the youth center took turns gathering grass. As winter progressed, they moved further into the meadow. They worked hard, fighting against the impending arrival of snow. As the days went by, Ping and her peers learned to rake the grass more efficiently. By the time they had collected a sizable pile in front of their center, each of them had frostbite, swollen shoulders, and chapped lips. Ping joined the team almost every day, and both of her wrists were covered with scabs that looked like rough fish scales, but her persistence and hard work earned the respect of her teammates.

"You are doing more hard work than any of us," one of Ping's roommates said to her. "You don't behave like an official's child."

Ping smiled. She wanted to prove herself. She noticed that even the peasants began to take her seriously.

Their efforts in gathering fuel proved worthwhile. When one snowstorm after another pounded the village over the course of the winter, they were repeatedly stuck in the center for days at a time. The grass they had gathered saved their lives.

Usually, a day's activity didn't end with the conclusion of physical labor. In the evenings, Ping and the rest of her group attended political study sessions with the peasants. They shouted slogans, sang revolutionary songs, and read Chairman Mao's quotations and newspaper articles. Since not all the peasants could read, the "educated youth" found they could play a more active role in such activities, but they were so exhausted that they had to make extra effort to show a positive attitude. The peasants came to the meetings with their smoking pipes or sewing, and didn't show much interest. They made a perfunctory appearance to avoid being singled out and criticized. But the political jargon had little impact on them. They chatted among themselves. Food, card games, or the next day's assignment received more attention.

The majority of the "educated youth" soon lost their enthusiasm. The day-to-day work was hard and repetitive. Besides, they realized that the peasants didn't want them there and viewed them as a burden. The peasants had lived in the countryside for generations and they resented the city teens for disrupting their lives. Their hostility disheartened Ping and her peers. Except for basic manual skills, they didn't feel there was much they could learn from the peasants. It was discouraging that all the work was done manually and in the most labor-intensive ways possible. It didn't take long for the "educated youth" to feel trapped by their circumstances.

Four months after their arrival, two young men from the center joined the army. They were the envy of the entire group. They had used their family connections to escape the countryside, and in the present situation, joining the army was the best alternative. After serving for two or three years, a discharged soldier would return to his hometown and be assigned a job. If he was capable, he also had the opportunity to climb the ranks in the military. The two boys' quick departure unsettled the rest of Ping's group.

The arrival of spring brought more demanding work, from removing the waste from the stables and pigsties to spreading the decomposed manure in the fields, as well as planting rows of crops. One after another, the young men and women at the center found ways to return home. Usually they sent back a doctor's note to request an extended leave. Zhao was supposed to supervise them, but he didn't care. The villagers worked on a point system. A man earned ten points for a day's work, while a woman, despite doing the same job, earned eight. The points were registered each day and the total sum was calculated at year's end. The value of each point was determined by the harvest. The village didn't need additional laborers, and the presence of the city youth only diluted the value of the points. As long as the "educated youth" were absent, they couldn't accumulate any points. Zhao didn't have a problem with that, but the "educated youth" cared about how the leader of the village and the peasants regarded them. A good appraisal could mean a ticket out, should the opportunity arise.

2

Each month, the "educated youth" picked up their ration of the unprocessed grains from the commune headquarters. They learned to operate the millstone and process the grain. The leftover husks were used as pig feed. Every day, one or more peasants came to the center to "borrow" grain husks. Soon enough, Ping and her peers realized they should keep the husks to raise their own pigs and chickens. During their first year, each of them received a small settlement subsidy from the state. In the spring, they used the money to purchase two piglets and a dozen little chicks. They were pleased to use the husks and their leftover food for their own livestock, but the peasants were not so thrilled. From time to time, they still came to "borrow" what they could get away with.

One job at the center that no one wanted was to cook for the entire group. Feeding a crowd of famished teens was hard work, especially with their limited supplies. Since cooking was considered a domestic chore, the job rotated among the young women. They decided that each girl was responsible to cook for a day, but when only two or three girls remained at the center, each had to cook two or three days a week.

Ping loathed the job. She had never liked cooking when she lived at home. At the center, she preferred backbreaking field work to preparing a meal. However, when her turn came, she carried out her task dutifully. She started working at the break of dawn. Breakfast was mostly the same every day: millet porridge and leavened cornbread. In the winter, her teammates ate at the center, before taking off for work. When spring arrived and the peasants started work before dawn, Ping, like the other cooks, carried two large pails on a pole over her shoulders, and delivered the food to her group in the field. One pail was filled with porridge, and the other with serving bowls, chopsticks, and cornbread. She took back whatever was leftover, and together with the saved dishwater, mixed them with the grain husks and fed the pigs and chickens.

As a cook, she was responsible for fetching water from the well and filling the water vat for cooking and washing. If she decided to serve coarse ground corn for lunch or dinner, she had to take a bag of corn kernels and grind them at the millstone. A donkey pulled the wooden bar that turned the grinding stone, and through a hole in the middle, she fed the corn into the grinder. The heavy, monotonous sound of the stone turning made her feel as if she was back in ancient times. When the corn was crushed, she scooped it up and sifted the powder for cornmeal. Then she put the rest onto a dustpan, one portion at a time, and tossed it into the air to blow away the thin chaff. By the time the job was done, her hair and clothing were all covered with dust. It was a relief when everyone returned to the center to have lunch. When the rest of her group left for the fields in the afternoon, Ping fed the hungry pigs and chickens again. Occasionally when her cooking duty fell on a Sunday, she cooked rice. That was a treat, since each person only received two pounds each month. At the end of the day, when dinner was served and the woks cleaned, she fed the livestock once more before retiring for the night.

There was another challenge for the cook. The teenagers had their grain allocation, but they had no vegetables. While the peasants stored root vegetables such as carrots, turnips, potatoes and pickled cabbages in a deep underground cellar, the "educated youth" had nothing of the sort. At first, they bought cabbages from a grocery in a small town not far away, but they had no place to store them. Kept in the bedrooms, the cabbages were quickly frozen solid and tasted like rotten pickles when cooked. During the first winter, they ended up eating their meals with salt water most of the time. Their stomachs burned from the rough food, and at one time or another, they all got sick.

As the work became more demanding, more and more people from the center left. But Ping stayed. As a child of purged capitalist roaders, she was supposed to receive a thorough reeducation. Besides, Mother wrote and encouraged her to take it as good training: "If you can overcome the difficulties in the countryside, you will become stronger and be able to deal with all kinds of challenges in life." Ping took the message to heart.

One day, Ping wrote with a request. She needed a suitcase. She had no place to store her clothing, diaries, and other personal items. A suitcase with a lock would not only provide her with a storage place, but also would give her some privacy. Having missed her last year in middle school, Ping had taken Yan's textbooks on math, physics, and chemistry with her, but she was afraid of being labeled as "Bai Zhuan," pursuing knowledge to the neglect of political orientation, and so she didn't dare read them. It was safer if she could lock up the books.

"Also," she wrote at the end of her letter, as if it were an afterthought, "Would you please get a pound of Lu Guo for me?" Lu Guo was baked biscuit made of flour, sugar, and oil.

Mother bought her a wood box instead. It was less expensive but sturdier than a suitcase. The box was especially made for the "educated youth." On its front, printed in thick red paint, were the familiar characters of the Supreme Directive. Underneath in smaller words was Chairman Mao's well-known phrase: "The vast land is boundless, and opportunities limitless."

Mother sent Wen to deliver the box to Ping at the center. Heeding Ping's request, Mother also put a pound of Lu Guo in the box, along with a scarf and a pair of mittens.

Wen took the long-distance bus to Ping's commune. She was surprised to see how dark and thin Ping had become in a matter of five months.

Wen spent the night at Ping's center. She squeezed into Ping's space on the Kang to keep warm. There were two large Kangs in the room. All the girls slept on one. The other one across the room was used for storage. They could hear the boys in the other room, but they didn't mingle much after dinner. The boys and girls stayed in their own rooms, bundled up under cover to keep warm.

Wen and Ping covered themselves with a cotton-padded quilt and murmured to each other. They turned on a small flashlight. Ping fished out two pieces of Lu Guo from under her pillow and offered one to Wen.

"I was dying to take a bite during the day," Ping said, smiling. "But I couldn't do it without sharing them with the girls," she murmured. She examined the piece of Lu Guo in her hand. It felt like a treasure. "I feel guilty," Ping added. "But I can't bear to share them."

"It's okay." Wen said. She watched as Ping carefully took a tiny bite, chewed, and rolled her tongue in her mouth. She relished it. Wen felt like crying. She pushed away Ping's extended hand with the other piece. "You have it," Wen said. "I can always get them at home."

"You won't believe it," Ping said. "I even dreamed of eating Lu Guo!" Ping paused, taking another small bite.

"I'm so homesick." Ping closed her eyes, lost in her reminiscences of home.

Wen told her home was no longer the same, but she didn't tell Ping how bad the situation was at the mud house. She didn't want to ruin Ping's sweet dream of home.

3

Ping persisted in her labors in the countryside. She chose to work side by side with the peasants and the other young men from the center. She learned to drive a horse-drawn cart, usually a man's job. She also joined the men in the village to spread manure on the field, flinging it with a shovel as far and as evenly as possible. The first time she did this task, she could hardly raise her arms the following day, but gradually she got used to it.

As soon as the ground thawed, Ping and her remaining teammates cultivated a vegetable garden. In early spring, they planted green onions, garlic, chard, chives, and lettuce. Later, when the weather turned warmer, they added green peppers, eggplant, green beans, and cucumbers. They could hardly wait to add some greens to their diet.

Ping learned to work in the fields, planting corn, red sorghum, and soy beans. As the season progressed, she weeded with a hoe, alongside the peasants. Facing the long row to plant or weed, Ping pushed herself to keep pace with the men and women working ahead of her. She didn't want to become a burden by falling behind, which usually required the others to turn back and lend a helping hand.

Summer came, but it made life no easier. Humidity and hot air filled their rooms, making it difficult for them to sleep. They folded away all the covers on the Kang, letting the heat from cooking dissipate, but the Kang still felt like an oven. During the day, they weeded under the burning sun. Their skin peeled off, layer after layer. There was no place to hide from the heat. At the end of each day, Ping and her group often doused each other with buckets of lukewarm water from the well before returning to the center.

Within a year, Ping learned to handle all the farm work, from planting and fertilizing to weeding and harvesting. The hard labor, however, didn't make her strong. Malnutrition took its toll on her. She was thin and suffered from anemia. But she stayed at the center. At times, only two or three people remained from her group. Ping was always one of them. Whenever she came home for a visit, she never stayed for more than two days.

Once, in the first summer when she was at the center, I went with Ping for a visit. She had stopped by at home while running an errand in the city. School was out, so she agreed to take me for three days. I was thrilled. I packed a small bag and eagerly left home with her. The bumpy bus ride made me ill, and I threw up, first on the floor and then into a dustbin someone handed us, until there was nothing left in my stomach. I was relieved when we finally arrived at the commune.

I had never felt so happy to put my feet on the ground. The bus left, stirring up a cloud of dust behind it. I sat down at the roadside and ate a steamed bun brought from home. I felt better.

"Our center is not far away," Ping said, reassuring me as we started walking.

Ping put my bag over her shoulder and led the way. I had envisioned more trees and hills in the countryside, but all I could see was flat plains in all directions. Ping walked fast. She wanted to get back to the center and help the cook with her chores. As we walked through it, the village looked deserted. Rows of single-story mud houses with large yards were scattered around. Ping pointed to an isolated building and told me that was their home. I followed her, curious to take in everything I could see.

The village horse stable was next to Ping's youth center. I noticed a horse with white stripes on its body and legs. "It looks like a zebra," I said, recalling images I had seen in picture books. To my surprise, Ping reacted to the sight by rushing over to the stable.

"What happened?" she asked.

"The horse fell into the well," an elderly man told her. "We had to use ropes to pull him out. It was quite a struggle."

The horse neighed as I moved closer.

"Sorry to hear that," Ping said, shaking her head in disbelief. She took me by my hand and led me away.

We entered the youth center. Chickens wandered through the disarray, pecking at the dirt floors. A girl was bent over the large wok, stirring corn. She looked relieved when Ping walked in.

"I'm glad you are back," she said.

"This is my little sister," Ping introduced me, but before I could say hello, Ping cut in.

"I'll feed the pigs and chickens."

"Thanks," the girl nodded.

Ping threw my bag on the Kang and told me not to wander away from the center. She rolled up her sleeves and set off to work.

The pigsty was behind their building. I could hear the noisy pigs and smell their stinky odor, which didn't seem to bother Ping. She carried a large bucket of pig feed and marched toward the sty. I watched her swing the bucket left and right as she quickened her steps. I ran after her. Ping poured the feed skillfully into a trough in the enclosure. I poked my head over the mud wall and saw two medium-sized pigs fighting for the food. Their bodies were smeared with mud.

The village consisted of nearly a hundred households. Ping promised to show me around. When her teammates came back from the field, we had a simple meal of ground corn, along with green peppers and cucumber that the cook had picked from their garden. I was tired from the journey and went to bed soon after dinner.

I woke up in the middle of the night with a terrible itching all over my body. I scratched in the dark and felt as if an army of mosquitoes had attacked me. The bites on my body seemed to grow as I rubbed them. My movements awoke Ping.

"What's wrong?" She asked in a sleepy voice.

"I'm itchy," I said. "Must be mosquitoes."

"Don't scratch," Ping said, fully awake.

She reached for the flashlight under her pillow and quickly turned it on under the cover. Several small black dots jumped around. Before I realized what was going on, Ping bolted up and caught one with her free hand.

"Damn fleas!" she said. She jumped off the Kang and dipped her clenched fist in a basin filled with water.

Seeing Ping's skill in catching the flea, I could tell this was a nightly exercise. Ping soon returned with a bar of soap and a small dish of water. She dipped one finger in the water and rubbed it against the soap. Then she applied the soapy water to my bites.

"That will help ease the itch," she said. It took her a while to cover all the bites on my body.

We repeated our battle with the fleas two more times during the night. They kept coming back. They must have liked my tender skin.

I didn't sleep much, nor did Ping. When we got up in the morning, even my face and neck were covered with bites.

"You poor thing," Ping said. "If you don't scratch, the itching will go away faster."

"We can't get rid of them," one of her roommates said, showing the bites on her arms and legs. "The last time we bombed the room with DDT, it only kept them away for a few days. But two of our chickens were killed."

"We can't use DDT anymore," another cut in. "It nearly choked us to death."

I tried not to scratch, but it was hard. Ping realized it had been a mistake to bring me to the center. The living conditions were too harsh and primitive for a little girl. The following day, one of the young men at the center was taking the bus to Baicheng. Ping asked him to take me home. She walked us to the bus station and waved goodbye as the bus started. I watched her from the rear window. She stood still, her hands hanging by her sides. She didn't move even when our bus picked up speed. I waved until her figure became a small dot. The injured horse and the fleas were all I remembered about Ping's village. Her sad face and still figure were carved in my mind. The glorious image I had of the vast countryside was replaced with shabby houses, deserted roads, and flat land.

4

In the winter of 1969, as the peak of the Cultural Revolution passed, Mother's situation improved considerably. She was no longer being targeted for abuse. She, Mr. Jiang, and Mr. He were waiting to be rehabilitated. When the new policy was imminent, she and Mr. Jiang made a trip to visit Ping's youth center. They were appalled by the living arrangements. It was much worse than it had been when Mother had dropped Ping off a year before. She had expected their situation to improve, not deteriorate.

A total of five young men and women remained at the center. It was lunch time, and everyone was in. They were thrilled to see Mother and Mr. Jiang. After they left school, they had stopped thinking about the revolution. On the contrary, they were nostalgic and often talked about the good times at school. They were overjoyed to see their old school Principal and Party Secretary.

"Mother, why didn't you write to tell me you were coming?" Ping shouted, running to the door to welcome Mother and Jiang. Mother held Ping's hands in hers and felt the calluses and frostbite. She wanted to take a closer look. Ping quickly pulled back and hid her red, swollen hands behind her back, but she smiled at Mother, genuinely happy to see her.

"Come on in," Ping said. "Take a seat on the Kang. It's warmer if you sit in the middle." Ping led the way inside.

Mother took a quick look around the room. Two sets of bedding were spread on the end of the Kang next to the stove, suggesting that only two girls were living there at the moment. Piles of extra bedding and quilts were folded away on the far end. A layer of dust covered them. The other Kang across the room was the same size. A few frozen cabbages rested on one corner. A flat of tofu on a wooden board was covered with a layer of ice. Mother's heart sank. She moved toward the storage Kang, wanting to take a closer look. A bed sheet on a clothesline blocked her way. Mother was surprised when the entire sheet shifted without bending as she tried to lift a corner to pass. It was frozen.

"Don't worry, Mother." Ping came over and led Mother away from the hanging laundry. "It will take a while to dry, but it will dry in due time."

Mother followed Ping to the Kang and put her hand under the quilt. She could feel barely any warmth. Jiang reached over and also put his hand on the Kang. They exchanged an uneasy glance. Mother didn't want to say anything discouraging in front of Ping and her roommate, but she was deeply disturbed. She took a deep breath. Over the course of the year, whenever Ping visited Baicheng, she had urged her daughter not to linger at home. "Devote yourself to the work in the countryside," she said. "Don't stay away because life is hard there." Mother knew the living conditions in the countryside were hard, but she had no idea that they were this bleak.

Upon returning to the city, Mother managed to acquire two tons of coal, a strictly rationed commodity, for Ping's center. The village sent two horse-drawn carts to pick it up. I don't know what strings Mother pulled. It was quite unusual for her to do such a favor for one of her children. The severe living conditions of Ping and her peers must have shaken her to the core.

Ping worked in the countryside for nearly four years. By the time she returned to Baicheng, she suffered from chronic back and shoulder pain. Her anemia often gave her dizzy spells. Sometimes it was so severe that she was lost in momentary darkness. She attributed later physical problems, including premature tooth decay, osteoporosis, and a persistent pinched nerve in her spine at the nape of her neck to the calcium deficiency she suffered during those years.

5

Yan's sojourn in the countryside was no easier than Ping's, but unlike Ping, Yan liked cooking. At first, the young women at her center took turns cooking for the group, as with the routine at Ping's. Yan did her share of gathering grass, collecting and spreading fertilizer, tilling and planting the fields. Gradually, though, she found herself cooking more and more often. When all the other girls were visiting home, Yan cooked for the five or six boys who stayed behind. Since no one else liked the task, Yan eventually became their designated cook. She didn't mind. She asked the older women in the village for recipes and tried to create a variety of meals with the limited materials available. She also took care of the pigs and chickens. She developed such an attachment to the animals that when the time came to slaughter a pig, Yan hid behind the center and cried. She heard others cheer in anticipation of a feast, and gathered her composure before rejoining the group. She didn't want to be criticized for bourgeois sentimentality.

Every bit of a pig, from head to toe, was treasured. At first, the "educated youth" were surprised that the peasants, upon learning of the slaughter of a pig at the center, descended in droves to "borrow" parts: a slice of meat, a chunk of liver, and a piece of intestine, which, it was soon realized, would never be repaid. This pattern recurred as long as the center had pigs to kill. They realized the peasants felt entitled to a free share of the center's larder, though they always used the word borrow. Ping had a similar experience. The peasants in her village borrowed the head of the first pig they slaughtered. The head was considered a delicacy. Ping and her teammates watched with regret as two peasants carried the pig's head away. They had excitedly planned how to make a few dishes out of the pig's ears, tongue, and cheek meat, but they couldn't reject the peasants' request—the teens were supposed to build a good relationship with them. They were appalled that peasants were taking advantage of them. "The peasants are so selfish and greedy," the city teenagers murmured among themselves, but didn't dare say in public.

One task that was hard for Yan to handle was fetching water from the well. A rope pulley was set up above the well. One had to turn the handle on the pulley to lower the attached bucket into the well. Tilting the bucket at just the right angle as it hit the water took skill. When Yan tried the maneuver, the bucket always seemed to sit on the water's surface like a little boat, and she couldn't get it to tip over. Over and over again, she pulled it up and dropped it. After many failed attempts, she eventually filled the bucket, but it was just as hard to pull it up without spilling and grab it to pour the water into her pails. Layers of ice encrusted the well in the winter, making the whole job even more difficult.

Since her village was not far from Baicheng, Yan visited home more often than Ping. Sometimes when she was in town to run an errand, she stopped by for an hour or so. She sniffed around and searched for food like a hungry wolf. Yan had a sweet tooth and always liked to snack. If Mother happened to be home, she'd offer her a few pieces of mung bean biscuits, or pack her some brown sugar, a rationed item. I watched Yan with resentful eyes. These items were reserved for Nainai. Yan knew that. She had a guilty look when she walked out of the apartment with one or two of these treasures, but that didn't prevent her from doing it again the next time she was home. "That is so selfish," I thought, but I bit my tongue. Nainai was willing to drink her milk without sugar and share the mung bean biscuits with her grandchildren. I didn't want to be the one to complain.

6

In January 1970, the coldest month of the year, Yan was the only female left at the center. The other young women had sought shelter in their parents' homes. Life was hard enough in the countryside, but the harsh winter conditions were much worse. The Kang turned ice cold soon after the fire went out. Yan lived in despair. It was not safe to spend the night alone in the women's quarters. She had heard terrifying stories of young women from the city who were raped in the countryside.

But an elderly woman in the village took pity on her. She liked Yan's good nature and ready laughter. She wanted to introduce Yan to Baofa, a young man from a local peasant family. If Yan was willing to marry Baofa, the woman reasoned, Yan could settle in his family and put an end to the ordeals at the center.

Yan knew Baofa. They had worked side by side in the fields, though they had never talked much. Baofa had received a middle school education and worked as a part time accountant for the village. He was the oldest child of a large family, with five younger sisters. His parents were pleased with the prospect of their son marrying a city girl. Father's disgrace didn't bother them. Their family had worked as peasants for generations. They didn't believe Yan's problematic family background could have much impact on their lives in the village. They extended welcome arms to Yan and readily invited her to spend time with the family.

Yan was touched. She started dating Baofa. Sometimes she spent a night at Baofa's home, sleeping on the Kang with his younger sisters. Baofa was a quiet man, the same age as Yan. A few years of education made him appear more refined than the other peasants. Yan and Baofa really didn't have much in common, but she felt Baofa was a kind person and trusted him. She also liked the security and friendliness of his family. Baofa's five younger sisters adored her. She felt at home with them. If Baofa was nice to her at such a difficult time in her life, she reasoned, she could always count on him. Simple kindness from another person was a luxury in her current existence.

Four months after Yan and Baofa were introduced, two "educated youth" from Yan's center left the countryside for good—one joined the army and the other returned to the city. Baofa's parents became worried. They were afraid Yan might leave as well. While it was easy to change residence from city to countryside, the reverse was nearly impossible. City residents received grain allocations, while people in the countryside earned theirs through harvesting the crops they planted. Baofa's mother proposed that the two should marry immediately. Yan was taken aback.

"We are so young," she told Baofa one day as he walked her back to the youth center. "Why don't we wait for a year or two?" she said. She didn't expect Baofa to object.

Baofa's face flushed red. He was silent for a moment, his pace slowing. Then he stood still. Timidly, he put his hand on Yan's right arm and turned her to face him.

"I don't want to lose you," he said, his voice trembling. "I want to marry you, as soon as possible."

Yan was surprised by Baofa's reaction. He had always been agreeable to her. Although he had never explicitly shown any passion, Yan knew he cared for her. She liked Baofa, too, and enjoyed spending time with him and his family.

"Don't be silly," Yan laughed. "I'm not going anywhere," she said. "Besides, I didn't say I won't marry you." She tugged at Baofa and urged him to keep walking. "We are both young. All I want is to wait a while."

She took a few steps and realized Baofa was not with her. She turned around and saw Baofa standing at the same spot, in the middle of the empty country road. He gazed at her intensely as if she was about to disappear.

Yan walked back to him. She was genuinely moved when she saw two streams of tears trickling down Baofa's face. No one ever had shown so much attachment to her. No one had loved her so much. Tears came to her eyes, despite her smile.

"All right," she agreed. "We'll get married."

Baofa was thrilled. "Really?" he asked.

"Yes."

Baofa wiped away his tears.

"Are you going to be good to me? Always? No matter what?" she asked.

"I promise."

Right there and then, they made the decision for their union.

Baofa's mother was delighted to hear the news. She set out to make arrangements for a dinner ceremony right away. Weddings were criticized as bourgeois and were officially regarded as one of the condemned "four olds." A revolutionary union in marriage didn't need extravagant ritual.

Yan came home the following week to break the news to Mother. She wanted to get Mother's blessing. Mother knew Yan was dating Baofa, but she had not met him. Although she understood life was very hard for Yan, she was against the marriage.

"You are too young, Yan." Mother reasoned with her. "Wait for a year or two." When Yan said she didn't want to stay at the center any longer, Mother pointed out the blunt truth: "If you marry a peasant, you may spend the rest of your life in the countryside. Is that what you want?"

Yan kept quiet. She had made her promise.

"I think life in the countryside is a transitional stage in your life. Be patient and wait a little longer."

Yan wouldn't hear any of Mother's words.

"Give it some more thought," Mother said the following morning. "We will talk more when I come back from work."

Yan stared at her, tears filling her eyes.

Father was still in detention. No one could ask his advice.

Yan paced back and forth in the room during the day, but before Mother's return, she wrote a note and placed it in Mother's bedroom. She left without saying another word.

Mother came home earlier than usual, but Yan was already gone. I told Mother about the note Yan had left. She quickly unfolded it.

Mother was stunned and disappointed. She read the note a couple of times and then crumpled it in her hand. It fell to the edge of the Kang as Mother stood motionless. I watched her nervously from the doorway, not daring to intrude. When Mother walked out of the room after a long pause, I stepped in and opened the note. It said:

"Mother, I am already twenty. I have made up my mind. I will get married with or without the consent of you or Father."

Mother was silent for the rest of the evening.

Yan went through with her marriage. A week later, a horse-drawn cart sent by Baofa's father came to take us to attend the dinner ceremony. Ping happened to be home for a visit. Mother didn't go, but she let Ping, Binbin, Wen, and I attend.

The bumpy dirt road swung us back and forth on the cart. We chatted and played, not quite understanding the significance of the event. "Yan is getting married. Can you believe that?" The concept of marriage sounded too strange to be associated with Yan.

We reached Baofa's family home, a one-story mud house with a large yard. I had never seen so many peasants together in my life. They all wore dark colored pants and sweatshirts. It was early in spring, and some of them wore light, bulky jackets, also in dark blue or gray. Most of them were smoking, either a short pipe or a hand-rolled cigarette. They spoke with a heavy northeastern accent and their voices were so loud that it sounded like shouting to my ears. Their laughter was hearty and pleasant.

Entering the crowd, I couldn't see Yan.

"Make way for Yan's sisters and brother!" someone shouted.

Many of them turned to gaze at us. They stepped back and let us pass through the throng. About six tables were set up in front of the house. Plates of roasted peanuts, sunflower seeds, steamed cornbread, and pickled vegetables were set on the tables. Nearby, Yan and Baofa stood side by side, both very shy. They looked happy. They served Baijiu to Baofa's parents, then to Baofa's aunts and uncles. Many households in the village had the same family name and were related in one way or another. Baofa and Yan made their rounds to propose toasts. The villagers poked fun at Baofa, urging him to kiss the bride. Yan kept a distance from Baofa. She was very self-conscious. A kiss in front of others, even at a wedding, was embarrassing. Baofa's parents were all smiles.

We stayed overnight with Baofa's parents. Wen and I squeezed onto the Kang with Baofa's sisters. There was not enough room. Ping and Binbin slept on a wood box and a long bench. The following day, the same horse-drawn cart carried us home. Mother didn't ask about the ceremony. She looked sad.

Yan was her firstborn. In our eyes, she always had a special affection for Yan. She was very disappointed.

As it turned out, Baofa and his family were kind and treated Yan well. They provided warmth and shelter when she most needed it, but despite her improved living conditions, Yan suffered from severe sciatic nerve pain. Not long after their marriage, she was immobilized by the affliction. Baofa and one of her sisters-in-law took her to a city hospital. All the doctors at the hospital had been condemned politically and were reduced to sweeping the floors. They were not allowed to treat patients. Self-taught, barefoot doctors had taken over, and, naturally, had no idea how to treat Yan. Baofa took her back to the village with a package of pain pills. Yan was bedridden for a month. The sciatica stayed with her, immobilizing her two or three times a year. Each time, the severe pain lasted from two weeks to two or three months. Yan often used a walking stick. Like Ping, she had chronic health problems for the rest of her life.

Yan's marriage turned out to be an insurmountable barrier that prevented her from going to college. A year later, the government announced the reopening of universities. Students were recommended from among workers, peasants, and soldiers, but married people were disqualified. Yan watched with envy as the other "educated youth" left for college or returned permanently to the city. She bit her tongue and endured, blaming herself for her shortsightedness. Later, she became a teacher at the village elementary school. She devoted her energy to the children, but the conditions at the school were poor and the teachers, Yan included, didn't have much in the way of qualifications.

By 1978, a total of sixteen million "educated youth" had been sent to the countryside. The Central Government finally changed the policy and decided to "explore every possible way" to help them settle back into the cities. Finally, these young men and women started returning to where they had come from. Yan took the initiative to move back to Baicheng as well. She had another reason to expedite the process. She gave birth to a son a year after she got married. She wanted him to receive the educational opportunities offered in the city. She had lost her chance for a college education, and didn't want that to happen to her son. Yan applied for an administrative job at the Normal College of Baicheng. With the new government policy in place, she was accepted. She found her colleagues at the college most sympathetic to her. A year later, she managed to get Baofa to work at a grain supply co-op. The young family eventually settled into a small apartment provided by the Normal College. Yan placed all her hopes and attention on her son.

Chapter Sixteen

Revolutionaries

1

In 1970, the government policy began to change and allowed the rehabilitation of purged officials and leaders at various levels. Mother was among the first to be "liberated." She was invited to join the Revolution Committee at the No. 3 Middle School. To our surprise, Mother declined. She was hurt, angry, and didn't want to be the leader for those who had lied and abused her and others. She also was concerned that she would not be able to work effectively—her actions could be viewed as retaliation. She asked for a job transfer.

The Municipal Government granted her request. In the spring of 1970, Mother was transferred to the Baicheng No. 1 Middle School, best known for its education quality before the Cultural Revolution.

As Mother started working at her new position as Deputy Director, Father's situation also began to change. For two years, the Revolution Committee at the Baicheng Prefecture had sent more than forty people to investigate him. They went to all the places Father had lived or worked, interviewing his former schoolmates, teachers, fellow soldiers, and colleagues at various government agencies and compiled pages and pages of reports on him. Father learned later that not a single person said anything negative about him. He was quite proud. There was no evidence to prove he was a traitor. The military representatives and the Revolution Committee at the Baicheng Prefecture eventually decided to release him. They sent for Mother.

Two military representatives talked to her about their decision.

Mother listened, mindful of every word they said. When she realized they didn't issue any conclusion on his release, she spoke up.

"What about a verdict on his case?" she asked.

"There is no official verdict for any of the released," one military representative said.

"That doesn't sound right," Mother said. "He deserves an official settlement for his release." She was calm and composed.

The military representatives were surprised by Mother's response.

"You should be reasonable," one said, shaking his head.

"I'm being very reasonable," Mother said. "My husband has been detained for two years. His name should be cleared at his release."

Mother wanted a verdict. She wanted them to admit the accusation against him was wrong.

"We have many cases to handle," the other military representative cut in. "An official statement will be issued in due time."

"I've waited for two years. I can wait a little longer," Mother insisted. She wanted to have a statement in writing, which, she hoped, would prevent the military or the Red Guard from taking Father away again should the political situation take another turn.

No agreement was reached. As Mother walked away unyielding, she heard the military representatives comment on her stubbornness.

Father was soon released without a verdict or the government admitting any wrongdoing. Mother's request was ignored. One afternoon, a military jeep dropped Father off at home, with his small bundle of belongings and his boxy radio. He returned unceremoniously to the tearful welcome of Nainai and Big Aunt. When we came home at the end of the day, we found him sitting on the Kang and chatting with Nainai as if he had just returned from a long trip.

Wen and I were thrilled to see him.

"Father!" we called out simultaneously and ran toward him. Father opened his arms and held us both against his chest. He pressed us so hard that I could barely breathe. I broke away from him and jumped over to the Kang. I climbed on his back and placed my head next to his. His unshaven face felt rough, and his familiar smell of cigarette filled my nose. Father laughed. He rocked me back and forth. The room echoed with his voice. I couldn't remember the last time I was so happy.

Our home, however, was no longer the same. Not only was the mud house a different world, but my sisters Yan and Ping had been sent away. There was so much we wanted to tell him. Wen and I clung to him as if he'd disappear if we didn't hold him tight. Mother's welcome was genuine, but subdued. She told him about the request she had made to the military representatives.

"They told me," Father said. "It would indeed be a relief to receive an official settlement," he nodded in agreement. "No one got it."

Nainai and I were the only two who were overwhelmed with excitement and believed this was the end of our separation. Father made no promise as we bombarded him with questions. He wouldn't comment on our living conditions either.

"I'm so happy to be home," he said again and again.

When dinner was ready, Mother proposed a toast for the family reunion. We chanted along. "Welcome home, Father! Cheers!" We put tea in our cups and clicked with Father's glass. "Bottoms up!" Father raised his glass as if it were real liquor. He gulped down the tea.

Father praised us all for our endurance, and again called me his little heroine.

"Our family is most fortunate," he concluded, taking a hard look at each of us. "Here is to our good luck," he suggested another toast.

"Good luck?" I asked. "What are you talking about?" I saw Mother throw him a questioning look.

As far as I could recall, I had never heard Father complain about anything. He was truly an optimist. He always chose to focus on something positive even in the worst situation. But talking about good luck under our circumstances didn't seem to be true.

I stared at him.

"Father, look at us. Look at the mud house. Where is our good luck?" Wen joined me.

"We have lots of good luck," Father said gently. He turned to me and took my right hand into his. He started counting my fingers.

"First, no one in our family was killed or committed suicide," he lifted my thumb. "Two, none of us was disabled or badly beaten," he moved to my index finger. "And three, we are together again as a family..."

Mother interrupted his counting and urged us to finish dinner.

We were relieved Father was finally home, but our joy was overshadowed by a sense of unspoken sorrow and anger. Binbin sat on the far end of the Kang, observing Father. He toasted with us and smiled, but was quiet most of the time. He was about to be sent to the countryside. Father's release would not change that.

Father's return, however, changed the political situation for all of us. We were no longer regarded as "shitty dogs." As if by magic, we were on the right side of revolution again. Father reported to the Revolution Committee at the Compound. He was anxious to start working again.

But they told him to wait.

2

One day, two of the investigators who had worked on his case stopped by to see Father. They congratulated him for his release.

"We risked our lives going to places where bullets were flying," one said, referring to the fighting among groups of Red Guards and rebels that they had encountered on their trips.

"You should treat us to dinner!" the other cut in, requesting Father to treat the forty or so people who were involved in his investigation. They were joking, but Father took their words seriously.

When Mother returned home, he told her about his intention. He asked her to prepare some food at home. The mud house apartment was small so Father suggested inviting them over in three groups.

Mother looked at him in disbelief.

"You want me to make dinner for the people who investigated against you?" she asked.

Father said they were doing a job they had been assigned to. Because of their work, his clean record was reestablished. Mother shook her head and gave him a flat no.

"I don't want to see any of them," Mother said. "No dinner from me. Not in my house."

She dismissed Father's attempt to argue his point.

In the end, Father paid one of the investigators and held a large gathering at his home. He didn't take their hostile digging into his past personally and didn't hold any grudges against them.

I was astonished. I found it hard to understand him. The government and the Party had abused him, but he didn't protest. Didn't complain. We had seen so many individuals, among them some of his investigators, reveal the ugly side of human nature— all in the name of revolution. Father seemed to forgive them as well, saying it was part of the consequence of a frenzied mass movement. I was angry about the injustice done to him, to us as a family, and to so many people around us; but Father, the person who was most entitled to such feelings, was calm and seemingly at peace.

When I asked him years later how he could possibly let go of all this, Father simply replied: "Liu Shaoqi, Chairman of the nation, died. Deng Xiaoping and so many other prominent leaders and generals suffered or died. Compared to them, what I had gone through was nothing."

"What about your own feelings?" I pressed on.

Father dismissed my question with the wave of his hand, saying he had endured it all because he had nothing to fear. "I never betrayed anyone," he said. "I had nothing to fear." But he made a mental note of how many times he was taken to the rally meetings and was "struggled" against, and he mentioned that to me. A total of seventy-two times. Yet he wouldn't complain, not then, not even to this day.

Seeing my incredulous look, he urged me to look forward, not backward. "Personal feelings were not important," he said. "Our country was in chaos. I didn't think much about myself."

Upset as Mother was, she held the same attitude. "The Party lost control," she said, as if the Cultural Revolution had suddenly dropped from the sky, out of nowhere. "We should all join our forces to rebuild China."

For a month, Father waited for his job allocation. When it came, we were dismayed. Instead of placing him with the Revolution Committee, they sent Father to manage a coal mine in Wanbao, a small town about a hundred miles away from Baicheng. Our family once again faced separation.

Father, however, accepted the position without objection. It was apparently banishment again. He took his belongings and got ready to leave for Wanbao immediately. I stood in the doorway, watching him pack his things, his cigarette dangling from his lips. I would miss him. It was both my blessing and my curse that I had parents who loved their country and their cause as much as their family. Or perhaps more, I sometimes thought. I looked after him as he left, and all that remained was the scent of stale tobacco.

3

With my parents restored to their leadership positions, albeit at a much lower level for Father, we were once more accepted into the Communist fold. Despite my anger and ambivalence, I wanted to join my peers. Mother continued to urge me to be Mao's good child, a request I took seriously.

The first thing I wanted was to join the "Little Red Guard," an organization for elementary school children. It used to be called the Young Pioneer League before the Cultural Revolution. Members of the Young Pioneer League wore a rectangular red scarf around their necks, which symbolized a corner of the red, five-star national flag. The Little Red Guard wore a small badge instead. It was modest compared to the Red Guard armband, but visible enough to make a statement. I wanted to be a member like my classmates. With Father's release, I was readily accepted.

We had been carrying out a required routine to show our devotion to Chairman Mao. Each morning, we started school by making three bows to Mao's portrait above the blackboard. This was followed by singing revolutionary songs and reciting quotations from Mao's little red book. Then we danced the "loyal steps" to Mao's portrait, simple movements with our arms stretching out to Mao and our feet stomping the ground.

"Our beloved leader Chairman Mao, you are the red sun in our heart. There are so many heartfelt words we want to say to you, so many ardent songs we want to sing in your praise..."

Our song echoed all over the campus.

"Mother is dear, and Father is dear, but no one is dearer than our beloved leader Chairman Mao..."

We stomped and stomped and stomped.

Soon, singing and dancing on campus were not enough. We organized ourselves into smaller groups of ten or so, and took to the streets to spread "Mao Zedong Thought." We set our stage at large street corners or marched into the one of the two department stores in town to give our performances. Wherever we stopped, a crowd formed. Everyone patiently watched us perform, adults and small clusters of children, despite having just seen another group doing a similar number. If we staged our performance in front of a store counter, no customer could reach it to make a purchase, but since we were carrying out our revolutionary duties, no one from the stores dared stop us.

The portrait of Chairman Mao in our classroom was a close-up of his face. He looked as if he was about to smile, and his eyes were gentle and expectant. He seemed to encourage us to live up to his expectations. Looking up at him, I felt he was keeping an eye on us all the time. Mao's gaze was so direct and engaging that no matter where I sat in the classroom, his eyes appeared to look at me.

I was always conscious of Mao's gaze. Sometimes, I stole glances at the portrait, as if he could catch me on the spot if I did something wrong. His omnipresent eyes overwhelmed my consciousness. Hard as I tried not to look up at his image, I found myself doing so numerous times a day.

Our studies at school were concentrated on Mao's works. In addition to the little red book, we also learned Mao's three long essays word by word. One was titled "In Memory of Dr. Norman Bethune," praising a Canadian doctor who served in the Communist Army during the Anti-Japanese War. He died from an infection from a cut when he operated on a wounded soldier. Another essay was titled "The Foolish Man Removed the Mountain." It was a fable in which an old man decided to remove a mountain that blocked his cottage. Leading his sons with baskets and shovels, he believed that generation after generation they would eventually accomplish the task. Mao applauded his spirit. And the last one was titled "Serving the People." It was about Zhang Side, a contemporary hero and party official, who, despite suffering from severe hepatitis, continued to work until his last breath.

We used these essays to guide our daily behaviors. A political campaign, which was called "creatively learning and utilizing Chairman Mao's thoughts," pushed us on, urging us to do more.

I was honored as a model student in this campaign. Together with five other children selected from different grades, we visited different classes, presenting our examples of how we utilized Mao's thoughts to overcome our shortcomings. Some talked about their effort in overcoming bourgeois thoughts by wearing patched clothing; others talked about how, by following Zhang Side's example, they gave up their seats on the buses to elders. A girl who had turned in the highest volume of horse manure as fertilizer for the school farm stated proudly: "My hands are dirty and my clothes smelly, but my mind is purified, and I am proud." My most prominent achievement was to put aside small change in a bank account to save the starving children in the capitalist countries. A manager from a branch of the People's Bank had come to our school and called upon us to put our savings in a bank account.

The money-saving campaign was the Bank's initiative to learn and utilize Mao's thoughts creatively. We were motivated to make our contribution to build our country and save the rest of the world.

After Father's salary was restored, Mother began giving me pocket money again. I used the money mostly for two things: One was to buy Nainai her favorite stuffed buns, and the other was to buy or rent picture books. These picture books, the size of half a brick, were read by both adults and children. They were black and white drawings of popular stories, or reprints of movie scenes. Each page was accompanied by a brief caption at the bottom, or sometimes a speech balloon within the panel. A picture book cost twelve fen. My ambition was to collect all the books that I could put my hands on. In addition to the ones sold at bookstores, small vendors also rented their collections at street corners for two fen a copy. The picture books were spread out on the ground. To keep them from being blown away, a long bamboo stick was placed over them. Readers could take their time to read, but couldn't take the books away. Customers picked their favorites, squatted down and flipped through the pages right there and then. A savvy vendor would provide a few stools to attract a constant flow of readers.

After listening to the bank manager who had visited our school, I decided to give up my hobby and save the money for a more noble cause. I also encouraged a number of my classmates to do the same. With twenty or thirty fen in our pockets, we stopped by a bank and proudly presented our savings. The counter at the bank was so tall that we couldn't even reach it. A teller had to reach out to us and dutifully register our deposits in our pocket-sized account books. It was not unusual that after months of diligent saving, the cumulative amount hardly reached one or two yuan.

As small as the amount might be, the children, including me, responded to the call with passion. For a while, there were more children than adults running in and out of the bank. We created a line, blocking the adults and, in our excitement, making a lot of noise. Apparently, the logistics involved in handling such frivolous amounts didn't pay. After a couple of months, the bank manager stopped visiting us in school. Most of the students stopped making their deposits, but I persisted, dutifully putting whatever amount I could save into my account. By the time I gave my speech, my account had reached a whopping twenty-two yuan, a significant amount. I was very proud, believing the money was put into a large pool and utilized to save the children suffering "in deep water and burning fire" in a capitalist society.

4

We also participated in various other activities that were supposed to train us to be the successors of revolution. The general slogan was to "learn from workers, peasants, and soldiers." To do so, the Municipal Government allocated a piece of land to each school and required all the students to work in the fields. To fertilize the land, we were required to collect animal manure. Every day, before or after school, we took our baskets and chased after horse-drawn carts for horse dung. There were so many children out there to fight for the manure that the moment a horse raised its tail, there were two or three children running toward it in the middle of the street. They shoveled manure into their baskets with the steam still rising. Each student was

227

supposed to bring a basket of manure to school every day. Piles of animal waste accumulated in the school's backyard. The fermenting manure gave out such a stench that it penetrated our classrooms, but no one showed any sign of discomfort. That was a demonstration of "bourgeois sentiment." From spring to the fall, we learned to plant, weed, and harvest the crops, mostly corn and soy beans. I saw ears of corn spread out in the schoolyard to dry, but never knew what happened to them afterward.

To learn from the workers, we made ink and fired bricks. The ink we made was like colored water. It wet the paper with smears of dark color, but couldn't register any distinct mark. We never sold a single bottle. The brick-making venture was somewhat grander. A furnace was built on our campus. We dug up clay and sand from our schoolyard and mixed them with water. Piles of half-fired bricks in red, yellow, or black accumulated around campus. They were too brittle to be used in building anything, but we kept making them. The result of our labor was not only measured by the quality of our output, but also by the process of working, an end in itself. From time to time, students were asked to move the bricks from one side of the campus to another, then back again. We needed to be trained to appreciate hard labor. Our hands turned rough with calluses, and our faces were smeared with mud and charcoal. We worked hard.

One day, our whole class gathered early in the morning and walked to a military compound on the outskirts of town. Our mission was to pick up unburned coals from a furnace slagheap at a military hospital. We needed fuel to fire our bricks. Yao, a quiet boy whose head was covered with thumb-size bald spots, overslept that day. By the time he rushed to school, we had already left. Determined to make a contribution nevertheless, he decided to collect sand for us from a big hole dug up by senior students. He had moved a few baskets of sand above the ground when it caved in, burying him underneath. By the time he was discovered, he had been dead for hours. We were shocked and couldn't believe he was dead.

I had never talked with Yao directly before. Boys and girls didn't socialize with one another in school. It was an unspoken taboo. We participated in group activities together, but it was socially unacceptable to mingle on an individual basis. Friendship between sexes was viewed with suspicion, even at elementary school. As we grew older, self-censorship and school requirements would only separate the two genders even further. Usually, boys grouped with boys, and girls with girls.

Yao's seat was two rows away from mine. His empty bench haunted me for a long time.

A funeral was held at school in his honor and he was made a Red Pioneer posthumously. His picture, framed with black ribbon, showed a childish, pale face and a pair of large eyes. His expression was shy, as if he was apologizing for his unfinished mission. He was an amiable boy. He had never been the center of attention. No one could imagine he would work on his own. How long did he suffer in the darkness? What went through his mind? We murmured and questioned, unable to overcome the overwhelming sense of loss. Soon after his death, our furnace was dismantled and the brick-making project abandoned.

To learn from the army, we marched back and forth on our track field, shouting "1, 2, 3, 4." We moved in unison like soldiers. The entire campus was filled with groups of marching students, each arranged by class. A grade was called "company," and a class "squad," as if we were military units. We learned about the Red Army's Long March and were deeply touched by their resilience and triumph.

The Long March took place in mid-1934, when the Communist troops embarked on an arduous journey to break free of the fierce attacks by Chiang Kai-shek's Kuomintang Army. There were ninety thousand men and women when the March started in the Jiangxi Province. They endured food shortages and harsh weather conditions, climbed snow-capped mountains, and plodded through grassy swamps. They were constantly attacked by the enemies. Their entire journey covered a distance of twenty-five thousand kilometers. When they eventually reached their destination in Yan'an, the Shaanxi Province, over ninety percent of the original troops were dead. But the surviving Communists were able to rebuild, and fourteen years later, defeated the Kuomintang.

What could we do to learn from them? The question lingered in my mind. One day an idea dawned on me. Since her marriage with Baofa, Yan had settled in the village and become a schoolteacher. I could take a group of students to her village, creating our own "long march." We could start early in the morning and make our way back by the end of the day. I was thrilled by the idea and proposed it to my study group. A dozen or so students volunteered. We were all ten or eleven years old, but there was no need to obtain parental permission—no one would stand in the way of a revolutionary act. I didn't even notify Mrs. Liu, our homeroom teacher. We wanted to impress her with our dedication.

On the day of our march, I gave a short speech in front of the group. We gathered next to the water platform close to my home. Thick clouds accumulated as I spoke. I told them that our "long march" would start right with our first step, and we should follow the examples of our heroic forbears. Each of us carried a blanket folded into a rectangle, mimicking the image of marching soldiers. Mother helped me pack mine, but she had left for work by the time we were ready to set out. Most of the children, however, had one or both parents seeing them off. They followed us, pushing their bicycles along our column. To put our will and determination to trial, I requested that no one should put their pack on a parent's bicycle. The Red Army didn't have such luxuries during their Long March, I reasoned. The parents walked with us in silence to the edge of town, and then reluctantly, waved us goodbye. We soon disappeared from their sight at the bend of the country road. No parents expressed their concern, but we could tell they were worried. I was feeling overwhelmed myself. Yan's village was about six miles away. I had been there a couple of times, but each time, I was riding on horse-drawn cart. What if I couldn't recognize the right exit and got lost? Didn't they say the class struggle in the countryside was severe and that class enemies were desperate to make counterattacks? What if we ran into one of them? I walked in the front, holding a red flag. I did my best to keep my worries to myself.

We took several breaks and pressed on. None of us had walked so far in one go. We soon felt tired, and our blankets seemed to gain weight with each step. The strings that tied them neatly cut into our shoulders. I cheered the team to sing revolutionary songs as we continued.

As if to test our determination, the clouds over our heads turned black and bore down. Soon big raindrops started to fall. We immediately took shelter under a big tree. When someone mentioned that we could be hit by lightning, we gathered our strength and ran the last stretch to the village. Yan and her mother-in-law were expecting us at the elementary school. By the time we got there, we were soaking wet, hungry, and tired. The soup noodles they prepared for us tasted so delicious that each of us had a second serving.

Yan's mother-in-law gave me a set of dry clothes, as one of her daughters was my age.

"Do you have thirteen sets?" I asked.

She looked puzzled. When she understood what I meant, she shook her head, looking tenderly into my eyes. She said she could try to persuade her daughter to loan us her only remaining outfit, but that could only take care of one more person. I handed the dry clothes back to her and said I would rather stay in my wet blouse and pants like my teammates. For years afterwards, she would praise me for my behavior, but not without a good tease and laugh.

We dried our clothes with our body heat and rested on the piles of straw set up for us in a classroom. Some took a nap by lying down on top of two desks placed together. Our blankets were wet and useless. We started to head back early in the afternoon. By the time we reached the edge of town, we saw most of the parents were waiting for our return at the corner where they had bid farewell to us, as if they had never left. We looked like a group of defeated soldiers. Our packs hung from our shoulders, and our clothing was dirty and wrinkled. I dismissed the group and let my exhausted teammates join their parents. I watched them as they got on the back seats of their parents' bicycles. My mother was not there. She wouldn't take time off from work unless it was something crucial. I was not expecting her. I was proud to walk home and complete the march on my own.

5

I had not been a healthy child, but I was active. In our school's annual sports meetings, I participated in the maximum number of events allowed per student, from short distance running, medley relays, to long jump. I enjoyed them all and did well in school competitions. I got stronger with each passing year, but from time to time, I still suffered from bouts of colds, high fevers, or occasionally pneumonia.

In 1971, when the city set up a spare-time athletic training center for speed skating, table tennis, and basketball, I applied to join the table tennis team. Table tennis was popular in China. We often played on concrete tables built on campus. We put a stick over two bricks to serve as a net and played during school recess. I was thrilled to be accepted by the center.

A dozen of us, six boys and six girls, were selected from different elementary schools. Mr. Li, a thin and handsome man in his early thirties, was our coach. He started our training with three sessions a week, sending us to run on the outdoor track field for strength and endurance. He also had metal paddles custom-made for us. Lifting the heavy paddle felt like moving a dumbbell. Our hands were sore and our fingers swollen, but we kept at it.

As we got better, we started training every day. The conditions at the center were poor. We had a large training room, with ten tables spread out. There were no showers or locker rooms. A pipe outside the building was our only source of water supply. But we didn't mind. We were lucky to be there. We all practiced hard.

When winter arrived, we practiced in the cold. A small stove at one end of the training room couldn't generate enough heat to keep the place warm. Sometimes it was so cold that we were reluctant to change into our sweatpants. We practiced in our cotton-padded clothing, which gradually became wet with sweat. As we stepped out of the door to go home, the cold wind assaulted our faces and made our pants stiff. We ran toward home as soon as we stepped out.

Coach Li often helped the girls, giving us a ride on his bicycle, two at a time—one sitting on the horizontal bar between his seat and the handlebar and the other on the back seat. We reached home faster with the ride, but our feet were numb and our pants frozen. Mother was amazed at my persistence.

When I first started with the team, she was not that enthusiastic, believing my health was too fragile to bear this exertion. As I continued, with Li telling her how hard I practiced and how much progress I had made, Mother nodded with approval. However, when I dragged my body into our apartment at the end of the day, completely exhausted, I often slumped into a corner. Despite feeling famished, I often felt too tired to move over to the dining table. Mother frowned at my "drop dead" behavior, calling me "a heroine outside, and lazy bones at home."

We watched documentary films of Zhuang Zedong, the three-time winner of men's singles championship in the World

Table Tennis Championships. We were in awe of him as we saw how fast he hit the ball and how much sweat flown from him. Father once asked me if I had ever dripped a puddle of sweat on my table. I shook my head, deeply ashamed of my lack of effort. I started pushing myself harder. When that didn't produce the desired perspiration, I nailed a few planks together the size of a half table and set it up in our front yard. I hung a string above the boards and tied a ball to it, so I could practice shifting my position in response to the swing of the ball. The string was short and the dangling ball came back too quickly, making me drip with sweat in no time.

I made good progress. A year later, the city held its first table tennis competition for elementary schools. Each of us at the center became a key player on our respective school team. For three years, I held the girls' singles championship in the city.

The table tennis practice not only improved my health, but also instilled in me a strong sense of persistence. Day in and day out, hot or cold, no matter how hard it was sometimes, I went to practice. "Back hand, one hundred repetitions!" When Coach Li gave us an order, we drilled until we accomplished the goal. If we reached ninety-nine and the ball fell off the table, we started from the beginning all over again. No lies. No exaggeration. I loved the sport. Mother looked pleased with my improvement.

"You must have good health to become a valuable contributor to the revolution," she said. In our family of revolutionaries, I certainly didn't want to fall behind.

Me, the red-scarfed Pioneer

Chapter Seventeen

Betrayal

1

Father visited home from time to time, mostly in passing when he was in town for a meeting. I observed him whenever I had a chance. His hearty laugh and upbeat attitude didn't change. The hardship he had endured seemed to have left no trace on him. The only concern he expressed was over Nainai's cataracts and her deteriorating health. The change in Nainai over the previous two years must have shocked him. To comfort her, he often sat by the Kang and chatted with her. When Nainai asked how he was, alone at the coal mine, Father rolled up his sleeves and showed her his muscles. "Touch my arm," he said. "Feel how strong I am." Nainai smiled. Father's presence always made her happy. She could no longer see her son clearly, but when she touched his arms, she could tell that Father had lost a lot of weight. The hair at his temples turned gray, as I had noticed. He also smoked a lot more, often using the burning end of a cigarette to light up another one. A layer of blue smoke cast a constant veil around him, separating him from me.

Despite the ordeal and mistreatments he suffered, Father kept his trust in the Party. "My case will be settled rightfully," he said when one of us brought up the subject. That sounded very much like what Mother had told us over the years. "Look forward, not backward," he repeatedly urged us. It was only when he was alone in the small bedroom that I sometimes found him deep in thought. He hardly noticed that ashes had accumulated on the tip his cigarette and fallen to the ground.

We started to have visitors at home again, most of them workers and managers from the Wanbao coal mine. They came to Baicheng on business or to run personal errands. Many of them stopped by our mud house apartment for a visit. Our humble dwelling must have brought them closer to Father. I resumed my role of serving tea whenever we had guests, but felt more ambivalent in dealing with them. I couldn't help looking at them with a skeptical eye and wondering which side they would be when another political storm hit us. I knew these people were not the government employees who turned against Father, but I found it hard to trust their friendliness and take their words at face value.

While Father worked at his new job with the same dedication, Mother was selected to head a special team consisting of people from several schools. For more than six months, they worked on the rehabilitation cases at the No. 2 Middle School. She was no stranger to abuse, but some of the gruesome incidents still shocked her. In one case, the Red Guards tortured an old math teacher. He was from a landlord family. At one struggle meeting, they made him stand half naked. Then they wrapped a towel around his penis and set it on fire. In another case, the Red Guards stripped their old principal of his pants and forced him to kneel on broken glasses. They pushed him and beat him, turning his knees into a bloody mess. No rehabilitation could heal the pains suffered by these people.

Chairman Mao had stated that the Cultural Revolution was a great movement and should be repeated every seven or eight years. Mother didn't want to subject herself again to the hands of the young who could be so brutal and heartless. She began to consider leaving the education system.

Shortly after she resumed her work at the No. 1 Middle School, Mother went to the Municipal Government and had a talk with Mr. Zhang, a deputy mayor. She requested a job transfer. "I've been working at a number of schools for a dozen years," she said. "I'd like to expand my horizon and have a career change." She tried to put it as positively as she could.

Deputy Mayor Zhang was no stranger to Mother. He was in charge of education and was rehabilitated from his persecution not that long before. He understood Mother's feelings. Soon after the meeting, Mother was transferred to the Department of Public Health at the City Government. She was to become a deputy director. The department managed two city hospitals, an infectious disease prevention center and the city's sanitation system. With mixed feelings, Mother bid farewell to her education career, once the dream of her life. She felt disillusioned and betrayed.

As my parents took on new jobs and spent most of their time away from home again, I was left much on my own. My brother Binbin was sent to the countryside in 1970 and my sister Wen left for a medical school in 1971. Wen was luckier than my other three older siblings. 1971 was the only year a new policy was implemented. Besides going to the countryside, graduates also had the option of receiving further education, becoming a worker, and even going to frontiers that bordered other countries. Father advised Wen to continue with her studies. "You are young," he said. "At this stage of your life, acquiring knowledge is more important than anything else." Wen listened. She applied for the Baicheng Medical School and was accepted.

I was lonely. All my older siblings were away from home. I found myself drifting between bursts of revolutionary fever and moments of confusion and doubt. I still wanted to be a successor of the revolution, but there were times I wavered—I didn't know what I was doing or what I should do to move forward. I missed my siblings and started sneaking back to the Compound to wander around. The familiar places brought me a sense of comfort. I climbed over the walls, dodging the patrolling guard, usually old Mr. Fan, who had worked as one of the gatekeepers at the Compound for years.

Sometimes I hid under the shade of the mulberry trees. It felt like ages had passed since we raised hundreds of silkworms and picked mulberry leaves to feed them. I had not seen a delicate silkworm since the start of the Cultural Revolution, but the mulberry trees still stood firm, their branches stretching out and their dark, large leaves rustling in the wind.

Such moments of reminiscence, however, didn't last long. Old Mr. Fan, gray-haired but still in good health, often came searching. Before our family was driven out of the Compound, I used to call him Grandpa Fan. He always returned my greetings in a deep, loud voice. That friendliness was long gone. He patrolled the Compound like a policeman, holding a club in his hand. He chased away the children as if they were flies.

"Out! Out! You shameless hooligans!" he shouted angrily, and ran after the intruders. Often, children living outside of the Compound jumped over the walls to get in there to play. They were after the dragonflies, grasshoppers, and crickets. There were plenty of them in the bushes and deserted areas full of grass and wild flowers. Some children also climbed trees to pick dates and berries, as my siblings and I had done before. But I was no longer interested in such activities. I was there to reclaim a part of my past. Old Fan, if he happened upon me, treated me as if he didn't know me. I ran away as fast as I could, like all the other children.

Once, a boy of my age from the same alley went in to catch dragonflies. He used a needle and string to tie his captured insects. When Old Fan appeared, he ran for the wall. In the rush to get away, he pressed his chest against the needle and it was driven inside. Panicked and in pain, he tried to pull the needle out. It broke in his hand. He cried and slipped off the wall outside of the Compound. Someone ran to his home to tell his family. His mother came and carried him to the hospital. The broken needle had moved dangerously close to his heart. He ended up going through two major operations to have the needle removed. Old Fan showed no sympathy.

"He shouldn't have been there to start with," he said.

I told Nainai my whereabouts and my encounters, but I never mentioned anything to Mother. I knew she wouldn't approve of my undignified behavior.

2

When I was eleven, I found myself accused of embezzlement. It happened like this: Two or three times a week, a few students and I would meet at my house after school to do our homework or study Mao's quotations from his little red book. I was the leader of our study group and thought it might be helpful if we could obtain a few copies of Mao's selected works for our group. There were four published volumes. One day I brought up the idea to Han and Bai, two of the most active girls in my group. Han was thin and small, but very articulate. She always spoke with great earnestness and clarity, narrowing her eyes and waving her hands for emphasis. I was impressed by her enthusiasm, but her bad teeth always bothered me. When she spoke, I had to make a conscious effort not to stare at her mouth. The other girl, Bai, was Han's best friend, but they had nothing in common. Bai was soft-spoken and good-natured. She never talked much. I told them about my idea.

"What would you think if we collected some money to buy copies of Mao's works for the entire group?" I asked.

Han and Bai clapped their hands in support. They calculated how much we would need and suggested we collect twenty-five fen from each student. "That should allow us to buy three copies," they said. I was encouraged.

I announced the initiative to our study group the following day, calling upon everyone to contribute. "Twenty-five fen each," I said, feeling confident that everyone would participate. A few students responded enthusiastically, while others remained silent. There was no objection. I looked at Han and Bai, realizing that in our excitement, we didn't consider that twenty-five fen might be a burden for some. Noting the hesitant response from some students, I added quickly that they could contribute whatever amount they felt comfortable with. I took out a small porcelain piggy bank my sister Ping had given me and led the group by putting in the first coins. Han and Bai, both prepared, followed with their contribution. There was a large hole in the belly of the smiling pig, blocked with a plastic plug. I could take the money out without smashing the piggy bank. To show their support, the rest of the group chipped in. The idea of keeping a record never crossed my mind. I was filled with pride.

Days later, just as I was about to count the money and see how many copies we could purchase, Zhao, one of the poorest students, came to me and asked to have her money back.

"My father said he could obtain a free copy of Chairman Mao's work from his factory," she said.

Zhao's father was a worker, and her mother did odd jobs at a co-op to make ends meet. Zhao was a pretty girl. Her large, beautiful eyes were kind and full of curiosity. Her request triggered others to follow suit. Soon, everyone asked for his or her money back. I was dumbfounded, but I knew the idea of obtaining free copies of Mao's works from their parents' companies or institutions, wherever they worked, was legitimate. Reluctantly, I took out the piggy bank and returned their money.

To my surprise, everyone asked to have twenty-five fen back. When I dug out the last coin, my own contribution included, I still owed several students their supposed shares. I felt my hair standing up on end. How could this be? Waves of shock and panic ran through my body. The world around me started spinning. I felt humiliated. My integrity was on the line. Even Han and Bai looked at me with questioning eyes. I didn't know how to clear my name without accusing others of being dishonest. I had no proof and I didn't want to point fingers. I could use my own small savings to dig myself out of the hole, but that meant I admitted my wrongdoing. Pride, dignity, and a sense of righteousness prevented me from doing so. I felt disgraced, as if I were exposed and paraded in the open streets. The word "embezzlement" murmured by my classmates brought tears to my eyes. Rumors spread quickly in school and the amount of money involved seemed to increase every day. I did the best I could to walk with my back straight, but I was keenly aware of the finger-pointing in the hallway.

Should I inform Mother of the situation? I hesitated. I was too embarrassed to bring up the issue. Besides, I was worried about Mother's reaction. While I was struggling with my dilemma, Han and Bai stopped my mother on her way home one day. They demanded Mother make up the amount embezzled by her irresponsible daughter. Mother returned home, quite surprised. I was shamed to tears as I explained to her what had happened. She listened quietly, viewing me with her intense, solemn eyes. To my relief, she only advised me to stay clear of issues involving money in the future. She gave me some coins and advised me to settle the matter. I swallowed my pride and gave twenty-five fen to each of the remaining claimants. I felt betrayed by my peers. It pained me to see Han and the others every day. When Han talked in class, her voice no longer sounded eloquent to my ears. Instead, all I could hear were lies.

I begged Mother to transfer me to another school. When she said no, I shed endless tears. I was miserable. Eventually, Nainai intervened.

"I don't want to see Jian so unhappy," she said to Mother. "Are you sure you can't help her to make a change?"

Nainai worked on Mother on my behalf. Before the end of the week, Mother stopped by my school and submitted a request for my transfer. The following Monday, Mother took me to Ming Ren Elementary School, which was about the same distance from home, but in the opposite direction. I was relieved. I promised Mother I would not make the same mistake again.

3

In 1972, half a year after my transfer to Ming Ren, Father was transferred back to Baicheng and resumed his Deputy Governor position. Instead of heading Light Industry, he was put in charge of culture and education, a jurisdiction that supervised public schools, colleges, and culture-related activities. Our family moved back to the Compound, not to our old apartment, which was now occupied by a fast-rising young official, but to a smaller unit.

The move back was simple and quick. The Administrative Office sent over a truck, along with many helping hands. Our belongings were not enough to fill up one truck load. A jeep came over and drove Nainai and Big Aunt over to the new apartment. Old Mr. Fan, who was still working as a guard, was friendly to us again. I enjoyed the convenience of running water and the indoor toilet, but I was not thrilled. The friendly greetings and smiles of the government staff seemed artificial to me. I responded politely, but I kept my distance. Besides, our ordeal had reduced Nainai to a bag of bones, and no amount of extra space could help her regain her strength and flexibility. She could no longer walk down the hallway and negotiate the toilet bowl. She had to use a bedpan next to the Kang, just as she had done in the mud house.

The few children of my age in the Compound all attended my former elementary school. I didn't reach out to them. I wanted to be left alone, yet I feared loneliness. Nainai was nearly blind with cataracts, and no doctor dared operate on her because of her age and frail condition. Big Aunt stayed by her side, providing companionship and taking care of her needs.

I refused to accept Nainai's aging. Whenever I was at home, I stayed close to her. "Nainai, I'm back," was my first sentence home. Every day, I found her sitting in the same place and in the same position on the Kang. Nainai could only see a shadow of my figure, but upon hearing my voice, she extended her bamboo walking stick to find me, as in the old days when we played hide-and-seek. Big Aunt and I helped her get down from the Kang to relieve herself. If it was a good day, I'd help her walk over to my bedroom, which was next to hers, or walk in the hallway for a few minutes. Her legs were getting weaker, but her mind was as clear as ever. She ate three meals a day on the Kang, leaning against her quilts and pillows. We took turns eating with her. Nainai made every effort to be independent and ate her meals on her own.

When Father got home, he stopped by her room and chatted with her. He often asked Nainai if there was anything she would like to have. Father's salary had not been raised for a decade, but he kept saying that each time one of his children became self-sufficient, it was equivalent to a pay raise. Our living conditions had improved, and Father wanted to do something extra for Nainai, but Nainai always said no. She needed nothing. She was happy and content. However, she did have one wish. She reiterated it whenever she had a chance.

"Don't burn me like a bird when I'm dead," she said. "Send me back to our village and bury me beside my husband."

It was the only request she had ever made for herself. At that point, Father changed the subject.

"Please think of something you can enjoy now," he said.

A burial was considered a feudal custom and was banned, especially in urban areas where all the policies were effectively enforced. As a government official, Father was obliged to observe the new rules, but he couldn't reveal that to Nainai. Growing up in the era of revolution, I had never seen anybody buried. I didn't give it much thought.

Early in the spring of 1974, Nainai's health further deteriorated. She ate little and could no longer leave the Kang. Big Aunt, Mother, and Father took turns staying by her side. For the first time I started to worry about her fragile condition. Nainai had been such a constant presence in my life that I never allowed myself to think that one day she would be gone. A few years before, I had seen Big Aunt sew a shroud for Nainai, putting it away for when the time came, but I refused to link it to Nainai's death.

Early one morning, Big Aunt took out the black shroud and yellow quilts. I was seized with fear. Black and yellow were the traditional colors of the dead. I started shaking. The night before, Nainai had been unusually quiet. I had held her hand and begged her to stay.

"Nainai, you'll get better. You must," I said.

Nainai opened her eyes slightly and tried to smile.

"I'm too old, Jian," she said, her voice hardly audible. "I'm useless now."

Then she squeezed my hand.

I always believed Nainai and I had a special bond. Just as she had called me back to life when I was a baby, I thought I could call her back from the dead. I kept whispering "Nainai", nearly choked with tears. I took her squeeze of my hand as a reassurance. All my life, religion had always been condemned as a superstition and "opium for the people," as Karl Marx had said. Except for scornful critiques of Buddhism, Judaism, or Christianity, I had never been exposed to any religious concept. But that morning, I felt the strong need to pray, to ask Buddha—or whatever being there might be—to let Nainai live.

"Our life has just started to get better," I put my palms together and murmured. "Please don't let her go."

My sister Ping came home before noon and took the rest of the day off. We all feared the worst for Nainai. To help her breathe, Mother and Big Aunt had arranged for her to lean against piles of bedding. Nainai rested her head against a pillow on the top. We were constantly around her, murmuring a word or two in hushed voice. We didn't want to disturb Nainai.

Suddenly, Ping cried out: "Nainai!"

She saw Nainai drop her head to the side. Her face suddenly drained of all color. Her startled cry sent Mother and Big Aunt rushing to Nainai's side.

"Niang!" Mother called out, her voice broken.

Big Aunt started crying.

I panicked. As everyone else rushed to Nainai's side, I ran away. I charged into the hallway and headed toward the bathroom, nearly colliding with Father, who, upon hearing the commotion, was rushing to Nainai's room. I couldn't bear to see Nainai go, nor could I bear to hear the cries. I was seized with fear. I started shaking. I pushed open the bathroom door and locked it behind me. I kneeled down on the cold, concrete floor. I prayed. I put my palms together and lowered my head. I prayed hard.

"Please, Buddha. Please God. Please!" I begged. "Don't take Nainai from me. Don't let her go." I repeated the same words again and again. I wanted, more than anything, to call her back.

4

Looking back, I have no idea how long I was in there. By the time I gathered enough strength to come out, Nainai was laid on a wood plank platform, fully dressed in her shroud. Her face was colorless, but very peaceful. Her lips were slightly parted, as if she was asleep. Her cheeks were hollow, giving her face the appearance of a smile. I inched toward her. My legs were weak and I was breathing heavy. Big Aunt was placing a piece of wafer and a coin in one of Nainai's hands, and a miniature whip with a red string in the other. She said that these items would protect her from going hungry or lacking money, and would drive anything harmful away from her in the next life. Only later I realized how extraordinary it was that Mother and Father let Big Aunt carry out the folk ritual, since any practice of this nature was condemned as superstition.

Eventually, I moved to Nainai's side. I was shaking, but I had no tears. Gently, I touched her hands, her cheeks, and her forehead. They were all cold. Big Aunt was sobbing and speaking gibberish, and Mother and Father were on the phone making arrangements.

"Nainai, this is not real," I said. I pinched myself to see if I could feel any pain, wishing I were in a nightmare, but the pain was real and sharp.

My sister Wen was with a medical team working in the countryside. She had been away for a week and was scheduled to continue the tour to treat villagers for another three weeks. The Administrative Office sent a jeep to fetch her. They followed her trail from village to village until they located her, more than a hundred miles away. By the time Wen was rushed back, Nainai had been gone for half a day. Wen and I were the two grandchildren who were brought up by Nainai, and we felt especially attached to her. Wen was overwhelmed with grief, because she hadn't been able to say goodbye. She kneeled by Nainai's side and let her tears flow. For the remaining two days of the wake, Wen hardly moved from Nainai's side. We all knew Nainai's only wish was to have her body returned to her village for a burial. And we were keenly aware that Father wouldn't be able to carry that out. Guilt and sorrow filled our hearts. Father sent for Yan, but decided not to tell Binbin, who was attending college in Changchun. Later he explained to Binbin that he didn't want to interrupt his studies.

"Nainai was already gone," he said. "There was nothing you could do about it. Besides, Nainai would have wanted you to concentrate on your studies."

Binbin swallowed hard. He would have wanted to be back and bid farewell to Nainai in person, even if it only meant standing by her body, but it was too late. Binbin sobbed. Nainai had been dear and close to each of us.

According to the custom, the deceased shouldn't be left alone at night. The Administrative Office sent Old Fan over to watch Nainai's body. When Old Fan arrived at nine o'clock in the evening, he was shocked to see that Nainai's body was placed in the middle of the Kang on a wooden board, with Big Aunt, Ping, Wen, and I arranged around her. He told Father that he carried out the task of watching the dead many times before, but had never seen such a demonstration of attachment and love. Father thanked him and sent him away. We didn't need a stranger to accompany Nainai on her final journey.

Three days later, a small group of family members and friends accompanied Nainai's body to the city's cremation center. Nobody said a word during the entire procession. I stepped away, as two men at the crematorium placed Nainai's body on a metal stand. I couldn't bear to see them push Nainai's body into the big hole in the furnace. I left the room, closed the door behind me and wandered back and forth in the yard. I could see the big chimney puffing out white smoke above the building. She was free now, free of this life and all its hardships. I imagined her up there in the sky. For the first time since Nainai passed away, I started to cry, silently at first, and then loud and uncontrollable. The tears and wail broke loose. I pressed my head hard against an old elm tree and felt the rough bark cutting into my forehead. The physical pain was easier to deal with than the echoing hole in my heart. I had never felt so alone.

After the cremation, Nainai's ashes were collected in a small box and put in a slot on a tall shelf that ran from floor to the ceiling. Rows of gritty shelves and boxes crowded the room, with a narrow passage not wide enough for two people to walk side by side. A photo was posted in front of each box. The size and shape of all the boxes were similar, and a family could identify the location of their loved one only by reference numbers. Reluctantly, we left Nainai's ashes in this dark, ominous place. A year later, Father arranged to have a relative take Nainai's ashes back to her village and quietly buried next to Yeye. It must have been painful for Father not to have fulfilled Nainai's only wish. None of the grandchildren was informed of Father's arrangement until "Qingming," a day in early April when people in old times swept tombs and paid tribute to the dead. We decided to go to the crematorium on this day to dust Nainai's ash box and pay homage to her. Father told us Nainai's ashes were no longer there. I was terribly torn when I heard this. On the one hand, I was relieved that Nainai was out of that dark, depressing place, and her wish had been at least partially fulfilled; but on the other hand, I regretted the burial had to be done so discreetly that none of her immediate family members was present. Nainai's hometown was in Shandong Province, a two-day journey from Baicheng via train.

We all missed Nainai. Each of us coped individually with the sense of loss. Father framed a black and white photo of Nainai, one of the few ever taken, and hung it above the desk in his study. Big Aunt kept talking about Nainai, bringing back memories of the old days in their home village.

And I continued to announce: "I'm home" every day, as if Nainai could still hear me. At first, I did this out loud, choking back tears. Later, I called silently, feeling somehow still connected to her. For years, I dreamed of Nainai. It was always the same dream. She was sitting in an armchair beckoning me to come closer. She looked at me tenderly from head to toe, but when I reached out my hands and tried to help her stand up, she faded away, smiling.

Chapter Eighteen

A New Start

1

It was a beautiful day early in the fall 1974 when I started middle school. I got up early and put on a pair of clean dark blue pants and a white cotton shirt. I stuffed my newly washed canvas school bag with notebooks and pencils, eager to begin my study at the No. 1 Middle School.

Mother joined me at the breakfast table.

"Ready for a new start?" she asked.

She put down her bowl of millet porridge and sat next to me. Mother had served as Deputy Director at the No. 1 Middle School for more than a year, and had more reason than ever to expect me to do well.

"It's important you set a good example for others," she said.

I nodded. After all, I was the daughter of Deputy Governor in charge of education for the prefecture. I had to be "Mao's good child," as my mother had frequently told me.

Mother's words reminded me of a birthday gift she gave me a year before when I turned thirteen. It was a rare occasion, and I was pleasantly surprised. In our family, the only birthday that was celebrated was Nainai's. When we were small children, our birthdays were acknowledged, but we never received any gifts. For Nainai, the celebration consisted of the entire family wishing her a happy birthday and good health for the future, accompanied by a bowl of noodles, symbolizing longevity. As for us children, our only treat was a hard-boiled egg for breakfast. And even such simple acknowledgement went out of the window when the Cultural Revolution started.

I was thrilled when Mother not only mentioned my birthday, but also gave me a birthday gift. "This is for you," she said, placing a copy of *Lei Feng's Diary* in front of me. "You should follow Lei Feng's example."

Lei Feng was no stranger to me, nor was his diary. I had grown up knowing of him as a hero and role model. The most popular image of him presented a glorified soldier, holding a machine gun across his chest. His head lifted high, his thick winter hat tilted upward, a faint but proud smile on his face. Lei Feng had been a truck driver in a military transportation unit. Being orphaned as a child, Lei Feng was brought up under the care of the Communists. He was very grateful and dedicated himself completely to the Party. He joined the army as a teenager. He lived a simple life, but gave all of the meager stipend he earned as a soldier to elders who had no family to support them. Lei Feng became known for his good deeds posthumously. In his diary, he expressed determination to become a nameless, rustproof screw in the construction of Communism.

In 1962, Lei Feng, at twenty-two, died in an accident. He was directing an assistant to back up his truck. The driver, young and inexperienced, was an apprentice. He lost control when he stepped on the gas. The truck jolted and charged to the side, knocking down a telephone pole. Lei Feng was not able to get out of the way and was hit and killed by the falling pole. After his death, his diaries were discovered and published. In 1963, Mao called upon the entire population to follow his example. He wrote in brush calligraphy: "Learn from Comrade Lei Feng," as he had done for Liu Hulan years before. Lei Feng immediately became a household name and his stories were repeatedly covered in books, newspapers, and magazines. A campaign to learn from Lei Feng spread across the country. The ideal of selfless giving and complete devotion to Chairman Mao and the Party was the core of the message. Feng's diaries went into print many times. Mao's calligraphy written in brush stroke was framed and hung in classrooms. We learned from Lei Feng when we denounced any selfish thought. We learned from Lei Feng when we visited elders to clean their homes and wash their clothing. Even a little kid turning in a coin found in the street would say he was learning from Lei Feng.

I knew Lei Feng's story and his diaries so well from repeated accounts, but I treasured the book Mother gave me—I took it as the demonstration of her care and love. I made extra effort to keep it in good shape. Only years later I realized how extraordinary it was that Mother gave it to me as a gift. She must have felt I needed more guidance as I turned into a teenager. I had never received a birthday gift from her before, nor would I ever after.

2

In addition to urging me to follow the example of Lei Feng, Mother urged me to learn from my older siblings. At the time, my sisters Ping and Wen were living at home. It was common that unmarried children lived with their parents out of custom and out of necessity because of a housing shortage. Ping was working at the Agricultural College when she returned from the countryside in 1972. And Wen, after graduating from the Baicheng Medical School, was assigned to work as a gynecologist at the City Hospital of Baicheng. They had both been admitted to the Party at a very young age, Ping at twenty and Wen at nineteen, an extraordinary achievement considering the stringent requirements for Party members. Mother was proud of them and expected me to embark on a similar path.

Ping started as a worker at the Agricultural College. She tended crops at the school's experimental plots, doing field work similar to what she had done in the countryside. She left for work early in the morning and returned home late at night, just like our parents. Her dedication was soon recognized with promotions to do office work, first as a typist, and then as a phone operator and announcer for the school's internal communication network. Ping was capable and efficient, and was able to handle all three jobs simultaneously. By the time I started middle school, Ping had been a Party member for two years, and was serving as Secretary of the Communist Youth League—an important leadership position.

Wen took a different path, but was equally, if not more, outstanding in her profession. At medical school, she excelled in both her academic studies and her overall performances. She maintained her good-natured personality and continued to speak softly, but under that amiable surface was a great deal of determination and dedication.

Most of the students at her school came from the countryside in the Baicheng Prefecture. The curriculum for the doctor program was for two and half years, and for nurses a year and half. As a Communist Youth League member, Wen started as a student leader. She was willing to help her fellow students, especially those who came from poor families in the countryside. Since their homes were far away, Wen looked after them when they were sick, bringing meals to their bedside and helping them make up for the classes they missed. Once, she noticed a boy in class tying a string to his shoes to hold them together. His toes were sticking out, and the sole and the upper level of his shoes were coming apart. Wen quietly started a campaign to collect money to assist him. She saved from her own food allowance and contributed a major portion. When she presented a pair of new shoes, a notebook, and a few pencils to the boy on behalf of the entire class, the young man burst into tears. Today, he is an official in charge of public health in Baicheng. He still talks about the incident. He says it touched him so much that he regarded it as a defining point that changed his life.

After their first year of academic studies, Wen and her classmates were sent to a county hospital to receive hands-on training for an entire year. They spent an extended period of time in each department, from internal medicine, pediatrics, to gynecology, surgery, and the emergency room. They lived in a shabby quarters at the infectious disease control center, with girls sharing one room and boys sharing another. They had their meals at the hospital's canteen. The hospital was short of doctors and the students were put to good use. Wen lived up to the challenges. She spent day and night at the hospital, eager to work and help. She was soon capable of handling simple operations such as appendectomy and sterilization. When other students shied away from blood and dying patients, Wen put herself to the front, dealing with the patients and their families with compassion. She particularly enjoyed working with women, especially in the gynecology department. She took delight in looking after the newborn babies and their mothers. She decided to become a gynecologist.

Before her graduation, Wen was admitted to the Communist Party. She was one of the two students from a pool of over three hundred in her grade who received such honor. When Wen graduated in 1973, she went to work at the City Hospital. Trained doctors were hard to come by. Wen had the luxury of choosing which department she would like to work for. She selected the Gynecology Department. To her surprise, she was met with a cold shoulder. Mr. Jin, the department head, didn't want her. He believed that daughters of high-ranking officials were pampered. "This is not a department for a young 'lady,'" he said sarcastically when Wen reported to him. Standing in his office, Wen was astonished. She was quiet for a moment, then, she pled: "Please give me a chance."

Jin was a short man in his late forties, a Chinese Korean who was well known for his stubbornness and straight-forwardness. He stared at Wen, seemingly deep in thought. After a pause, he decided that if he assigned enough difficult tasks to Wen, she would request a transfer to a different department. "All right," he said to Wen. "Here is our work schedule." Jin pointed to a chart nailed to the wall and filled in Wen's name for night shifts and assisting duties. He felt certain Wen would leave in a week. He observed Wen from a distance and was surprised by her endurance and effort. Wen not only did what Jin requested, she did more. She had a compassion for her patients, especially those who didn't have family members to accompany them. She went out of her way to look after them. She served as their doctor during the day, and in the evening, she spent time in their wards, helping them to wash their clothes and emptying their chamber pots. She did more than a nurse would normally do. Wen's dedication soon won over Jin. "She is willing to do the most difficult work," Jin told Mother during one of her visits to the Hospital. "She has no traits of a pampered young 'lady' from an official family," he smiled.

Once he was convinced of her commitment, Jin took Wen under his wing, training her to be a good gynecologist. He placed Wen by his side when he performed major operations. Sometimes, he let Wen be the surgeon and he served as her assistant, guiding her each step of the way. Occasionally, he even held her hand to go through a difficult procedure. Wen's skills and knowledge improved quickly.

In the 1970s, medical services at the countryside were very poor. Each year, the City Government required city hospitals to organize mobile medical teams and sent them to the countryside. A team usually spent one or two months, going from village to village to treat patients. They carried their own bedding and spent their nights at village schools or in homes of peasants, sharing a corner on their Kang. Conditions were primitive, and no one in the Hospital liked to go. As doctor in chief and department head, Jin always took the lead to join, but another member from the department was needed. Wen volunteered. "I'm young and single. I'll go." She raised her hand at a department meeting where the staffs were staring at one another, wondering whose turn it was this time. For those who had families, especially with small children, it was a long time to be away. They were relieved to hear Wen volunteer.

Jin and Wen joined other doctors from the Hospital and left to carry out their mission. They rode horse-drawn carts from village to village, treating patients with various diseases. Jin and Wen focused on their specialized area, treating women and performing sterilizations and abortions. At the time, the Chinese Government implemented the "one couple, two children" birth control policy, which would later be changed to "one couple, one child" when China's population continued to explode. In the early 1970s, those who had given birth to two or more children were required to have their tubes tied. Each village organized their women to come forward, some with willingness, some with reluctance. It was not unusual to hear incidents where women were forced to go through the procedure. Jin and Wen were taken to each location. Two desks were placed together to serve as an operation table. Sometimes, they operated on as many as thirty or forty women a day.

The job Wen enjoyed doing was to treat women and their children who had medical problems. They were poor and mostly neglected, and they freely came to Wen and Jin for help.

One night, the medical team slept at a village school. Wen shared one classroom with two other women doctors. They each placed two desks together and put their bedding on top. They were used to such conditions.

In the middle of the night, Wen was awakened by an urgent knock on the door. "Wen, wake up. An emergency." She heard Jin's voice. Wen jumped up from her bed and put on her clothing and shoes in the dark. When she stepped out, she saw Jin ready to take off. A woman in another village was suffering from difficult labor, and a peasant had rushed over with a horse-drawn cart to ask them for help. They loaded their medical boxes on the cart and left immediately. It was two o'clock in the morning. A thick layer of clouds blocked the moon, and the vast field along the road was dark. The peasant was familiar with the surrounding and he whipped the horse to speed up.

"Why don't you get some sleep," Jin said to Wen. "I'll wake you up when we get there." Wen thanked him. After a long day of performing operations and treating patients, Wen was exhausted. She put her light jacket on the surface of the wooden cart and lay down. The wooden boards of the bouncing cart cut into her body. Wen closed her eyes despite the discomfort. Jin leaned against the larger medical box and put the smaller one under Wen's head to use as a pillow.

She fell asleep, and was awakened only by the anxious voice of a man. "Hurry, please hurry up." Wen realized they had entered the village. The man rushing toward their cart was the husband of the woman in labor.

As soon as the cart stopped in front of a mud house, Jin jumped off and charged toward the entrance. He grabbed the two medical boxes in his hands. Wen followed him. The woman in labor moaned weakly on the Kang. Sweat soaked her shirt, and her lower body was covered with a sheet. A self-trained barefoot doctor was by her side. He was a man in his early thirties. He looked pale and his forehead was covered with sweat. He gave way to Jin and Wen, sighing with relief that they had come.

Jin took a quick look at the woman and announced they had to perform a Caesarean section immediately. The woman, who appeared to be in her early thirties, was semiconscious. Wen removed the bedding from the Kang and spread a clean sheet on its surface. She quickly spread some liquid disinfectant and took out their equipment from the boxes. As Jin injected anesthesia into the woman's body, Wen instructed the barefoot doctor to place the dim ceiling light hanging on a wire closer to the Kang. The wire was not long enough. Wen took out a flashlight from the large medical box and asked the young man to hold it.

Jin quickly started the operation. Wen stood by his side, bending over the Kang to hand him the tools and wiping away the blood with gauze pads. As they worked with intensity to save the baby and the woman, they realized the focus of the flashlight shifted to the side. "Light," Jin shouted out of habit. "Stay on focus." The light faded away instead. Wen turned to look what was going on and caught a glimpse of the barefoot doctor falling backward. He had passed out at the sight of blood.

The husband of the woman had to drag him outside to recover.

Fortunately, Jin and Wen made it there on time. They were able to save the woman and the baby. When daylight broke and the condition of the mother and the baby appeared stable, Jin and Wen took the horse-drawn cart back to where they came from. More patients were waiting for them.

During the time when she worked at the City Hospital, her colleagues selected Wen as a model worker every year. When the required period for work experience was fulfilled, Wen applied to go to college. She wanted to get more formal medical training. Under the policy of the time, once her application was submitted, Wen needed to face her peers at a department meeting for an appraisal. She had to obtain more than half of their votes for her application to pass on to the top-level management of the Hospital, and then to the City Government. Wen was the only person who received overwhelming support at her department and the Hospital, and the only graduate among her classmates in Baicheng to go to college that year.

Mother was pleased with her performance. As Deputy Director of Public Health, her responsibility included managing the City Hospital where Wen worked. One evening over dinner, Mother sat by Wen and looked pleased.

"You did well," Mother said to Wen. "Keep up with the good work in college."

Wen nodded. Her eyes beamed with excitement.

I observed their exchange of words with envy. For Mother to say "good work" was no small compliment. I understood that Wen's outstanding performance had brought her honor. Mother would expect me to do just as well.

3

I had passed the No.1 Middle School many times, but had never been inside before. The arched double doors at its main entrance always attracted me. The gate was set between two connecting buildings, with a reception on the side of the entrance hallway, visible from the street. Walking through it for the first time that morning, I felt the excitement of being a student.

Many people arrived early that day. Greetings and laughter echoed in the air. I was surprised to see a flower garden, usually regarded as bourgeois sentimentality. Echinacea, marigolds, and morning glory bloomed in gold, pink, and purple, filling the air with a sweet fragrance. I noticed an old man who was tending the plants with a watering can. He was short, and his face was dark brown and full of wrinkles. Some students greeted him as Grandpa Zhang. He waved and smiled, seemingly happy that the campus was full of life again after the summer break.

The No. 1 Middle School was established in 1954. Before the Cultural Revolution, it was regarded as the best middle school in town, with the highest rate of students going to college. Although the option of attending college was no longer available, the school still commanded respect from the local residents.

I joined a group of freshmen and found my classroom. Most of the other students were already seated. I sat down at a desk and looked around. I didn't know anyone, except Yang, a student leader from my elementary school, Ma and Du, two faces I recognized from the first school I attended.

Soon, a middle-aged woman entered the classroom. Stepping behind the podium, she examined the stack of paper in her hands, and from time to time threw a glance at us. But she said nothing. She was less than five feet tall, and her complexion was dark. Her small, round eyes were penetrating. Her poise and silence had a magical impact on the students. A silence fell over the room. Finally, when the bell rang the woman raised her head and spoke:

"I am your homeroom teacher," she said. "My name is Wu." Without any ceremony, she raised the roster and began to call everyone by name. Each student responded with a formal "Dao" and dutifully stood up. Wu fixed her gaze on each of us, forcing eye contact. She seemed to say, "I can see right through you." The relaxed feeling I had upon seeing the flower garden disappeared. When I stood up, Wu gave me an unexpected nod of acknowledgment. It made me uneasy. When I passed Wu during recess, she stopped me and asked how my parents were doing, as if she knew them both. I was puzzled by her behavior. I didn't want to be treated differently. I wanted to start out on equal footing with everyone else.

As our regular classes commenced, I made efforts to stay on top of each subject. It wasn't very difficult, since we covered only the basics in our curriculum. The emphasis in school was not on academic studies, but rather on political campaigns. There were eight classes of freshmen, each consisting of sixty to seventy students. As in elementary school, two or three students shared a bench and a narrow, rectangular desk. Mrs. Wu taught us

Chinese. As our homeroom teacher, she was also in charge of our political studies and ideological campaigns. She was responsible for the day-to-day administration of our class and our overall behavior.

Wu divided us into four groups, appointing a team leader for each. She also organized a committee of seven students to help her manage the large class. Since we were all new, Wu made her selection of the committee members based on our elementary school appraisal. I became one of the committee members. Ma, a small boy—very social and energetic—became our class monitor. Du, a girl with a talent for drawing and calligraphy, became deputy monitor. Wu appointed Yang, the only student who had been admitted to the Communist Youth League in elementary school, as our overall student leader. Yang was tall. Despite her two girlish ponytails, she seemed more poised and confident than the rest of us.

The Communist Youth League was an organization for children fifteen or older. During the Cultural Revolution, the Youth League had stood in the shadow of the Red Guards, but it had since made a comeback, reestablishing itself as the most important organization for the young. The Red Guard, meanwhile, had become an empty shell. Almost everyone was a member. We wore the red armband, but there was no more organized activity. The Communist Youth League was much more popular. One had to pass through a probation period and receive two member recommendations to be admitted.

Mrs. Wu wasted no time in turning the class into a collective unit. She was tiny, but possessed an inexhaustible amount of energy. She walked in and out of the classroom swiftly, ready to tackle any problem that might rise. She led us right into the "Anti-Lin and Anti-Confucius" movement that had been going on in the country.

Since his death in September 1971, Lin Biao, Vice-Chairman and Commander of the Army, had been condemned for his attempt to overthrow Chairman Mao. He once was Mao's heir-apparent; now he was considered the most notorious conspirator in China. We were told Lin tried to assassinate Mao. When his plot failed, Lin attempted to flee to the Soviet Union with his wife and son, but his plane crashed in Mongolia. We were in elementary school at the time. Totally shocked by the turn of the situation, we repeatedly denounced Lin and swore our loyalty to Mao. The Anti-Lin campaign continued. Early in 1974, the

Central Party Committee upped the ante, calling upon the nation to carry out the "Anti-Lin and Anti-Confucius" movement.

"Throughout our history, all counterrevolutionaries adored Confucius," an editorial from *The People's Daily*—the official mouthpiece of the Central Government—declared. Articles criticizing Lin and Confucius appeared all over newspapers and magazines. Wu voiced tremendous enthusiasm for the campaign and encouraged us to participate.

We had a hard time linking Lin with Confucius. Our generation had entered school at the beginning of the Cultural Revolution. We had never learned any classical Chinese prose, which was substantially different from the simplified Mandarin we were brought up with, nor had we been exposed to any of the teachings of our ancestors, including Confucius. They belonged to the four olds—"old ideas, old culture, old customs, and old habits," and as such, were eliminated from our curriculum. We couldn't even read the writing of Confucius in its classic form, but that didn't stop Wu from leading us onto a vigorous anti-Confucius campaign.

Wu selected Du and another student to create a bulletin board in our classroom. Posted excerpts from newspapers guided us. We held endless denunciation meetings against Lin and Confucius. We were so conditioned to political campaigns that no one questioned the absurdity of the situation. One of the students, a girl named Wang, who was eager to join the Communist Youth League, always started her speech with the exact same sentence: "During the Great Proletarian Cultural Revolution that is unfolding on a magnificent scale, we should all..." It was a line that frequently appeared in newspapers. Since everyone mimicked the official statements, no one laughed at her. We spent more time compiling criticisms from various sources than we did studying.

Soon, the "Anti-Lin and Anti-Confucius" movement took another turn. The Central Government declared a village in the Hebei Province as a role model in carrying out the campaign. Jiang Qing, the last wife of Chairman Mao, personally visited the village and called upon the entire nation to follow its example. Madam Mao, twenty-one years younger than Mao, was a very ambitious woman. She had been an actress in Shanghai in the mid 1930s. In 1937, she went to Yan'an, in the Shaanxi Province, to join the Communists. Yan'an was where the Red Army settled at the end of the Long March and the headquarters of the

Communist Government. In Yan'an, Jiang Qing caught the
attention of Mao and married him in 1938. She had played a
peripheral role in the government, but ever since the start of the
Cultural Revolution, she took center stage in the political
campaign, persecuting many officials and professionals in the
literary and performance fields. She became a controlling force in
cultural events. Madam Mao set up the village in Hebei as her
showcase. Peasants in this village wrote poems in praise of Mao
and sang songs from the "eight model operas" handpicked by
Madam Mao. For more than a decade, these "model operas" with
modern, revolutionary themes, were the only shows performed on
stage throughout the country.

When the call to learn from this Little Jin Village in Hebei
reached our school, Wu's eyes sparkled with excitement. Wu was
a good singer. She immediately put her talent to use. She selected
a group of students for a choir, and appointed Ma and Du as the
male and female soloists. We started with "Odes to Jin Xunhua."
Jin was an educated youth from Shanghai who went to the
countryside in the Heilongjiang Province. In a severe flood, Jin
jumped into the swirling river in an attempt to save a tree log. "I
must protect the state property," he shouted. The roaring water
swallowed him instantly and he drowned. His act was praised as
noble and he became a national hero. A long poem was written in
his honor, and we sang it to hail the spirit of self-sacrifice.

Then Wu led us to perform the Long March Series of
Songs. The Long March in the 1930s was regarded as the
historical event that preserved the lifeline of the Communist
Army. The songs were a tribute to their heroic acts and spirit.

"Boundless snow, and endless plain;
The highland is cold, the supply is cut short.
The Red Army soldiers are made of steel and iron,
Thoroughly tempered, they fear none.
Snow-covered mountains bent to their arrival,
Grass and mud became the blankets of their camping
ground.
Piercing wind and rain hardened their bones,
Weeds and hunger strengthened their wills.
Officials and soldiers shared weal and woe,
Revolutionary ideals were held above all."

A series of ten songs chronicled the key events on the Long March, showcasing the unimaginable challenges faced by the Red Army and their extraordinary persistence. We rehearsed the songs again and again until we were able to recite all the lyrics. We were as touched by the power of the words as by the bravery of the Red Army. A poetic monologue between each song provided the background information and set the transition from one episode to the next. Ma and Du took turns reciting the monologue. To memorize the long narrative, Wu encouraged them to skip classes to practice. We took the performance seriously.

Our hard work paid off. Our performance was recognized as the best in school, and Wu was honored as one of the school's model teachers. We found ourselves the center of attention. Other teachers in our school came to sit in Wu's class and watch our performance. Then, principals of other elementary and middle schools came as well, learning from our success at carrying out the political campaign.

I had continued to practice table tennis at the city's training center after entering middle school, but with so many rehearsals and meetings under Wu's leadership, I found it impossible to keep up with the daily practice. Wu often kept us in school long after students in other classes went home. I couldn't excuse myself all the time from class activities. I decided to quit the table tennis team and devote myself to our class activities. I felt guilty facing Coach Li's disappointed look. I had practiced table tennis on a daily basis for nearly five years and had become a good player. Li was reluctant to let me go, but he understood the political pressure. To his credit, Li allowed me to keep my paddle and uniform as souvenirs. "Practice when you can," he said, bidding me farewell. I nodded. I left the center with a mixed feeling of regret and anticipation.

I threw myself into Wu's activities. Before the end of our freshman year, Li, a tall, hard-working boy and I became the first students in our class to be admitted into the Communist Youth League. I felt honored. With three Youth League members in our class, we formed a branch committee, with Yang as secretary. We set out to organize students to participate in more political studies, including reading works of Marx, Engels, Lenin, Stalin, and Mao. We required each student to write commentaries on their readings and explore means to apply these socialist theories. We didn't understand much of our reading materials, but we pressed on.

4

In 1973, a young man named Zhang Tiesheng wrote a letter on the back of his examination paper, criticizing those who had spent time studying while people like him had dedicated themselves to farm work. He condemned academic tests as "a return to the old ways that were designed to keep peasants and workers out of college." His exam paper was otherwise blank. *The Liaoning Daily*, the official newspaper of the Liaoning Province, published his letter with an editorial titled "A Thought-Provoking Answer." Zhang was immediately hailed as a "go-against-the-tide" hero. Not only was he admitted into college, but also accepted as a Communist Party member.

Similarly, Huang, a fifth grader in Beijing, wrote to a newspaper to denounce her teachers, calling their authority over students "repressive." She received similar attention and was praised as a young heroine. Another girl, aged twelve, went even further. She was from a middle school in a commune in the Henan Province. She did poorly on her English examination. Unwilling to accept her failure, she wrote a "poem" on the back of her test: "I am a Chinese, why should I learn a foreign tongue? Without ABCD, a successor of revolution I can still be. Carry on the revolution and bury the imperialists, revisionists and reactionaries." After being criticized in school for her attitude, she jumped into a river and killed herself. A peasant committee was sent to the school to take over its management. The girl was seen as a victim of the resurgence of the old education system and a heroine for fighting against it, even sacrificing her own life.

The curriculum at our school changed frequently, based on the political barometer at the time. Foreign language was a subject that was prone to such changes, as reflected in our teacher Mr. Han. Han had been trained to teach Russian when the Soviet Union was regarded as China's "big brother." In the 1950s, Russia provided China with financial support and technical know-how to many large industrial projects, but Stalin never trusted Mao and the two countries' relationship deteriorated as Mao wanted to establish himself as a superior leader in the socialist countries. In 1960, Russia withdrew its financial support and all the technicians working in China. By 1969, the conflicts between the two countries escalated to battles at the borders. Russia became China's enemy and Russian was dropped from school curriculum. English was offered instead, which created a severe shortage of English teachers. Han, already in his fifties, was learning and teaching English at the same time. Han was an awkward looking man. He was tall and seemed as if he didn't know what to do with his long limbs and thin body. Most of the students didn't take him seriously and ignored him in class. Han spoke English with a heavy "r" twisting in his mouth as if he was speaking Russian. He seldom asked students questions. As soon as the bell rang, he put the textbook under his arm and quietly walked out. The open denunciation of English study made his class even more chaotic.

I, however, liked to study English. Ping had exposed me to the alphabet when I was a child. I did well. But to my disappointment, English was dropped from our curriculum not long after the country girl's suicide.

As I exerted my utmost efforts in school to become an outstanding student, my older siblings went through a transitional period in their lives as well. After he left for the countryside in 1970, Binbin spent a year in a youth center, together with his friends Yongbing and Dongsheng. By then, there was no illusion left for the so-called reeducation in the countryside. The three of them stuck together, like they had done in the most turbulent years of the Cultural Revolution. They helped one another working in the fields and didn't care much for the political studies. They didn't like the peasants either. They were convinced there was not much to learn from them. The village leader considered the three troublesome, but couldn't manage them. In about a year, Yongbing left for the army, Dongsheng became a driver back in Baicheng, and Binbin, after Father's further banishment to Wanbao, moved to the same town. He became a worker at a small factory and lived close to Father, visiting him from time to time. In 1973, having fulfilled the two-year work requirement, Binbin applied for college and passed the appraisal by his coworkers and the Revolution Committee at the factory. He went to study in Changchun, the city where he had spent his early childhood.

Ping worked at the Agricultural College until 1974. Then she left for college as well. She studied mechanical engineering at a college in Harbin, capital of the Heilongjiang Province. Students had no choice for their major. Once their applications were accepted by colleges, they were assigned to different departments. The requirement for the students, as for everyone else, was to listen to the Party. The motto that "The Party's wishes are our desires" was carried out at every level. The assigned major set the stage for Ping to become an engineer.

My sisters and brother were the lucky ones who had the opportunities to attend college, but the quality of college education for these "worker-peasant-soldier students" was poor. Their already condensed three-year curriculum was further eroded with numerous political activities, physical labor, and military training. After 1977, when the college entrance examination was restored and the four-year formal program resumed, the education received by those "worker-peasant-soldier students" was considered inferior. Many of them had to take make-up courses or go to graduate school to rid themselves of the "worker-peasant-soldier" label.

Chapter Nineteen

Second Thoughts

1

When Deng Xiaoping resumed his top-level position in the Central Government in 1975, China embarked on the road to restoration. Building the country's economy became the top priority, and individual competence was more important than classification of family background. Father, who had rarely made any comments on the endless political campaigns, cheered for Deng's resurrection. "Deng is the man who can save the country," he said, making a toast over dinner.

With the overall atmosphere in the country changing, attention shifted to academic studies at school as well. Father, who had never finished middle school, always emphasized the importance of schooling. I listened to him. I also listened to my siblings. Ping and Binbin were both in college in 1975, studying hard to catch up on their lessons, especially Binbin who had hardly learned anything in middle school. We frequently wrote each other letters. I knew they were frustrated by the long time they spent working at college farms or going through military training. They wrote to me, urging me to focus on my studies.

In one letter, Binbin wrote: "Don't be swept away by political campaigns. Your duty as a student is to study."

His words spelled out the thought that was lingering in my mind, but never dared to be expressed. He gave me the direction I needed.

"Our golden years were wasted," Ping wrote in one of her letters. "Don't stumble into the same trap!" She underlined the sentence to emphasize her point. "I'm having a tough time studying English," she continued. "You should keep at it now. It's much easier to learn a foreign language when you are younger."

I was interested in English and found her advice encouraging and timely. The Roman alphabet system, from pronunciation to word composition, was very intriguing to me. The Chinese often referred to Westerners as "big nose." I had never met one my life, but we saw many short documentary newsreels, usually five to ten minutes long, shown before the start of a feature film. Many of them showed meetings between Chinese top officials and visiting dignitaries from foreign countries. Sitting behind them were interpreters. I was always fascinated by their quick wit and the function they played in communication. Even the way they carried themselves impressed me. I dreamed of becoming an interpreter someday.

I put more effort into my English studies, but when the middle school student from Henan condemned the study of foreign language and committed suicide, English was dropped from our curriculum. I was disappointed, but I continued on my own.

Binbin had left behind a few records of English lessons and a thick textbook titled English 900. I dusted off the old record player and started from the beginning. "I'm a teacher. You are a student..." the clear voice of a foreign instructor speaking with a heavy British accent echoed in my room. I repeated every expression. A radio station in Changchun also offered English lessons. The half hour broadcast started at five thirty each morning. Since I was no longer practicing table tennis, I spent my early morning in front of Father's beat up old radio and listened. One of the two knobs was missing, and I had to use a handkerchief to hold the bare stick for fine tuning. The long distance from Changchun provided very poor reception. Sometimes I had to press my ear against the speaker to catch the words out of the overwhelming noise. Du learned of my endeavors and joined me. The reception on her radio was even worse than mine, but after a couple of weeks, she dropped out. It was difficult to get up at five and be over at my place by five thirty. Besides, there was a sense of uneasiness about our effort since school no longer offered the subject. But I persisted.

Word leaked out in school, however, and Wu learned of my morning ritual. One day, Wu criticized the surge of bourgeois tendency among "a selected few" students in our class.

"They worry more about what to wear than what was going on in their minds," she said. She scanned the classroom with a disdainful look. "I suggest they do some serious self-reflection and get rid of the tendency before it's too late." Wu rarely criticized anyone directly. The term "they" effectively separated those who had problems from the rest of "us," and her method was very effective, since no one in our class wanted to be "them."

Then Wu changed the subject. "I'm also aware that someone in our class is pursuing a forbidden subject," she said. "To me, it indicates an interest in pursuing a bourgeois lifestyle." She paused, letting her words sink in. "Let me warn you: Worshiping anything foreign is dangerous." She threw a glance in my direction. "Stop it now. Stop studying English before your mind is polluted!" She raised her voice.

Wu didn't mention my name, but everyone knew to whom she referred. My face burned and my heart pounded. This was a serious denouncement from Wu. I had brushed shoulders with her before, but she had never exposed me in the open. I leaned forward, pressing my chest against the desk for support. It was hard to keep my composure. I was fully aware of the stares from the other students. I hated Wu for putting me on the spot. Without looking up, I could tell Wu's eyes were on me. I clenched my hands in my drawer and accidentally touched the notepad that had my scribbles of English. I wondered if someone had seen it and reported to Wu or if Wu had checked my drawer and found it herself. I realized I could no longer bring anything linked to English study to school. Wu's warning and scorn didn't stop me. I was more cautious, but I continued, supported by the words of my older siblings.

The shift of attention from politics to academic studies brought me relief. The majority of students in our class began making more efforts in their studies, but for many, catching up—especially on subjects such as math, physics, and chemistry—was difficult. Seeing this, I teamed up with Liu, our study representative, to help them. Liu, one of the tallest girls in our class, was the daughter of a college professor. She was smart and eloquent. Together, we selected a group of students who were lagging behind and kept them after school for tutoring. We helped them with their homework and reviewed materials we had learned before. Liu was a natural teacher. When she noticed an issue that more than one student had a problem with, she would walk up to the blackboard in the front and explain the concept to the entire group in detail. I worked tirelessly, going from one student to another. In the process of helping others, we both learned more. We enjoyed the mission we gave ourselves. Wu left us alone as long as we didn't interfere with the other activities she organized. We kept the program going for a semester, but when Deng Xiaoping was purged by Mao from office for the second time toward the end of 1975, we had to drop the program. A strong political campaign against Deng, which was called "the Anti-Right-Wing Revival" movement took over everything else. Once again Wu plunged us into denunciation and slogan shouting.

One day I returned from school to find Father sitting at his desk. A few layers of newspapers spread before him. From the cigarette ashes accumulated in his ashtray I could tell he had been there for a while. He didn't want to be disturbed, saying he had to give a speech criticizing Deng at a large meeting the following day. I tiptoed away but observed him from the hallway. He was deep in thought, and the notepad in front of him was blank. Father had always admired Deng. He had been enthusiastic about Deng's return not that long ago and had pushed hard to carry out Deng's policy on education. It dawned on me that Father was reluctant to denounce Deng, but had no choice. When I brought him a cup of tea later in the evening, I saw he had pasted a few excerpts cut out of newspaper articles to his notepad. He didn't even bother to copy the paragraphs to the pad in his own handwriting. Cigarette butts piled up in his ashtray; he still had one between his fingers. Father took a deep draw and slowly exhaled. A gray cloud surrounded him. I couldn't see his facial expression in the dim light. I realized Father, who had always appeared assertive and positive, was torn and unsettled. He was in a dilemma, struggling between his belief and respect for Deng, and his political obligation to criticize him in public. I felt his pain and became aware of my own resentment against these endless political movements.

2

My view on Mrs. Wu started to change. My admiration for her enthusiasm and strength was replaced by my doubt of her integrity and motivation.

As was the custom, students often visited their teachers at their homes, especially their homeroom teachers, as a show of respect. We paid our due visits to Wu. Something I saw during these visits started to bother me. A couple of boys from our class seemed to spend most of their after school hours at Wu's home. They were both quiet, and somewhat mediocre in their studies, but they were physically strong. Whenever I visited Wu, I found them there, helping Wu with her household chores or playing with Wu's small children. Once I saw them arrive with a cartload of coal, with one drawing the cart from the front and the other pushing from behind. Apparently they did Wu a favor by fetching her allocated coal from the supply center. Their faces and hands were covered with black dust. They grinned when they saw me, their teeth whiter in contrast to their dark faces and lips. Each of them scooped a ladle of water from the vat and gulped it down in one go. I felt Wu was taking advantage of them. Soon afterward, I noticed one of the two boys started giving Wu a ride to school on the back of his bicycle every day. Wu seemed to be proud that she had such loyal support from her students. She grinned and waved when she passed other students on her way. I was disturbed. Du, Liu, and a few other students expressed their distaste for Wu's action as well.

Wu was a complicated person, and I found it hard to integrate her various dimensions into one person. On the one hand, she was smart and driven. She was capable of organizing all the activities that got everyone in our class involved and was the driving force to get our class recognized as the "model" for the entire school. Her talent in music and singing led us to numerous performances. Despite the propaganda nature of the shows, we learned to sing, and three or four students learned to play flute or erhu, a traditional Chinese instrument. On the other hand, she was extremely aggressive in her pursuit. She never provided guidance for our studies. All her efforts were political. Her relentless push for us to outperform other classes created an unspoken tension between her and many students, including me. I feared her and resented her at the same time. She was the authoritative figure we faced on a daily basis.

There was another side of Wu, however, that was humane and triggered sympathy. Wu had three young children, a boy and two girls. She appeared to be sweet and patient with them. Her husband, an art teacher at another middle school, sometimes came to our class to help her direct our rehearsals. He acted like a professional and coached us in staging monologues, singing and dancing. He was thin and handsome. We adored him, and he was patient with us, but he was rude to Wu sometimes.

Occasionally, Wu arrived in school with her face and arms covered in black and blue. The first time it happened, we were shocked. A couple of students asked if she was all right. We thought she must have had an accident of some sort. Wu's answer was cold and terse. She looked so upset that we tiptoed around her. The next time it happened, we whispered among ourselves, guessing what might have happened, but no one raised any questions. Wu was quiet for a couple of days. Then, she would bounce back and resume her controlling role. Her vulnerability remained a mystery to us.

I began to resist Wu, in a subtle and silent manner. When we first started school, Wu told us all to keep a diary and write regular self-reflection reports. To ensure that everyone would carry out the task, she appointed me to check the diary entries of my classmates on a weekly basis. I felt ambivalent about this. Personal diaries had never been respected in China. During the chaos of the Cultural Revolution, confiscation of personal journals was a common practice, and what had been written privately was often exposed to the public and used against the writer. We all knew of a personal diary's potential danger, but we obeyed Wu. We didn't have a choice, but to openly require turning in the diaries was a different matter. How could we put down our true feelings when we knew what we wrote could be used against us? Sure enough, as I flipped through the pages, I saw that some jotted down events that happened during the day; some recorded daily trivialities that bore no connection to their opinions; and others used the entries to make progressive statements, hoping to score a few points for their appraisal.

Wu was very strict about collecting the diaries for inspection. If anyone stated that he had left his diary at home, Wu didn't hesitate for a second to send the student home to fetch it. It didn't matter that the student would end up missing a class by running back and forth. Wu wouldn't accept any excuses. Once I had to go home to retrieve mine in the middle of her Chinese class. By the time I returned, the 45-minute class was over. I loathed the practice and was reluctant to carry out her instructions. When Wu was engaged in other activities and left the diary inspection completely to me, I let it go. Wu soon noticed my reluctance and took action. Without notifying me, she ordered a group of students to turn in their diaries to me, all at once. I watched as notebooks piled up on the narrow space of my desk. Wu made it clear that we should keep our minds pure with revolutionary ideas. "There should be nothing to hide from others. If you are reluctant to have your dairy checked, that means you have something bad going on in your mind," Wu declared, looking at us sternly. "No matter what it is, it should be purged from your thoughts. Like removing a tumor."

I was cautious about my entries. My passive resistance to her request was cause for concern. When the inspection of diaries became a regular activity and students no longer made the entries personal, I learned to go straight to the last page and make a 'checked' mark. I put a date beside it, in case Wu would check on me. She did randomly select a few to take a look for herself. When she found problematic issues, Wu would mention them to the entire class, requesting us to conduct deeper self-reflection and get rid of these unhealthy ideas.

One day, Father told me of an encounter with Wu. The incident further lowered my opinion of her. It took place at a citywide education conference, which was held in the largest auditorium in town. I knew the auditorium well. We often went there to watch movies. Whenever there were feature films showed in town, our school would block-book entire screenings for the students. We paid for our own tickets, but we went to the show in one group. Each time, we gathered on the playground in school and then marched, class after class, to the auditorium, singing songs along the way. Once inside, students in each class were seated in a designated area. Waves of songs continued as we waited for all the students to take their seats. A music teacher stood on the stage, asking one group to sing, and then the other, by class, or grade, before the show started. It was a major event in our school life and we looked forward to it.

Father's mention of Mrs. Wu at such a large setting immediately caught my attention.

"Did she approach you at the meeting?" I asked, wondering what Wu could possibly do

"Oh, yes. Teacher Wu is quite a character," Father said.

Seeing I was eager to hear the details, Father continued: "During our conference at the auditorium today, she came up to me on the stage and introduced herself. 'Governor Hou,' she said, 'I'm Jian's homeroom teacher.' There were a dozen officials sitting on the platform, and hundreds of people in the audience. Mrs. Wu was certainly not shy." Father laughed.

The attendees of the meeting included principals, administrators and teachers' representatives from all the schools in town. I refrained from making any comment, but I was appalled. Why did she take such an extraordinary step to meet with Father in this manner? I wondered. Getting on the raised stage would expose her in full view of the audience. Did she want the people, especially our school principal and the other administrators to see she was well connected? Did she want to give the impression that she had some political clout? What else could have prompted her to do so? Despite her status as a model teacher, Wu had not been admitted to the Communist Party. Was she trying to push the case? Many questions flashed through my mind. I was not certain what her intention was, but I began to see her as an ambitious opportunist.

3

Ever since 1966 when the Cultural Revolution started, the destination for middle school graduates was the countryside. Those who joined the army were seen as lucky. In addition to avoid the fate of "fixing the earth" in the countryside, the army had a special allure. Our generation had been brought up admiring soldiers, from heroes like Wang Cheng who died on the battlefield, to Lei Feng, the "selfless servant to the people." Joining the army was a glorious and trendy choice. I watched with admiration as several older children in the Compound put on their grass green uniform and left. I knew, however, Father would not use his relationship with the commanders in the military for me, so I kept my longing to myself.

One day, the Political Commissar of the army stationed in Baicheng came to see Father at home. As I served tea to him, he asked how old I was.

"Fifteen," I said.

"That is a good age," he responded, nodding his head. He was a man in his mid-fifties. He was friendly and had a booming voice.

"Would you like to join the army?" he asked, a big smile crossing his face.

"Why, yes, of course!" It took me a moment to comprehend what he was saying. Once the question hit home, I nearly lost my composure. "Very much so!" I raised my voice.

I was so overcome with excitement that I spilled his tea on the table. I felt like shouting. I wanted to call Father to discuss the matter right there and then. I was so overjoyed that my hands were shaking. He patted me on my shoulder and promised he'd talk with my father.

I left the room feeling elated. I kept the door slightly ajar so I could hear their conversation. Father had gone to his bedroom to look for a document. I waited anxiously for his return. I closed my eyes and wished Father would let me go. I wanted to be away from Baicheng—to be in a place where no one would judge me as a Governor's daughter, and to be away from Mrs. Wu. Besides, seeing what my older siblings had gone through, I had no desire to go to the countryside upon my graduation.

I heard the Commissar's cheerful voice when Father returned to the room.

"Governor Hou," he said. "I didn't know you had a teenage daughter. Fifteen is the perfect age to join the army." Getting no response from Father, he continued: "I can take care of her. At her age, she doesn't have to go to the regular units. We have openings for younger girls to be phone operators, or if she wants, she can join our song and dance ensemble. She is a good looking girl, and I am sure she can learn quickly."

The song and dance ensemble was a special unit in the army. It consisted of handsome young men and women who toured the troops with shows to "convey greetings and appreciation" for the soldiers.

The Commissar sounded casual, but full of confidence. He seemed certain that my father would take his offer as a favor. I locked my hands in front of my chest and silently begged Father to say yes.

"You mean Jian?" Father's voice sounded absent-minded. I peeped in and saw Father flipping through the documents he held in his hands. He didn't seem to pay any attention to what the Commissar was saying.

"Thank you for your consideration," he said, eventually lifting his eyes to look at him. "Jian is still in school. She should complete her studies first." With that, he changed the subject.

"You know, my door is open if you change your mind," the Commissar said. Then, the conversation turned back to work,

I stomped into the kitchen and slammed the teapot heavily on the stove. Tears rolled down my face. What a golden opportunity! But

I knew Father had always been proud to be an official of integrity. He would not allow me to join the army through the back door. Besides, a good education had always been important to him. I should have known better.

"Father, please," I pleaded in spite of myself. I couldn't bear to see the opportunity slip away. "Several students from my school have left for the army. I want to go, too! Please," I begged.

"Your task right now is to study," Father said in a firm voice. He left no room for arguments.

I cried for a week. Father repeated the same remarks over and over again. "Education is very important. You don't realize how lucky you are. Concentrate on your studies and get all the other fancy ideas out of your mind." His tone sounded more and more unyielding as my standoff continued. He said one of his greatest regrets in life was not having the opportunity to receive a better education, but I was stubborn. I persisted. Mother stayed out of it. I didn't know if it was because Father had made his decision and she didn't want to contradict him, or because she agreed with him. Nainai had passed away a year before, leaving me with no ally. I eventually stopped crying, realizing my effort would not get me anywhere. Father's word was final.

The subject was never brought up again. It would take me more than two years to appreciate Father's unbending integrity and foresight. When the college entrance examination was resumed, I became the first and only beneficiary of the new policy in our family. I was very grateful that I didn't go to the army. Those who quit school earlier for the army didn't acquire enough knowledge to pass the exam. They would miss the opportunity for further education.

"Knowledge is power. No one can take that away from you," Father said when I thanked him for making me stay in school.

4

I started pulling back from Wu. I visited her less. When I felt compelled to show my face at her door, I teamed up with a couple of other girls to go together. I dreaded the expected visits and regretted that I had abandoned my table tennis practice. I longed for a way to do something more constructive, something that would enable me to stay away from Wu.

One day, Wu didn't show up at school. The homeroom teacher in the class next to us filled in for her. He said Mrs. Wu was sick and he would be available for us during her absence. We felt obligated to visit Wu. After school, I teamed up with two girls and headed toward Wu's home. It was not far away from school, a typical two-room apartment in a single-story brick building, with a large Kang in the bedroom. As we approached her home, we found ten or so students from our class were standing in the yard, with boys in one group, and girls in the other. They were whispering among themselves. Wu was lying in bed, we learned, but she covered herself completely under bedding and refused to speak to any of us. Two girls, who had arrived first, murmured that when they got there, Wu was crying.

"She is black and blue all over again," one of them said.

We didn't go in, but didn't leave either. As we were hesitating about what to do, Wu's husband returned. His face was gloomy and he was not pleased to see us. Wu's youngest son was crying at the door, and he yelled at him to stop. We were alarmed by his temper.

"You can go home now," he said to us. "I'm sure your teacher will be well enough to show up at school tomorrow."

We quickly took leave.

The following day, Wu did show up at school. She was quiet and timid. She casually put a scarf around her head, but the black and blue marks were still visible. The truth soon leaked out. Wu was beaten by her husband. We were astonished. How could a strong person like her be abused by her husband? But her vulnerability struck a sympathetic chord in our heart.

Wu said nothing about her personal life. A couple of days later, when the visible signs on her face faded out, and she regained her strength and spirit, the old dominating Wu resurfaced. Her sharp voice of criticism echoed in our classroom again.

There was a photo of our class taken in 1976. A total of eighty-three students all dressed in buttoned up attire, with boys in Mao suits and girls in dark-colored or square-patterned tops. Only three girls were wearing flowery blouses over their cotton-padded jackets. Everyone looked serious. Wu tied her hair into two pigtails and was wearing a plain, dark top and a pair of baggy pants. She looked more rustic than tyrannical and manipulative. Yet, all the awards we had won bore witness to the recognition we had received. Prominently displayed in the laps of students in the front row were ten award certificates—for our outstanding performances in sports, political campaigns, singing, and overall excellence. I find it hard to link these passive faces to the vigorous actions that led to such recognition.

When English was offered in school again, only a boy named Li and I paid much attention. No one else bothered to answer Mr. Han's questions. Wu's criticism of studying foreign languages still lingered in the minds of many. The overall attitude toward English study was disinterest, and a notion prevailed that those who wanted to study English must have a tendency to "fawn on foreigners." Eventually Li succumbed to the pressure and gave up. To avoid being called by Han to answer a question that he would no longer be able to give, Li sometimes hid himself under his desk during a class. Han looked around. He wanted to have someone other than me, the single volunteer, to answer some questions. Having finished the radio lecture series on English, I was way ahead of everyone else in my class. I was Mr. Han's favorite student.

In early 1977, I learned that the city was about to set up a spare-time military sports training center for school children. The center would be at the same location where I used to play table tennis, and would start with two teams: one for shooting and the other for airplane models. The word airplane immediately caught my attention. I remembered the first time I saw a fast moving object in the sky when I was a child and someone told me it was an airplane. I looked up and saw the plane reaching higher and higher in the air, leaving a thin, white vapor trail. I stared at the plane in awe of the free and fascinating world above that was beyond my reach. Ever since, whenever I heard someone shout: "Look, an airplane!" I'd stop in my tracks and look up at the fast moving plane until my neck hurt. Sometimes there were two or three of them flying side by side. They were all military jets.

Flying airplane models, while incomparable to taking an actual flight in the sky, was as close as I could get to explore the world of aviation and open sky. I was excited and wanted to join the airplane team. Besides, it was also a good opportunity to get away from Wu and her endless political activities.

Wu told us our class, as a model in school, could recommend one student for a team. I became restless. After much thinking, I approached Wu and expressed my desire to apply for the airplane model team.

Wu said it was okay with her if I wanted to join, but she would run it by the class committee.

Two days later, Wu held a meeting with all the student leaders in our class. She explained the situation and stated that one of us could join a team. The classroom became deadly quiet. Apparently, most of the students, if not everyone, wanted to go. Unlike other meetings in which we had heated discussions, no one said a word. I found the atmosphere stifling and was worried that Wu was playing games with me. After what seemed an unbearably long time, I raised my hand.

"I'd like to go," I heard myself saying, my voice quivering. "I'm familiar with the training center," I continued, clearing my throat. "I practiced table tennis there before and would love to go back to be trained in another sport." My voice trailed off. I bit my lower lip and waited. I could hardly believe I blurted it out just like that. I must have been desperate. I knew I was selfish in doing so and was embarrassed. The silence continued in the room. I could hear the beating of my heart.

"Well, if no one has any objection, it's all right with me," Wu said. She threw a glance over the group. Seeing no response from anyone, she ended the meeting. The matter was decided. The awkward silence stayed with me for days. Yang would later criticize me for being selfish at our year-end review meeting. I bowed my head and humbly accepted her criticism, but I didn't regret my action.

I joined the airplane model team, a group of two girls and five boys. I was relieved that I could get out of our classroom with a legitimate reason as the last bell rang in the afternoon. I spent two to three hours each day at the center, making airplane models with balsa wood and carved propellers, as if I were a carpenter. We made everything from scratch from a blueprint. Mr. Lan, our coach, was a very pleasant and caring person. He was chubby and his clothing always appeared ill-fitted, but he didn't seem to care. He was in his late thirties, but still single. A broad smile showed on his face whenever he was pleased with our work. I was fascinated with the plane models and learned eagerly. Most of the team members worked on gliders, but Lan assigned a boy and me to work on a model with a small motor. Two strings attached to the model controlled the maneuvering of the flight. When the weather was nice, Lan showed the two of us how to fly the model in the stillness of the early morning. The high-speed motor and a hand-carved wood propeller made a roaring sound. It was odd that no one complained about the noise.

I felt lucky that another window had opened in my life. It provided me with fresh air and relieved me from the endless political campaigns I was no longer interested in.

Chapter Twenty

Out of Baicheng

1

In 1977, the government restored the regular four-year college education system and the comprehensive college entrance exam. The reinstatement of this policy meant a change of fate for millions, especially the "educated youth," who had been laboring in the countryside or factories for nearly a decade. For the first time since the start of the Cultural Revolution, college applicants were able to take the entrance exam without having to pass a political evaluation or meeting the minimum two-year work requirement. Test scores were once again the sole criterion for admission.

November 1977 marked the start of the first exam. Even though each province had its own version of the tests, it was held at the same time all across the nation, covering the same subjects. Nearly six million young men and women took the exams. Competition was fierce, and the admission ratio for the first year was a steep twenty-nine to one. The lucky ones who passed the tests found themselves starting college in January 1978. The nation couldn't wait another half a year to train its youth.

This change also meant that middle school seniors were eligible to take the exam the following year, scheduled in July 1978, less than eight months after the first one, with entrance to college in October. This time the test was standardized across the country. The seniors at our school scrambled to get themselves ready, facing a daunting challenge. Years of political movements and neglected schoolwork had left them poorly prepared. They had watched the first college entrance exams anxiously.

Afterward, they moved quickly to obtain the tests from every province, nearly thirty in total. They pored over them, trying to ensure their success.

A shakeup took place in our school. Awakened from a long political nightmare, our school administrators worked enthusiastically. They reorganized the senior classes and set up academic competitions on various subjects to push the students to study harder. The reactions from the seniors, however, were mixed. While a small number were anxious to have a jump start, the majority were overwhelmed. Faced with this situation, the school put the focus on those who had the potential to succeed. Advanced classes for science and liberal arts were set up. Students in these two classes received dedicated help from the best teachers. They had eight months to make up for their education deficits. Electrical lines were wired to their classrooms, and tutorial sessions extended late into the evenings. Even weekends became regular school days.

Meanwhile, our school also stepped up its management of us juniors. This time, the main goal of our studies was defined for the short term—to pass the college entrance exam. Political movements and ideological campaigns were put aside and students eagerly shifted their focus. Mischief in class that had been ignored before was no longer tolerated. The school administration even broke up a class in our grade to separate a group of troublemakers. Eight students were allocated to our class, among them, De Rong and Zhi Qiang, two brilliant young men who would later bring honor to Mrs. Wu. The other newcomers dared not attempt to make any waves in our class. Wu's heavy hand and our conditioned conformity left them no room to step out of line. Besides, the change had turned former heroes such as the "blank-paper" Zhang Tiesheng into fools. For the first time in our lives, academic studies were the top priority.

As we became more engrossed, many students sought the help of teachers who had college degrees and rich teaching experiences. We were requested to consider our focused area of study in college—majoring in science or liberal arts. We would be divided into two groups in our senior year. The subjects offered to each group were determined by the upcoming exam. There were no elective courses, and fewer students chose liberal arts. Years of political movements had taught us to stay away from potentially dangerous areas involving self-expression. Majoring in science meant a future in a technical or research field, a much safer bet.

The exciting changes compelled me to study hard, especially English, my favorite subject. I solicited the help of Mr. Wang, one of the best English teachers in our school. Although his teaching responsibility didn't cover our class, Wang was most willing to help. He lived on campus in a tiny apartment with his wife and two small children. I often stopped by during school days or weekends, and he was always patient and helpful, glad to finally have a serious student.

Right after the winter break in early 1978, De Rong and Zhi Qiang excelled in a school-wide competition in physics. They jumped a grade and joined the seniors in their preparation for the college entrance exam. Mrs. Wu beamed with pride since the two star performers were from her class. It didn't matter that they had joined only three months before. Mr. Han, my Russian-turned-English teacher, suggested I apply for the impending exam as well, majoring in English. He felt my English was good enough to pass the test, but I dismissed the idea without a second thought. I was preoccupied with something else.

2

I had been on the airplane model team for more than a year. The first competition for airplane models in the Jilin Province was to take place in the spring of 1978. I wanted to compete. I had made great progress building and flying my motorized models. Using a handlebar, I was able to manipulate the strings and make my model fly in various patterns. I crashed a couple of balsa wood planes when the motor choked in mid air. The challenge lifted me as if I had wings.

When the agenda for the competition was displayed, however, I was disappointed. No event allowed for motorized models, which were regarded as too advanced for the new sport. But that did not deter me. With the help of Coach Lan, I shifted to fly a glider. The model he assigned me to handle had a slender body and two long wings. Compared to a motorized model, a glider was much easier to fly. No maneuvering was involved. All that one needed to do was keep the glider aloft as long as possible.

Twenty days before the competition, all the team members were excused from regular school. We went to an old pilot training center in the suburb for intensive preparation. Before long, I realized it was where my sister Ping had studied for several months before the Cultural Revolution. It was still not in operation.

I made two glider models with meticulous accuracy from a specified blueprint. One was to be used for the competition, the other as a backup. I was immersed in the craft and practice, ensuring the balance and smooth surface of the gliders, to reduce air resistance. With a thin layer of coating, they glistened smartly under the sun. Coach Lan was so pleased with my progress that he rewarded me with a specially arranged ride on a real glider.

On a beautiful spring day, I sat on a big glider with an instructor by my side. A heavy-duty cable propelled by a motor clanked and rolled, pulling the glider forward. I was very nervous and tightly gripped the wooden bar in front of me. The glider moved faster and faster, then suddenly left the ground and soared into the sky. The arched shield in front of me hardly blocked the strong winds. Streams of tears spread across my face as we picked up speed.

"Are you all right?" the instructor asked, seeing me wipe away tears.

"Yes!" I shouted. I was not certain whether my flood of tears was caused by the wind or my excitement. I grinned at him, letting him know that I was not afraid.

As the glider reached its peak, the instructor released the cable. All of a sudden, the violent shaking stopped. Then, after a sudden jolt and drop, the glider stabilized. We started gliding smoothly, high above the ground.

For the first time in my life, I was up in the sky, living my childhood dream. In front of me, extending into the horizon, were endless grass meadows. Beyond the runway and the training center were rows of farmland, as far as my eyes could see. It was a moment of wonder. A moment of complete freedom.

I took a deep breath. I could hear the cheering of my teammates. The land shifted back below me. The long, yellow grass waved elegantly in the breeze. I kept my eyes wide open despite the wind in my face. My thoughts turned to Ping. If it were not for the Cultural Revolution, she would have been a pilot. At the moment, I understood her eagerness to follow such an exciting career.

Time lost its proportion and eventually the glider touched down smoothly on the ground. I had relished each moment in the air. The grand view from high above not only exposed the vast landscape in front of my eyes, but also ignited my desire to explore the larger world.

When the competition started, I was very nervous. The top three winners of each event would be granted a ten-day trip to a summer camp in Beijing. Beijing! The capital of China! The city I had seen numerous times in newsreels. I wanted the success of my model glider to open the door for me to the outside world.

Two hours before my event, I conducted a last minute trial flight to make sure everything was in good shape. To my surprise, a strong current suddenly came and took my glider off-course. I ran after it as it flew faster, wishing I hadn't released the string attached to the tow hook. I watched in horror when it crashed into an electrical pole. Tears filled my eyes as I picked up the broken pieces. Coach Lan ran over.

"There is no time to do anything about it now," he said, his voice subdued. "Get your back-up model ready."

I nodded.

Each person had a chance to fly his or her model three times, and the sum of the cumulative gliding time, in the order of duration, decided the winners. My back-up model did well in the first two rounds, but in its final flight, it landed on the steep roof of the training center. It lay flat on the tiles like a dragonfly resting on the tip of a plant. It was at least twelve feet above ground. If it had the chance to fly its natural course, it would have easily lasted another thirty seconds in the air, a crucial period of time.

Coach Lan was with me during my event. His brilliant smile faded when my model settled on the roof.

"You did well earlier," he said, trying to comfort me. "You may still have a chance."

I did my best to maintain composure. In such a competitive event, thirty seconds was a long time. Unless others suffered a similar misfortune, I knew I didn't have a chance to win. I watched silently as Coach Lan climbed a ladder and retrieved my plane.

I was terribly disappointed.

3

Baicheng is located near Inner Mongolia and Russia. Since the border skirmishes with Russia in 1969, China had taken extensive measures against potential air raids by the Soviet Union. The call from the Central Government was to "dig deeper shelters and store more grain." The Baicheng Municipal Government established an ambitious plan to build air raid tunnels throughout the city. Every year, the government specified tunnel sections for middle schools, government agencies, and factories to dig. The backbreaking work was done manually, with spades and pickaxes. Each spring, when the ground thawed, large sections of the city streets were closed.

We dug open the ground and competed with one another to accomplish our task. We had to dig a ten-meter wide, five-meter deep trench to provide enough room to build the tunnel. Once we finished digging, construction workers took over where we left off. They set up wooden boards and metal bars and poured concrete into them, to create the floor and sidings, then sealed the whole structure with an arched roof. After the concrete dried, we moved mounds of dirt to cover the finished tunnel. For years, we took turns at the hard work, fulfilling our mission to defend the nation. Red flags flew to keep our spirits high, and loudspeakers wired to the nearby trees announced our progress, broadcasting stories of extraordinary achievements. Later, tar roads were paved over its top, leaving no trace of the tunnel underneath.

In addition to the miles of concrete tunnels, the underground shelters accommodated a city hall, thirty-one storage places, four stores, three clinics and other facilities. A special department in the Municipal Government maintained them. Years later, these underground constructions would become obsolete, and then obstacles to the future development of the city.

In order to set a good example for our peers, Yang and I always worked at the most challenging locations. As the tunnel deepened, we created layers of terraces, three feet wide and four feet high, to support one or two students. We lined up and moved the clay, gravel, and sand from the bottom to street level. We worked like a human conveyer belt. Most of the students worked on the ground level. They shoveled the heavy material way back to the side, making room for more dirt and gravel, creating a small hill in the process. The sticky clay covered our shovels with heavy mud, making the upswing more strenuous. Yang and I were the only female students working at the lower level. Our shirts were drenched with sweat, which dried up when we took a break, only to be soaked again as we resumed digging. Salt stains marked our dark shirts and pants. Many times I pushed myself so hard that I felt nauseated. It was not unusual for students to pass out on the site. Their dedication and hard work were immediately hailed as heroic over the loudspeakers.

That year, however, I discovered I could no longer work that hard. Building airplane models didn't make me physically strong. I was not in good shape. Two days into the digging, I felt on the verge of collapsing. I sweated easily and profusely. My face burned, and my legs felt like they would buckle at any moment, but my mind refused to give in. As usual, I took the leading role with Yang. I watched Yang out of the corner of my eye. She was competing with a boy, apparently proud of her endurance. My heart pounded and I gasped for air. I didn't want to pass out on the site, yet didn't know how to retreat without feeling guilty.

I took a break to use the outhouse. I noticed that the senior classes were not with us. They must have been busy with their preparation for the college entrance exam. I imagined De Rong and Zhi Qiang at their desks, studying hard. Mr. Han's suggestion to take the English test flashed through my mind. The college exam was in two months. If I could take the test, I believed, I would be rightfully excused from the work site.

Whenever we worked on large projects for an extended period of time, we kept a student or two behind to watch our classroom. Li was the girl in our class who always stayed behind. Despite being the tallest and biggest student among us, she suffered from various chronic diseases, including an irregular heartbeat and hyperthyroidism. I thought I could go back to school and join Li. While keeping the classroom clean, I could also prepare for the exam. I worried about failing the test, but decided to press on. As Mr. Han said: "You have nothing to lose."

I went to Mr. Gu, chief administrator of education at our school. I asked for permission to take the exam a year before my graduation. If I applied for an English major, I needed to take tests on history, geography, Chinese, English, and politics. Math was optional. I had not learned much in history or geography, but the school had put together enough review materials. Mr. Gu was impressed by my initiative and approved my request without hesitation, not aware of my intention to escape from the hard labor. With his approval, Wu sent me back to watch the classroom. I was relieved that she didn't voice any objection. I went back to school, only to learn that the feeling of relief was temporary. I was instantly buried under piles of books and review documents. It was not a review, for most of the information was brand new to me.

Every day, I went to our classroom early in the morning and left when it became too dark to study. The review materials were formatted mostly in question-and-answer style to cover questions that might come up in the exam. I first browsed through the readings on each subject, and then read them repeatedly to memorize as much information as I could.

When my fellow students returned to school a month later, I found it impossible to attend regular classes and prepare for the approaching exam at the same time. I obtained a special permit to study at home, with the promise that I would make up for the lessons I missed. My regular courses did not concern me. I had the whole summer to catch up, and at the moment I was single-mindedly engaged in review. The seniors had been tackling the questions and drills for six months. I had a total of eight weeks. I doubted that I could succeed, but I wanted to give it my best.

My parents initially encouraged me to study hard. As the exam drew closer, however, Mother urged me to slow down for my health. I had moved my morning wake-up alarm from five a.m. to four a.m., and at night, when the lights in all the other rooms were off, mine was still on, and would remain so till the wee hours of the morning. Many times, I fell asleep with my head lying on top of the paper pile, a big ink spot underneath my pen and saliva on my notepad. Mother came to check on me from time to time, helping me get into bed and turning off the light. I hardly woke up and couldn't tell the following morning if I had dreamed of her presence or if it had been real.

Soon, I found something to relieve the tension. I borrowed a rifle-length BB gun from a friend and loaded it with small lead pellets. During the day, I took down a window screen and set the gun up in position. When I heard sparrows chirping on a pine tree in our backyard, I aimed and pulled the trigger. In the late 1950s, sparrows were one of the "four evils" along with rats, flies, and mosquitoes, accused of eating too much grain. Chairman Mao declared war on them. Country and city folk, from adults to children, were organized to go after them. They smashed their nests and chased them around, drumming gongs or knocking on pots, to prevent them from landing. I heard stories from my older siblings about how sparrows dropped dead from the sky, exhausted by their continuous flight, and how worms, after their near extinction, flourished in the fields and devoured many grain plants. As it turned out, the war against sparrows had been waged on flawed intelligence. Chairman Mao later received reports that they hardly ate any grains at all, only during a few weeks in the fall, to supplement their usual diet of worms and insects. The sparrows were rehabilitated and removed from the list of the four evils. They were replaced by bedbugs. The war against the "four evils" waged on.

By the time I was preparing for my exam, sparrows were all over the place, on the tall branches of big poplar trees and singing side by side on long sections of electrical wires. At first, I was utterly amazed that I could hit a bird. I had never even touched a toy gun before. Perhaps there were so many of them that even if I had just fired into a tree, one would drop to the ground, but in due time, I got better and could actually aim at a sparrow in a tree, pull the trigger, and watch it drop like a rock from the sky.

Big Aunt, who continued to live with us after Nainai had passed away, shook her head as I ran to the back yard with excitement to pick up a bird, but she became my conspirator, as the sparrows accumulated in a basket by the door. She plucked their feathers as she did with chickens and cooked them for me. They were all bones except for the meat on the breasts, but they tasted delicious to me.

"They will give you the energy you need," she said.

There were certainly more sparrows than pork, which was strictly rationed.

The time came to take the college exam, with each subject lasting for more than two hours. For three days, we took the exam, two subjects a day, one in the morning, and the other in the afternoon. A question with multiple choices or blanks to fill in felt like a treat. Many topics required written essays. I moved my pen frantically, writing down whatever I deemed relevant. Many parents accompanied their children to the exam hall. They waited outside during the tests and eagerly provided their children with food and drink between test sessions.

"Was it difficult? Were you able to answer all the questions?" the parents asked. There was no such fuss over me. I went to the exam in the morning by myself, taking off on my bicycle shortly after my parents had left for work. Seeing me study so hard over the last few days, Father asked me to take it easy, but he praised me for my persistence. "You have the spirit of an ancient scholar," Father said. He quoted an ancient phrase dating back to imperial times: "Tou Xuan Liang, Zhui Ci Gu." It referred to how hard applicants, who prepared for the imperial court exam, had studied. To prevent themselves from falling asleep, they hung their pigtails to roof beams or poked needles into their flesh. My parents were amazed by my determination, but didn't seem to take my efforts to go to college too seriously.

When the exam was over, I had no clue how I had fared. I rushed back to school and started to make up for the classes I had missed. To my relief, we were soon sent to our school's farm to work in the cornfields for a week. I worked with my classmates side by side during the day, but at night, lying on the Kang, I heard the other girls' even breathing. I had a tough time falling asleep. I was excited and nervous as I waited for the exam result.

4

The extended period of exertion, lack of sleep, and anxiety finally got to me. Upon returning home from the farm, I came down with a high fever. Ever since I had entered middle school, my health had improved significantly. The five years of daily table tennis practice played a key role in strengthening me. Only occasionally did I suffer from a high fever or pneumonia, though I remained anemic. Mother was so used to my frequent bouts of illness that she seldom took time off from work. She played doctor, giving me pills to reduce my fever, and sometimes, even antibiotics when I had a whooping cough, but she went to work as soon as I had swallowed the medicine. No amount of begging could keep her at home.

She gave me the same treatment when I returned from the weeklong farm work. I threw my bedding and other belongings into a corner of my room and collapsed. I had not been feeling well the previous two days. I was light-headed and weak, but chose to ignore the symptoms. Over the two months of my preparation for the college exam, I had slept little and often suffered from dizziness. My remedy was to put my head against my folded arms on the table and rest for ten or fifteen minutes. I thought my feeling of exhaustion was a result of the hard, physical labor and believed I would be fine once I got some rest.

But my fever got worse. The evening I returned home, my temperature reached 103 degrees Fahrenheit. Despite drinking a lot of water, my mouth was dry and my lips cracked. My body and joints were sore. Mother's pills failed to keep the fever down. I shivered one moment and burned hot the next. The following day, my fever climbed even higher. I was so weak and dizzy that I couldn't walk to the bathroom on my own. I stayed in bed, covered by layers of bedding. I tried to sweat out the fever. It didn't work. I drifted in and out of sleep. Mother put her hand on my forehead from time to time to check my temperature, as if she didn't believe the thermometer.

I had no appetite and declined to touch any food.

"It will help if you eat something," Mother said, bringing to my bedside a bowl of soup and a steamed bun.

I shook my head, but Mother insisted. She put down the food and propped me up against two pillows.

"Listen to me," she said. "Be a good child."

She dipped a piece of the steamed bun in egg drop soup and put it in my mouth. After three or four bites, I couldn't continue. Mother picked up the soup bowl. She used a spoon to stir it, cooling it off. Then she scooped up the soup and lifted it to her mouth first to make sure it was not too hot.

I watched her every move. I couldn't remember when Mother had ever shown such care. Each time she put the spoon to my mouth, I obediently opened and swallowed. Tears came to my eyes.

"Don't cry," Mother said. Her voice was tender. "I've sent for a doctor. You'll be fine soon."

My crying had nothing to do with my illness. I had often questioned Mother's love and longed desperately for her affection, but she always bore the look of a schoolmaster. And yet, here she was. Just when I needed her the most, she became the mother I had always wanted.

Dr. Ma from the Compound clinic came to see me. I had known Dr. Ma since he treated my broken toe when I was a child. He was a short man and always good-natured. We ran into him all the time, calling him Uncle Ma. He was in his forties. For years, he had served as the doctor for all the employees and the officials' families in the Compound.

Ma put his cold stethoscope on my chest and asked me to take a deep breath. He examined me carefully, and then gave me a shot for my fever. He asked Mother to consider sending me to the hospital if my fever persisted. I drifted into sleep. I had another restless night.

When I woke up the following morning, I was surprised to see Mother sitting on a chair by my bed. She looked tired, and her eyes were red.

"Mother," I called out, trying to sit up. "How long have you been here?"

"Sh..." she put a finger on her lips and gestured me to lie still. "You were talking in your sleep."

A cold, wet towel had been placed on my forehead. Mother used it to keep my temperature down.

Seeing I was awake, she rubbed my arms and chest with cotton balls dipped in alcohol. My fever was still dangerously high.

I liked Mother's touch and her undivided attention. I smiled at her. Mother smiled back. She repeated that I would be fine soon. I must have drifted off to sleep. When I came to, I saw Dr. Ma in the room, along with another man whom I didn't know. Picking up bits and pieces of their conversation, I figured out he was a doctor from the No. 1 City Hospital. I was surprised to see a drip attached to my right arm. The doctors were discussing whether to apply a stronger dose of antibiotics. They were concerned my body would develop resistance to the medicine. Should I fall seriously ill again, the antibiotics wouldn't be as effective anymore, but they were anxious to get my fever under control, afraid it might cause other problems.

"Dr. Ma," Mother called. "She is awake!"

Mother sounded nervous. I stared at her.

The doctor standing next to Mother was not Dr. Ma. I felt dizzy, but my mind was clear.

"Mother," I murmured. "That's not Dr. Ma."

To my surprise, Mother smiled through tears.

"She is alert," Mother said.

Her statement puzzled me. To my amazement, Mother patted me on my cheek and two streams of tears rolled down her face.

Mother stayed with me for two days.

As soon as I was out of danger, however, she was gone.

Too weak to move around on my own, I felt disheartened. The wonderful Mother I had for three days disappeared. The connection I had felt with her faded. It was like waking up from a dream. Big Aunt was home to keep an eye on me, but I wanted Mother. I buried my head in my pillow and cried. I felt her absence. I knew when she returned from work, she would be the schoolmaster figure again. I shed bitter tears, as if Mother had abandoned me.

As was the custom, Mother's colleagues stopped by after work to visit me, bringing me fruit and biscuits. In my anguish, I asked Mr. Liu, another Deputy Director at the Public Health Bureau, if he would like to adopt me. Mr. Liu often visited us. He had three sons. He and his wife had always wanted to have a daughter. Liu had joked with Mother before about taking me to his home, saying his wife would be so pleased to have me.

"Take me with you," I said to Liu. "My mother won't notice if I am here or not." I raised my voice. I wanted Mother to hear.

Mr. Liu smiled. "Jian," he said gently. "You don't know how worried your mother was. I'm sure she won't let you leave the house now." He laughed.

I gave a deep sigh. I believed him, but I wanted the mother I had seen over the previous few days. The mother who was full of love, care, and tenderness. I turned to look at her. She was sitting in a chair at the far end of the room. She looked at me, a faint smile across her face, and she shook her head slightly. With a wave of her hand, she dismissed my remarks. I fought back the tears.

5

As I gradually recovered, five or six girls from my class also visited me at home. They filled me in on school news and told me what Mrs. Wu was up to. One day, I was surprised to find Zhi Qiang at my door, all by himself. My association with boys was limited to our class committee meetings. As a member of the branch committee for the Communist League, I conducted one-on-one talks with boys who had applied to join the League. It was all carried out in our classroom, in the presence of others. The topic of the discussion was strictly focused on how to improve their performance.

Zhi Qiang had been in our class only for a short period of time. He was smart and eloquent. He got along with Wu and fitted easily into the group of student leaders. I was impressed by his high test scores, especially in physics and math. He was short and his skin was dark. He looked very serious when he tried to make a point, but when he relaxed, he smiled readily, narrowing his eyes to a thin line. We had only exchanged a few words with each other in our classroom.

He grinned awkwardly as I stood at the door.

"I heard you were sick," he said, seeing no sign of welcome from me. "I thought I'd stop by to pay a visit."

I let him in, but I was ill at ease.

Why was he here by himself? Why was he so daring? Did he know that his behavior could create a scandal in school? As students, we were required to focus on our studies and school activities. Association with anyone of the opposite sex was discouraged. There was no such thing as friendship between boys and girls. Even our own physical development caused embarrassment. Many girls in school wrapped long strips of cloth around their chests to hide their emerging breasts.

When it came to boys, I was naïve and simple-minded. I played table tennis and engaged in making airplane models, which gave me more opportunities to associate with boys than most of the other girls in school, but I had never spent any time with a boy in a social setting. "Tan Lian Ai,"—or "talking about love,"—was strictly forbidden and voluntarily self-censored. Gossip or rumor could ruin a person's reputation and put one to shame. Girls shied away from boys, and vice versa. Even curiosity about the opposite sex was scorned as something dirty, especially for a girl whose chastity was considered one of her most important virtues.

I felt relieved I had never developed any interest in boys, and I took caution to keep my distance, so that no "abnormal" thoughts would creep into my mind.

The year before, a boy named Yi had handed me a note after class, which I thought was his regular "thought report." I didn't pay much attention and put the note into my pocket. Yi was a handsome and quiet boy, a team leader in our class. I had served as one of the two members in introducing him into the

Communist Youth League. To help him pass the initiation period, I had talked with him in our classroom a couple of times.

I forgot about the note and didn't open it until a couple of weeks later. I was shocked to see his request for a meeting, at a specified street corner outside of school. The day had long since passed.

Yi's note was simple. "I like you," he declared. "Please meet me at 4 o'clock." He listed the location. My initial reaction was rage—"How dare he!" Instead of feeling flattered, I was upset. I paced up and down in the classroom, wondering how he dared approach me. Yi sat in front of me in class. A couple of times when I stretched my feet forward, I accidentally kicked his feet. I quickly withdrew my legs, but never gave much thought to it. Did he take it as a signal of my interest? I felt insulted. A mixed feeling of anger, embarrassment, and humiliation overwhelmed me. I didn't know what to do with the note. For a moment, I thought about turning it in to Mrs. Wu, but I worried about Yi being condemned as a hoodlum. I didn't want that to happen, nor did I have any desire to be the cause of a sensation. After much thought, I tore up the note into tiny pieces and threw it away. I didn't tell anyone about the incident and didn't face Yi either. He avoided me ever after.

Looking at Zhi Qiang in front of me, I was even more at a loss. I found it incredulous that he was so bold as to come to my home alone.

"Your English is so much better than the rest of us," he said. "I wonder if you can help me."

He couldn't possibly have come all the way to the Compound to get help for his English, I thought. I bit my tongue. I wanted to say you should have knocked on the door of an English teacher.

"We can study English in school, if you want to," I said after a pause.

Zhi Qiang blushed, but he didn't leave. He talked about his experiences studying with the seniors, and he inquired about the plans I had for college. He rattled on, trying to fill the awkward silence. My cold reception didn't seem to bother him. In the following three weeks, he stopped by two more times. He didn't make excuses anymore. He said he enjoyed talking with me. I was alarmed. Even his friendly smile made me nervous. I couldn't ask him to leave or not to come again, feeling it was too rude. Yet, I didn't want him to come. I feared that gossip might soon start in school.

"Your classmate is here," Big Aunt announced one day. "That boy again!" she laughed. I found my face turning hot. If Big Aunt suspected something was going on, what about others?

I stayed in my room. I heard Big Aunt tell Zhi Qiang I would be out soon. I kept him waiting for twenty minutes. When I eventually emerged from my room, I was so unfriendly that he apologized.

"I'm sorry," he said. "I must have come at a bad time." He quickly took leave.

A week later, he stopped by again, this time in the company of another boy. Three people constituted a group. He hoped that would relax me. Instead, I became more conscious. I kept my distance. Zhi Qiang never visited me at home again. After he stopped coming, I found my thoughts turning to him, and sometimes, even hoping to see him. His courage seemed to have awakened something in me. A curiosity. A vague desire. I couldn't express the unsettling feeling. Eventually the school rules and fear got the better of me. I knew I shouldn't enter any dangerous territory. A scandal, even based on rumor, could ruin both our lives.

6

One day late in the summer of 1978, the results for the college entrance exam were posted in front of city hall. I jumped on my bicycle and raced to the site. So many people stood before the posting that all I could see was the header: Results of College Entrance Exam, 1978. Everyone was busy writing down their scores. I tried to get to the front, but found no room to squeeze through. No one was leaving. No one was speaking loudly. Greetings among friends were exchanged in whispers, as if to sustain the solemnity of the situation. My heart pounded with anxiety. The names were listed in phonetic order, written in black on red paper that covered the six-foot wall from ground to the top. I finally lost patience and pushed my way through the crowd. My name caught my eye right away, but it took me a moment to let the results sink in. My scores were far above the cut-off line for admissions. Most likely, I would be accepted by Jilin University, the best university in the northeast of China.

I quickly squeezed my way out and rushed home in record speed to share my news.

I could hardly believe my good fortune as I pedaled hard toward home. The constant ringing of bicycle bells didn't bother me, and the honking of the few motor vehicles on the streets sounded even further away. I gave a courtesy wave to the guard at the entrance of the Compound, without making the required stop. I could picture Old Fan shaking his head behind the window.

My mind was racing along with my pedaling. I could hardly believe I would get out of Baicheng before graduation. How I longed for a new place, a new world! I wanted to have a chance to stand on my own.

"I'm in," I shouted as I ran through our front door. "I'm going to college!"

Father was in the living room. "That's what we've heard," he said. When I entered the room, he patted me on the shoulder. "Hao!" he said, clearly delighted. His exclamation was music to my ears. I was so happy to see the big smile on his face. Father looked at me and raised his right thumb. "Hao. Hen Hao!" He said again. It meant "very good."

Mother's reaction was less dramatic, but she looked equally pleased. "I'll make a special dinner tonight, to celebrate your success," she said. That was high praise from her.

By the time I reached home, Mother had received two phone calls from her former colleagues in school. They had been among the first to see the posting of the exam results. The news that the Governor's daughter had achieved high marks traveled fast. It meant much more than just my acceptance into a college. With the previously required recommendations for attending college, acceptance had been a matter of "back door" politics and manipulation. Any official's child going to college was subject to gossip, and suspicions of favoritism. Finally, with test scores serving as the only deciding factor, Father was freed from any suspicion of interference, even indirectly.

When the wave of initial excitement was over, however, Father sat me down and asked me to think about the regular school courses I would have to miss for the final year. Eventually, he put his concern and suggestion explicitly to me.

"Do you think you should stay for one more year and finish your middle school?" he asked. "If you were able to pass the exam this year, you will surely do well in next year's exam," he said.

Father always regretted he never had the chance to finish his middle school because of the Japanese invasion. Was he asking me to stay so I would finish the fundamental education he believed to be crucial? Or was he worried that I was not ready to take off on my own? Or did he simply want to keep me at home for another year? I couldn't tell. I didn't want to know. All I wanted at this moment was to leave Baicheng, to get out of the shadow of politics, and to cut myself off from the past suffering. I had been treated like a little princess, abused as a "traitor's" daughter, and praised as the Governor's bright child. I didn't want any of that. I longed to be regarded as an individual, and evaluated on my own merits. I wanted to embark on a journey that would lead me to a life of my own.

My bewildered look must have given him the answer. He paused for a moment and murmured, more to himself than to me: "The feathers on the little bird have grown strong enough to fly away."

Soon afterward, I received the admission notice from Jilin University.

7

Late in September, shortly before I left for college, Mrs. Wu invited me to a farewell photo session with the rest of my classmates. I felt ambivalent. Since it was announced that De Rong, Zhi Qiang and I had been accepted into college, Wu had acted like a model teacher again. A huge outdoor blackboard at school posted the names and scores of the students bound for college. In the liberal arts section, my name came in second, and my English score was the highest. Teachers and students still stopped at the board long after it had been set up, as if to savor the taste of their success. Four out of the seven juniors who had taken the exam had succeeded. Considering that only thirty-five students, about 18% of the seniors from our school, were accepted by a college or trade school, we had fared very well. Wu's cheeks turned red as she received all the compliments. Her eyes sparkled, and she acted as if the results were her achievement. Her behavior disgusted me.

After much hesitation, I decided to join the photo shoot. After all, I was the only student from Wu's original class, and our classmates had been split, one group majoring in science, the other in liberal arts. This might be our last opportunity to get together.

When I arrived at the studio, Wu was at the door, talking to the photographer, a middle-aged man.

"Three of my students are leaving for college before their graduation," she said, looking proud. She passed a note to the man and instructed what to print on the photo. The note said: "Farewell to De Rong, Zhi Qiang, and Jian Ping for going to college early. September 27, 1978."

More than sixty students from our original class showed up. I was touched. I knew that most of them would not be able to make their way to college. I had spent four years with them, participating in political campaigns, farm work, and construction projects. They worked hard, following directions. Most of them came from working-class families. They were intelligent, they were strong. They were the future. And how different their future might have been, if politics had not robbed them of their youth. What if Mrs. Wu had directed her energy and dedication to actually teach them, to guide them in life? I turned to look at Wu. She was standing among ten or so students, taking center stage. I couldn't hear what she was saying, but her arrogance, even her grin from ear to ear, angered me. She took pride and credit for what the three of us had achieved. She had always required us to do self-reflection. I wondered if she ever did any herself.

Then, I heard Wu call everyone to line up for the photo. She directed a few students to arrange the stools and benches, and asked each one of us to take our place. She was in command again, as if she was on stage, ready to start another show.

As everyone started filing into position, Wu sat down in the center of the first row. She beckoned De Rong, Zhi Qiang, and me to come over. I saw De Rong and Zhi Qiang settle on Wu's right, but I didn't move. I remained where I was, hesitating. The seat to Wu's left was reserved for me.

A moment passed. I could feel the uneasy glances of the students around me. Wu extended one arm over Zhi Qiang's shoulder, smiling broadly. The deliberate gesture sickened me. She would never change. She rode with the waves, siding with the tide that she believed would carry her far and high. The three of us were her latest triumphs. I didn't want to sit beside her.

I walked to the second row.

"I'll take a center position," I said, faking a cheerful voice. Wang, the leading female singer in our class, happened to stand to Wu's left. I pressed both hands on her shoulders and asked her to sit down. Wang protested and insisted I come to the front. I whispered into her ear and begged her to sit down. She hesitated for a second and then quietly took the seat next to Wu. With a strong flash brightening the room, an instant of my silent resistance was recorded on film. I had an anguished look, while Wu showed no emotion. De Rong and Zhi Qiang stared into the camera solemnly, and no one else smiled. As I examine the photo today, looking at all those youthful faces, frozen in time, I feel a pang of pain. In the end, only eight students, the three of us included, out of a class of over eighty, succeeded in going to college.

The winds of life had scattered us all. A few years ago, I learned that Cheng, a girl I had promised to stay in touch with, but lost contact for years, was in the United States. I tried calling her, but the line was busy. When, after a few attempts, the phone was finally picked up, I heard the voice of her son.

"My mother died ten years ago," he said. "Breast cancer."

I was silent. Then I mumbled my condolences and hung up.

To this day, the class photo is a wistful reminder of all that once was and all that might have been.

8

Early in October, I was ready to leave for Jilin University in Changchun, the city where I was born. I could hardly conceal my excitement. To my surprise and delight, Mother gave me a Shanghai wristwatch on the day of my departure. The watch cost her nearly two months' salary.

"You are on your own now," she said as she handed me the watch. "This will help you keep track of your time. Make sure not to be late for your classes."

I felt like jumping up to give Mother a hug, but she took a matter-of-fact approach to the situation. She went on to tell me I should learn to be better organized and maintain good relationships with my roommates.

Mother must have given much thought before she made such an expensive purchase. The watch weighed heavy in my hand. It certainly revealed her care and love, yet, Mother, as usual, wouldn't show any emotion. I swallowed hard. "Thank you, Mother." In the end, that was all I managed to say.

Father lifted my luggage to check its weight. It was the rectangular wooden box my sister Ping had used in the countryside. The red print of the Supreme Directive and the two lines underneath—the promise of the vast land—were somewhat scratched, but still clearly legible. Ping, not wanting to be reminded of that episode of her life, had abandoned the box when she left for college.

"It's quite heavy," Father said. "You should have packed less."

I told him not to worry. My brother Binbin and sister Wen were both in Changchun. Binbin had become a physicist and was working at a research institute, and Wen had graduated from the Bethune Medical College four months earlier, and had become a gynecologist at the People's Hospital of Jilin. They had offered to meet me at the Changchun train station.

"I've asked your brother and sister to keep an eye on you," Father said. "Go to them if you need any help."

I nodded.

Father, who never allowed us to use government vehicles for personal purposes, had arranged for a car to take me to the train station. I was shocked.

"Yes, Jian, a special treat for you," Father said as he saw the surprise on my face. "Baicheng has changed so much over the eighteen years of my stay here," he continued. "I want to take you for a ride in the city. You should remember the place you grew up in."

I bit my tongue. I couldn't tell Father how much I wanted to move away from here. I didn't have the resolve Father had for the cause he'd committed his life to, or the faith he had for the Government and the Party. I wanted to get away and to explore a new life.

The driver pulled the car up in front of our apartment. Father shook hands with him and thanked him for his help.

"My pleasure," he said. "You've got a smart kid." He smiled, looking at me.

I had seen him many times before. He usually sat in the car and waited for Father. He wore a pair of gloves and a dark blue shirt. He loaded the heavy wooden box and my bedding roll into the trunk.

"Is that all?" he asked. I laughed, telling him my father thought it was too much.

We drove through the main streets, passing the two department stores, the movie theater, and the city stadium where the center for table tennis and airplane models was located. Right before we reached the train station, I saw the gate to the Military Compound where Father had been detained for two years. My heart skipped a beat. I turned to look at Father in the back seat. He was pointing out something for Mother to see. I didn't want to bring his attention to the painful past.

We pulled up at the train station. It had been remodeled since the time I wandered around while waiting for my chance to visit Father. The two-story building was crowded with people. The train to Changchun was already at the platform. Our driver helped Father carry the wooden box to the train. Mother and I watched them from the platform. They found my seat and placed the box on a rack directly above. Mother smiled at me. "Are you ready to take off?" she asked.

I nodded.

She took me by the shoulders and turned me to face her.

"Be good," she said. "Write to us."

"I will." Suddenly I was seized by sadness. "I'll miss you."

"Changchun is not that far away," Mother said. "Winter break is in three months. You will be back in no time."

Mother, as always, had her emotions well under control.

Father and the driver came down from the train. I realized how much he had aged. At fifty-seven, his hair had turned gray and deep wrinkles had appeared around his eyes.

"Now you are really flying away from us," he said. He squeezed my arms with his hands, as if he was testing if my wings were strong enough to carry me.

"I'll be fine," I said.

"I know you will."

Hugging was not the custom in China. Father extended his right hand before me, ready to shake hands and send me on my way. I pushed it away and threw myself against his chest. I wrapped my arms around his waist.

"Oh!" Father staggered back. He laughed and patted me on my back.

I stayed in his arms for a moment. I could hear his heartbeat and feel his breathing. Even his strong smell of cigarette smoke felt soothing. From the corner of my eye, I could see Mother, a wistful smile on her face.

Then I broke away. I ran to the train before they could see the tears in my eyes.

Binbin, Ping, Yan, Me and Wen in 1982

Epilogue

A thick layer of clouds obscures the world below me. I hear the hum of the Boeing 747, but I can't sense its movement. Chicago is far behind, and with each passing minute, China draws closer. The clouds remind me of the smoke that obscures my father as he holds his ever-lit cigarette.

My long-ago dream of freedom, of flight, has become real. So real that freedom is commonplace now. I fly on business all over the United States or to visit my family in China. This time, my husband Francis and my daughter Lisa are with me. This journey is special. It's a family reunion—a pilgrimage to my past.

In 1982, my parents moved from Baicheng to Changchun. That same year, I graduated from college. Three months after they settled down in an apartment provided by the government, I was assigned to work as a translator in Beijing, leaving my parents behind a second time. Two years later, I got married in Beijing. In 1985, I gave birth to Lisa. A year after that, unhappy at work, I decided to pursue my graduate studies in the United States. I received a scholarship from Ohio University, and was thrilled about the opportunity. When I went to Changchun to bid farewell to my parents, Father remained silent. He didn't show much enthusiasm in my pursuit of further education.

"Beijing is not big enough for you?" he asked.

I couldn't understand his resistance.

All my life, I wanted to know him better, to understand him, but gradually, as I grew up, I began to see him in more human than authoritarian terms, as a man whose life was forged by the events of his times.

I knew he wasn't keen for me to go abroad, but I had been exposed to the outside world through business travels and foreign films. I wanted to explore the larger world in more intimate terms than through business and film.

I still wanted to fly.

We land in Beijing, and after a couple of hours, boarded another plane heading toward Changchun. After the flight attendant welcomes everyone to the capital of the Jilin Province, I exchange a quick smile with Lisa and Francis. Our plane touches down smoothly, and I feel myself getting closer to home, closer to Mother and Father. I, however, can't help feeling a sense of loss. My years in America had changed me. I had become more independent. I remember my first taste of freedom. A professor at Ohio University advised me on my selection of courses for registration: "Do what you think is best for you," he said.

I was shocked. I could choose what I was interested in, and in the sequence I saw fit. I marveled at the concept and opportunity.

One year after I had gone abroad, my husband followed me to the United States. Alone in a new and foreign culture, our differences became more apparent. Shortly after our daughter joined us in New York City, we divorced. In 1994, I moved to Chicago with my daughter.

Two years later, I married Francis, who had fled with his family from China to Hong Kong in 1953. Overnight, his family had turned from well-to-do landlords to penniless refugees.

"We would have been enemies if we were in China," we joked, but there was truth in it.

Times have changed, and my parents welcomed Francis into their family. I close my eyes, as the plane touches the ground.

Father meets us at the door of his new apartment. I immediately recognize the familiar smell of his Red Pagoda cigarettes. I know I am home. I watch the smoke rise and drift away with the breeze, hoping the veil that separates us will also be lifted. For years, I've resented the clouds that engulf him and choke me. And yet, today, at this particular moment, I wish I could be inside the blue circles with him.

Later, sitting with my father in his study, I examine him closely. His hair is white. His thick, long eyebrows, which I sometimes pulled and played with while sitting on his lap as a child, are also white. His wrinkled and worn face tells of years of hard work. His eyes, however, still radiate light and energy, revealing an indomitable spirit and an alert mind. He is as sharp as ever. He reads two or three newspapers a day to keep up with the happenings in China. As always, the cigarette smolders between his tobacco-stained fingers.

Many items clutter his desk: a small television, piles of classic Chinese literature bound with twine, textbooks of calligraphy and painting, and scattered papers covered with his own brush writing and drawings, evidence of hobbies he has taken up since his retirement in 1983. Beneath the glass cover on his desk are family photos. On the wall above the television is a small, framed photograph of my grandmother, Nainai. Over the years, her image has faded into the gray background. With each passing day, the lives we used to lead become less real.

Lisa, my sister Yan, and Mother are in the kitchen, preparing dinner. Father leans toward his desk, and fixes his eyes on the wall before him, as if he were watching episodes of his life playing out in front of him. His unwavering devotion to his cause has remained incomprehensible to me. I ask him about the Cultural Revolution, hoping to better understand him. He simply exhales a mouthful of blue smoke and says that the party made a mistake.

I still become enraged to think of the sufferings we endured, but Father continues to dismiss his suffering—and ours. Perhaps that is the key to his forgiveness, his inner peace. Would I have done anything differently if I had been an adult then? Are we better off if we remain bitter and angry about the past? Does it sacrifice our humanity to deny or dismiss it? Father looks at me, and I avert my gaze. I don't have a clear answer. After all, I'm the one who left the country.

Then, he places one elbow on the glass cover over his desk, his eyes closed. The silk shirt I gave him from my trip last year looks big on him. He must have lost twenty pounds since then. The weight loss worries me. At eighty-six, he is diagnosed with lung cancer. The news hit us hard. I spend endless hours talking over the phone with my sisters, checking on Father's health.

He says he has a headache. I stand behind him and massage his temples. His breathing is heavy, but my touch seems to soothe him.

Mother says he stopped smoking for a week when he first learned of his diagnosis. He was quiet and spent hours walking in a nearby park. Then he resumed smoking. No doctor can persuade him to put out the ever-lit cigarettes between his fingers.

"Each day I have is a bonus," he always says. "I'll live it to the fullest."

Instead of following the doctor's advice, he announces three "NOs": No operation; no chemotherapy; and no hospitalization. His remedy to illness is to go to the playground in the neighborhood and exercises.

"Life is motion," he says.

My parents recently moved into a new apartment. Ever since their retirement, the government has neglected the maintenance of their old building. The roof was leaking, and black mold grew on the ceiling and walls. There was no elevator, and to climb up four flights of stairs had become increasingly difficult for Father. With China's economic boom, new high-rises were built all over the city. I offered to buy a new apartment for my parents, but for a long time, Father declined, saying he was content with his living conditions. At heart, he was still a stubborn country boy from Shandong. When my sister Wen purchased an apartment in a new development, I bought a unit in the same building for my parents.

"It will make it much easier for Wen to look after you," I reasoned with Father and Mother. Mother liked the idea, but Father continued to say no. For a long time, he refused to settle in. He had always taken pride in living simply. Only shortly before this family reunion did Father finally agree to move.

The new apartment is simple, but very inviting. The living room is bright and open, and the three bedrooms all have large windows, allowing the smoke from his cigarette to waft away quickly. What's more, there is an elevator in the building. Mother was delighted when she first saw it, and Father, after living here for two weeks, cautiously expressed his appreciation. What he likes the most, however, is not the new facilities, but that Wen and her husband are close by. Every day, they bring him his newspapers and check on him and Mother.

Dinner is almost ready. Wen rushes back and forth to make sure everyone is taken care of. She is still working as a gynecologist, and serves, at the same time, as our parents' personal doctor. Yan is in charge of cooking. A number of dishes have been spread on the table: spicy beef, stewed chicken, stir-fried tofu, green beans with pork, and leafy pea pod sprouts. I can hear the sizzling of the cooking pan and smell the grouper braised in soy sauce. Yan is still an excellent cook. Two years ago, she retired. Yan and her husband live in Baicheng, but spend most of their time in Changchun, to be close to our parents and their son, who also lives in Changchun. Ping, as always, is the most eloquent one. She talks with Father about the economic changes in China, and from time to time, argues with him. Ping, suffering from occasional dizzy spells, had retired early, in her mid-forties. She lives with her husband in Shenyang, the capital of the Liaoning Province. Since the Shanghai and Shenzhen Stock Exchanges were established, she has become a day trader.

My brother Binbin lives with his family in Rochester, New York. He has recently started a new job and cannot take time off to join us. My half-sister Wei is also absent. She and her family live in Shenyang. She sees Ping from time to time, but she has severe asthma, which prevents her from traveling.

Lisa is amazed by her extended family. She has not seen her Laoye and Laolao—my parents—and her aunts and uncles for more than ten years. She has been brushing up on her Chinese since we decided to make the trip and is eager to put it to use. We sit down at the dinner table.

"I'd like to make a toast to Laoye and Laolao," Lisa clicks her wine glass with a spoon over the dinner table and speaks as if she is about to continue with a speech.

"Wish you good health and happiness!" she says loudly, her measured tone tainted with a foreign accent. I'm pleased at her progress. She is beginning to embrace her heritage.

Everyone joins in. After we quiet down, Father raises his glass.

"This is a happy day for our family," he says. "I'm a lucky man." He takes a look at each of us. Then he focuses his attention on Lisa.

"Let's make a toast to welcome Yieyie home," he says, calling her by her Chinese name. "And all of you, the younger generations," he adds.

Lisa's cousins, one child from each of my sisters' families, are present at the reunion.

I let the word "home" linger in my mind's ear. It is a complicated notion for me. I've been in the United States for twenty-one years, longer than the time I spent in Baicheng, the place of my childhood. The US is one kind of home for me. When I am with my parents, seeing them taking center stage at family gatherings, I feel another strong and sweet sense of home. Mother is looking at me, smiling. She has become more affectionate in her old age than she was when we grew up.

I join the cheers. My eyes scan the people who represent the different lives and generations of our family at the table. I think back at the mulberry trees in our Compound, and how, each year, their shoots would produce fresh leaves, bringing a small patch of green into our gray world, even as the old branches were dying. I look at my father, and I wonder how much time we have left. We savor every single moment.

I close my eyes, and in that instant but also for all time, the past and the present become one, and I'm grateful for all that we've had, and all that we carry in our hearts.

Mother, Big Aunt and Father

Nainai and Father

Acknowledgements

To write this story of my childhood, I visited China once or twice every year over the course of eight years, talking to my parents, my sisters, and my middle school classmates. Like all memories, it is deeply personal. In some cases, characters' names were changed to make it easier for Western readers. In other instances, small visual details were added to create a more well rounded narrative.

Revisiting our life, especially during the ten years of the Cultural Revolution, is a very difficult undertaking. Mother tells me to this day she changes channels if a television show about the Cultural Revolution appears on screen. "It's too painful," she says. My sister Ping is equally adamant. "A single image of the Red Guards at a struggle meeting can ruin my appetite and sleep for days," she says. But despite the emotional toll it levies on them, they go back in time and share with me the vivid details of their experiences. My brother Binbin still clams up when I broach the subject, but in our phone conversations and occasional meetings, incidents in the past inevitably surface. Our lives are marked forever, and there is no escape from it. I want to thank each of my family members for taking the journey to the past with me.

I would also like to thank my school teachers and classmates, in particular, Gu Changkuan, Liu Yuqin, Wang Hongguo, Ma Xubo, Du Xiuyan, Liu Ying, Wang Huanzhi, Sun Lihua, Liu Derong, Wang Zhiqiang, Zhou Runzhi, Huo Yingjie, Zhang Limei, Wang Yisu, Liang Xiaojuan, and many others who welcome my return and share with me many unforgettable moments of these turbulent years. I'm indebted to and humbled by them, their resilience, and continued hard work. Most of them are still in Baicheng.

I am very thankful to my friends in the United States. Their interest in my story and encouragement for me to write helped me through this long, sometimes difficult process. My heartfelt thanks go to Ellis M. Goodman. Without his unwavering support, belief, and help, this book would not have been in print.

I am deeply indebted to Steve Fore, Frank Shen, Rita Dragonette, Laura Grill, Larry Engelmann, Vincent Fan Yuan, Joe Scarry, Lana Quinn, and Susan and Fred Mardell. Their repeated reading and editing, or their feedback at various stages of this writing, have significantly improved the narrative and language of this memoir. Special thanks go to members of my writing group: Timothy Gray, Sharon Stangenes, Susan Myrick, and Phil Woollcott. Over the past eight years, they've tirelessly worked as my sounding board, providing input and raising the writing to a higher level. Their support and friendship are invaluable. I'd also like to thank my instructors at the creative writing programs at Northwestern University and the University of Chicago: Mary Cross, Jim O'Laughlin, Sheila Donohue, and Dina Elenbogen.

I'd also like to thank the following friends for their assistance: Barbara Starr, Cindy Chu, Joellen Desautels, Daniel Kinghorn, Steve Danemayer, David Weksel, and Jill Yang. And of course, George Semsel, who helped initiate my new life in the United States. He and his family always provide me with generous help when I most need it. And special thanks to John Apgar for his dedication and wonderful work on the cover design; and Timothy Gray for his meticulous proofreading of the manuscript.

My heartfelt thanks to my editor Emanuel Bergmann. The structure, voice, and every single line and word in the story bear witness to his dedication and tireless work. And thanks to my publisher Brian Forbes for giving me the opportunity to release the book.

Special thanks to the Ragdale Foundation and the Florence Bear Picker Fellowship.

And finally thanks to my daughter Lisa, whose future inspires me to tell of the past, and my husband Francis, for his constant support and encouragement.